UNWIN UNIVERSITY BOOKS

1

Social Foundations of Wage Policy

BARBARA WOOTTON

The Social Foundations
of Wage Policy

**A STUDY OF
CONTEMPORARY BRITISH WAGE
AND SALARY STRUCTURE**

LONDON
UNWIN UNIVERSITY BOOKS

First published in 1955
Second Edition 1962
Second Impression 1964

This Second Edition
© *George Allen & Unwin Ltd. 1962*

UNWIN UNIVERSITY BOOKS

George Allen & Unwin Ltd
Ruskin House, Museum Street
London

Printed in Great Britain
in 10 pt. Times Roman type by
John Dickens & Co. Ltd., Northampton

Acknowledgements

NOW that this book is written, the amount of help that I have had in preparing it seems altogether out of proportion to the finished product. For many reasons the work has hung about for a long time, and has never been able to enjoy more than a low-priority claim on its author's time. In the course of these delays, ambitious designs have continually had to give way to more modest ones in which some of the material contributed by those who helped at earlier stages could not find a place. But the work would never have been begun without the help of a generous grant from the National Institute of Economic and Social Research; and it would never have been carried through even on its present limited scale without the co-operation of many colleagues and assistants. In particular I have to thank for various forms of research assistance Dr. Ivy Pinchbeck; Mrs. Joan Clarke (now Jaksch); Miss Rhona Ross (Mrs. Cyril Sofer); Mrs. Marion Mead; and Miss Hilda Kahn. To Miss Kahn a special debt is due for assistance freely given long after she had vacated her post in the Social Studies Department at Bedford College, and any right to claim her services as a research assistant had come to an end. On the subjects of job analysis and job evaluation, Mr. J. H. Arkell, Controller of Staff Administration at the BBC, has been most helpful in keeping me up to date; and on points of detail I have pestered—either directly or indirectly through Miss Kahn—more Government Departments, Trade Unions and other organizations than it is possible to record here.

To these and many others I am glad to acknowledge my indebtedness —not less gratefully for the knowledge that those who have helped me would dissent from some of my interpretations of the facts here presented. For those interpretations as well as for any mistakes of fact that may have eluded detection I alone, of course, am responsible.

B. W.

Bedford College
University of London
August 1954

Contents

Introduction to the Second Edition[1]

THERE is always a sour satisfaction in being able to say: 'I told you so'; and in introducing the second edition of this book the temptation to do so is irresistible. In the seven years since the first edition appeared the trends which are analysed in these pages have continued fast and furiously, with the result that the consequences that are there foretold have now begun to be appreciated.

On p.161 of this book I described the wage and salary structure of this country as 'the accumulated deposit laid down by a rich mixture of social and economic forces operating through considerable periods of history', and I was at pains to emphasise the growing importance in contemporary wage and salary settlements of conventional and social, as contrasted with purely economic, forces. In the intervening years the retreat from economics has become even more pronounced. Perhaps the outstanding example is to be found in the Report of the (Pilkington) Commission on Doctors' and Dentists' Remuneration.[2] This Commission listed, in entirely orthodox fashion, a number of factors (fourteen in all), which may be regarded as influencing the balance of 'net advantages' in any profession. Instead, however, of attempting a specific assessment of the significance of those factors in relation to the medical and dental professions, the Commissioners merely gave an assurance in completely general terms that they had 'given particular attention to the advantages and disadvantages inherent in the lives of doctors and dentists'. Even comparisons with other professions might, they suggested, be misleading, as 'the relationship between earnings in different professions is determined not only by considerations of precise justice and logic, but also by tradition and economic pressures of various kinds'. Without, therefore, revealing any of the mental processes which led them to this conclusion, the Commission roundly declared that the earnings of doctors and dentists were too low, and proceeded to recommend substantial increases, particularly in the higher ranks. And then, as if to deal the final death-blow to old fashioned theories of supply and demand, they followed this up with the remarkable observation that, since the future supply of doctors seemed likely to be

[1]Some passages in this Introduction have already appeared in my Eleanor Rathbone Memorial lecture 1961, *Remuneration in a Welfare State*, and are reproduced here by kind permission of the University of Liverpool.
[2]Cmnd 939 (1960). See especially paras. 149-155.

'reasonably close to requirements', 'the question of using remuneration as an instrument either for encouraging a greater flow of potential doctors or reducing the present flow does not arise'. An economist would, of course, have drawn the inference from this estimate, not that the question did not arise, but that the answer to it was that the existing level of doctors' pay must be about right. Nor is this by any means an isolated example. Indeed there have been hardly any signs of improvement in the meagre quality of the statistical evidence adduced in support of claims that particular industries or occupations are seriously undermanned, to which attention is drawn on pp. 154 ff. of this book. It is indeed odd that empirical studies of the supply side of wage equations should have been so generally neglected by economists.

Equally strong, too, in the past few years, has been the continued emphasis upon traditional and conventional relativities. When the Royal Commission on the Police in 1960[1] proposed to raise constables' pay to a level approximating to that of teachers, this raised an immediate outcry from the teaching profession; and ominous words in similar vein are to be found in the Pilkington Report also. 'We have taken no account in reaching our recommendations' write the authors of that document 'of possible repercussions in other fields. We fully recognise that there may be such repercussions and that other groups . . . . . may argue that the implementation of our recommendations . . . . . ought to be accompanied or followed by increases in their own remuneration'.[2] In the race for higher pay, it would seem the positions of all runners are still fixed beforehand, and poor indeed for those who have fallen behind are the chances of catching up on the leaders.

At least until very recently, that is. But now, at long last, the first hints are appearing of a breach in the long-established autarchy of income determination. When in 1955 I wrote (p.166) that 'The pattern of income distribution is essentially a political question', this was heresy indeed, To assert that 'the place for the discussion of wage policy is on the agenda of the political conferences' and that 'the responsibility for consequent action must lie on governments' was to challenge the sacred doctrine of the divine right of collective bargaining or at least of the divine rightness of every collective bargain. Yet only seven years later the Government itself brings out a White Paper with the title *Incomes Policy: The Next Step*.[3]

[1] Cmnd 1222 (1960).
[2] para. 167.
[3] Cmnd 1626 (1962).

This Paper does not, to be sure, contain much that can be called a policy. But even if it has nothing else to offer, it does concede, in a negative fashion, the inappropriateness, or at least the insufficiency, of the criteria of wage determination which I have criticised in this book. 'Arguments derived from the increased cost of living', we are now told, 'or from the trends of profits or productivity cannot in present circumstances be regarded as providing of themselves a sound basis for an increase' in pay. Nor, it is added, is more reliance to be placed on shortages of labour within a particular industry or firm. As for our old friend, 'comparisons with levels or trends in income in other employments'—these, it is said, 'will still have a part to play'; but they are now to be subsidiary to 'general economic considerations'. Even what Sir Walter Monckton (as he then was) called 'the scrupulous respect for the independence of arbitration' is now challenged. To suggest to-day, as I suggested on p.170 of this book, that arbitration tribunals can no more function properly without guidance or instruction than Her Majesty's judges could dispense justice without benefit of statute or case law is no longer to hint at 'tampering' with the independence of arbitrators. On the contrary, it is now said to be a matter of 'crucial importance' that arbitrators should be 'conscious of, and interested in, the wider implications of their awards'; and they are therefore to be given 'an opportunity to consider all the information necessary to put the particular case before them in its proper perspective against the background of wage movements elsewhere and other factors affecting the national economic situation'.

The White Paper is not an Incomes Policy. It is merely the promise of a policy; and it is significant, and also sinister, that it has practically nothing to say about incomes other than wages and salaries except that 'the same principles apply', and that 'continued restraint in profits and dividends is a necessary corollary' of the proposed policy for incomes. In view of the Chancellor of the Exchequer's estimate that between 1950 and 1960 total wages rose by 87%, total salaries by 119%, gross ordinary dividends by 145% and total company profits by 70%, such restraint can hardly be said to have yet begun.[1] All that we have had so far has been a few months of a wage standstill broken by a few unrepentant and unpunished recalcitrants, and followed by a period in which $2\frac{1}{2}$% all round seems to have become the approved standard figure for wage and salary increases: while the last-minute settlement of a threatened national dock dispute in May 1962 on terms involving

[1]House of Commons Debates, 13 February 1962 col. 1099.

an increase in earnings of something like twice this amount suggests that, if the divine right of collective bargaining has been challenged, its brute force has not. As *The Times* has commented in a leading article[1] 'the result is an object lesson in the insufficiency of a combination of 'guiding light' and admonition to achieve the objectives defined in the Government's incomes policy'.

Of any serious discussion of priorities there is as yet no sign. Only one small hint is to be found in a speech by Lord Hailsham to the London & Westminster Conservative Association on 7 May 1962[2] in which he admitted that one unpopular aspect of the $2\frac{1}{2}\%$ 'which cannot be allowed to continue indefinitely' is 'the rigidity between one calling and another'. 'Some professions', he went on to say, 'in particular those which demand long periods of training and a high degree of personal devotion and self-sacrifice have been persistently undervalued in the past and must be better valued in future'. Even on this, however, the Government appears to be a house divided against itself, for only a month earlier the Minister of Health is reported to have told a meeting of Young Conservatives that the reason why he could not pay the nurses' claim in full was not that he did not 'consider them worth more than another two and a half per cent compared with everyone else', but that rejecting the full claim was 'part of the whole and continuous policy, compliance with which is required from the economy as a whole;'[3] and at the conclusion of a Parliamentary debate on the subject, the Financial Secretary to the Treasury unequivocally declared that 'any question of any increase out and above $2\frac{1}{2}\%$ could not be implemented at the present time'.[4]

However, the important thing is that a policy for incomes is now definitely on the agenda of politics. Now is the chance for the political parties to sketch the broad outlines of the rival patterns of income distribution which they hold to be at once socially desirable and economically feasible. Now is the time for them to make their proposals for remedying the ingrown injustices which the increasing rigidity of our wage and salary structure has allowed to harden. That the Conservative Party will hardly be disposed towards a policy with so strong an equalitarian bias as that outlined in the final chapter of this book may be taken for granted. But the

[1] 14 May 1962.
[2] Reported in *The Times* of 8.5.62, but the above quotations are from the full text kindly supplied by Lord Hailsham.
[3] *The Sunday Times*, 8.4.62.
[4] House of Commons Debates 14.5.62 col. 1056. See also the Lord Chancellor's uncompromising observations on the same subject. House of Lord's Debates 28.6.62 col. 1032-1045.

opportunity is wide open for their rivals to consider and to publicise some of the facts from which an incomes policy that was infused with a sense of social justice would need to start. Within the professional field, at the time of writing, a Civil Service Principal at the top of his scale gets a salary of £2070 p.a., a University lecturer £1850, the Matron of the largest hospital in England £1643 and a staff nurse £656. Are we satisfied that these relativities bear any relation either to the responsibilities involved, or to any rational criterion whatsoever? In the manual working-field are we satisfied with a situation in which nearly $1/5$ of adult men in full-time employment earn less than £11 a week, while the earnings of more than 93% of women in full time industrial employment fall below that figure?[1] Real poverty still persists, amongst fully employed persons as well as amongst the aged and sick. Mr. Peter Townsend has calculated that more than one-third of the members of households living at standards not more than 40% above the level of National Assistance allowances are to be found in families in which the head is in full-time employment; and that altogether some 4 million persons in the United Kingdom (29% of them young children) were still scraping along on this level at least until 1953-4[2].

For too long has a supposedly affluent society turned a blind eye to the contrasts of wealth and poverty by which it is disfigured, and by which it must always be disfigured so long as the present rule of grab-what-you-can-devil-take-the-hindmost does duty for an incomes policy. For too long have the social scientists (and the politicians), to quote Mr. Townsend again, allowed themselves to sink into a state of 'dazed euphoria'. The pattern of incomes moulds the shape of social life and sets the limits of social intercourse; and everywhere that pattern bears the marks of greed and envy and of ruthless bargaining. Now is the time to show that in a civilised society those marks need not be indelible.

[1]Ministry of Labour Statistics on Incomes, Prices, Employment and Production No. 1, April 1962. Figures relate to October 1960.
[2]As yet unpublished paper on *The Meaning of Poverty* read to the British Sociological Association Conference 1962.

Introduction to the First Edition

THIS study owes its origin to two incidents. The first occurred shortly before the Second World War when I happened to visit the Zoological Society's park at Whipsnade and came across an interesting brochure full of facts and figures about the Whipsnade Zoo. From that I learned, amongst other things, that the big elephant which gave rides to children there was then earning at the rate of £600 per annum. This fact struck me with peculiar force because £600 happened to be exactly the salary that I was myself receiving at that time as Director of Studies to the University of London Tutorial Classes Committee —a job which involved the supervision of adult education under the University throughout a wide area in and around London. I found myself wondering what other occupations stood upon the same rung of the ladder as the elephant and myself, which would be above us, and which below, and why—a train of thought which soon led far beyond the trivial personal coincidence to fundamental reflections about the social and economic forces which determine the valuations which our society sets upon different kinds of work. The coincidence itself was, indeed, shortlived: not so the reflections. About twelve years afterwards, when I was able to return to the subject, the secretary of the Zoological Society courteously treated a request for information about the elephant's post-war remuneration as the serious inquiry that it was intended to be; and I learned from him that in 1949 two elephants were helping each other out, working together in the busy season, and alternating at other times; and that their joint earnings amounted to £1,355, or only £677 10s. per head. In the meantime, I myself had changed my job and enjoyed sundry promotions with substantial increases in salary, so that any personal comparison at the later date would have been out of step with that of pre-war days. On any basis, however, the elephant was left far behind, for the 1949 salary of the post most nearly comparable to that which I had held before the war (the title had been changed and the scope of the post considerably enlarged in the course of reorganization) was £1,350; and so remained in 1953.

The second incident occurred a year or two later, on the first occasion on which I took part, as one of the members of an

2

Arbitration Tribunal, in an adjudication on salaries in a branch of the public service. After hearing the arguments of the parties concerned, the Tribunal retired and the Chairman outlined a possible decision for consideration by his colleagues. I recall with great vividness how, when asked whether I agreed with his proposal, I was aware only of a sensation as of a great void opening; for one cannot decide whether the salary of a particular post should or should not be increased, or how great any increase should be, unless one has some principles from which to start. But I, at any rate, was distressingly conscious of having no principles at all: I determined then and there to look for some. In the intervening years the search has had continually to give way to more pressing obligations; but it has continued intermittently ever since these incidents occurred.

CHAPTER I

The Economists' Theory of Wages

I

'THE theory of the determination of wages in a free market is simply a special case of the general theory of value. Wages are the price of labour; and thus, in the absence of control, they are determined, like all prices, by supply and demand.'[1] With these words Mr. (now Professor) J. R. Hicks opens his study of the theory of wages, first published in 1932; and in these words he presents the classical economic approach to wage problems.

It is indeed remarkable that so little attention has been given, by English economists in particular, to wage theory in its own right. The fact that the level of wages and salaries is a matter both of grave public importance, and of acute personal interest to every individual amongst the millions who work for their living, might well have induced great concentration upon this branch of economics. Yet, whereas the literature on other specialized topics, as for instance monetary problems or international trade, is impressively large, studies of the specific problems of wage theory are, by comparison, few and far between. In this country, Professor Hicks' work, now more than twenty years old, has had no comparable successor. A seminal study of a few years earlier,[2] by Mr. J. W. F. Rowe, which handled the subject in a—for that period—unusually realistic way fell on stony ground. Only in the past few years have any conspicuous advances been made by American writers—particularly by Professor A. M. Ross of the University of California, to whose original work I am indeed myself much indebted.[3] In contemporary economic textbooks, however, on both sides of the Atlantic wage theory is still treated strictly as a 'special case of the general theory of value'.

This general theory has itself been constructed with the aid of elaborate artificial models. Indeed, so fascinating have these models proved that economic theory has been slow to emerge from

[1] Hicks, J. R., *The Theory of Wages* (London, Macmillan, 1932), p. 1.
[2] Rowe, J. W. F., *Wages in Practice and Theory* (London, Routledge, 1928).
[3] Particularly in his study of *Trade Union Wage Policy* (Berkeley, University of California Press, 1948).

11

dependence upon them: analysis of the working of these constructions has too long and too readily done duty for observation of the actual world of which they are a highly simplified image. Wage theory, in particular, has suffered very much from this inability to move forward from theoretical abstraction to concrete reality. As Professor Hicks, whose own work is itself extremely abstract in character, has justly remarked: 'A long road has to be travelled' before the 'abstract proposition' embodied in current wage theory 'can be used in the explanation of real events.'[1] In practice this road seems to have been not only long, but so exhausting that few travellers have attempted it.

The abstract models used in wage theory naturally share the characteristic features of the more comprehensive structure of which they are a part. In particular, they postulate a world of pure acquisition and of pure competition. The men and women who people this world are deemed to be free of all the bewildering complexity of human motivation which occupies the science of psychology. They respond instead to a single motive—the urge to get more money, or more of the things that money will buy. In this imaginary world, also, every employer bids against every other employer in the attempt to buy labour as cheaply as possible, while every worker competes with every other worker in the struggle to sell his labour on the best possible terms. This fairyland is indeed only a first approximation, the artificial nature of which is constantly emphasized; and the very language in which wage theories are expressed may help the student to keep this artificiality in mind. Thus, in the archaic vocabulary still in use even in studies of quite recent date, workers of all grades are commonly referred to as 'labourers'—although in common speech today this term is used only of those who have not attained more than a low level of skill. Nevertheless, innocent though these models are of any claim to representational accuracy, the fact that they are used as the point of departure has, as I hope to show, profoundly affected the conception of the real world that has resulted from their use.

In their classical—pre-Keynesian—shape, wage theories have also another characteristic in common with other branches of the general theory of value: they neglect the cumulative effect upon the whole economic system of any changes in the general wage-level or in the total volume of outlay. While a place is found for various forms of frictional unemployment, these theories take no heed of what has come to be known as the 'general' unemployment that results from insufficiency of public and private spending.

On this basis of competition-plus-acquisition-plus-substantially-full employment the parent theory of price or value branches, first,

[1] Hicks, *Theory of Wages*, p. 10.

into a general theory of distribution which seeks to explain the share appropriated by each of the various factors of production in the total output for the creation of which they are all jointly responsible; and, second, into specific theories of rent, interest, profits and wages dealing with the rewards of each of these factors in turn. Finally, the theory of wages is itself adapted to explain the wage and salary rates pertaining to particular occupations. For present purposes I propose to attempt a summary only of the later and more specific stages of this whole logical process: these are admirably elucidated in the first half of Professor Hicks' work.

This classical individualistic pre-Keynesian wage theory proceeds by a succession of orderly steps from one level of abstraction to another. At the first level we are required to assume that the available supply of labour (that is, either of 'labour' in general or of a particular class of 'labourers', according to the degree of specificity of the theory in question), is for the time being fixed. So also are both the number and the ardour of the potential employers of this labour force. In these conditions a central 'equilibrium' wage-rate emerges, defined as the figure at which supply and demand are equated. The term 'equilibrium' is appropriate inasmuch as, on the assumptions already indicated, if wages happen to have been fixed above this level, economic forces will operate to push them down to it; and if they happen to fall below this equilibrium figure, similar forces will drive them up to it again. The operative mechanism is supposed to function as follows. In the event that employers find themselves paying more than the rate that is in this sense appropriate to a given supply of labour, some workers will fail to find employment, just as goods remain unsold if they are priced too high. If, conversely, employers are offering less than the equilibrium rate, an unsatisfied demand for labour will appear, comparable to the unsatisfied demand of bargain-hunters who arrive too late. In that case, competition between employers bidding against one another in order to get hold of the limited supply of workers available is the force that pushes wages up to the point at which both demand and supply are neatly matched.

It should perhaps be added that, in the terminology of technical economic theory, this equilibrium rate of wages is said to be equal to the 'marginal product', or 'marginal net product', of the labour force available in the particular market involved. The 'price of labour', as Professor Samuelson puts it in a textbook published in 1948, is equal to the 'marginal cost of output × marginal product of labour'.[1] These are indeed highly elusive concepts: but they have played so

[1] Samuelson, P. A., *Economics* (New York, McGraw-Hill, 1948), p. 536.

large a part in economic thinking on the subject of wage determination that it does not seem right to leave them out of the picture altogether. Perhaps the best short interpretation would define the 'marginal net product' of any worker as equivalent to the difference that it would make to the total output of the industry in which he is employed, if his (but only his) labour were withdrawn. Theoretically, this quantity can be expressed in terms either of the physical product that is created by a man's work, or of the economic value of that product. In the present context, it is the latter that is relevant. Such a definition is admittedly a very rough and ready affair. To achieve real accuracy it would need to be hedged about by all sorts of qualifications as to the interchangeability of 'labourers', the constancy of methods of production and so forth. I can only hope that it is near enough to the mark to give a tolerable idea of the basic notions contained in classical wage theory. What that theory is really trying to say is, it would seem, that in a fully competitive market people tend to get out of the productive process just about what they put into it. Readers who would like something more refined will find their needs abundantly catered for in any of the works to which reference has already been made.

At the next stage we have to remove the dual assumptions that both the supply of labour and the demand for it are fixed. They now become variable items. The demand for labour (or, alternatively, for any specific class of labour), is liable, for instance, to be increased or diminished by factors which are external to the present theory, and must, for the purposes of that theory, be taken as given. A rearmament programme will, for example, increase the demand for the skills of trained engineers. Increased demand, as everyone knows, spells rising prices. We must therefore expect the wages of these engineers to rise, until a new equilibrium rate is reached which is appropriate to the new intensity of demand. Conversely, a change in the conditions of supply, such as an influx of new workers into any labour market, will tend to bring wages down: things are cheap when they are plentiful, and increased supply means a new and lower point of equilibrium.

All this is very simple; and very close, it may be added, to common experience. The parallel, too, with movements in the prices of commodities will be apparent to everybody. Labour, like other things, goes up in price when it is in much demand, and falls in value as it becomes more abundant. One peculiarity, however, which the price of labour shares with some, but by no means all, commodities, needs to be noted at this stage. The demand for many kinds of labour, other than personal services, is an indirect one, in the sense that it is derived from the demand for the things that that labour makes, or helps to make. Moira Shearer's dancing is prized (as is also a basket of strawberries) for its own sake. The same is not, however, true of the services of riveters; these are required, not for themselves, but as a derivative of the demand for ships. This peculiarity, as will appear later, assumes great importance with the development of what is known today as economic planning.[1]

At the next step, we become aware of the essentially circular nature of all economic theory. This circularity, incidentally, is what makes economics so difficult to present intelligibly: you cannot understand any part of it unless you have already understood the rest. In the case of wage theory the circle leads from movements in the demand for, or supply of, labour to wage changes, and from wage changes back again to further movements in demand and supply. Thus a rise in the remuneration of any occupation will (subject always to our original assumptions) tend to attract additional workers into the calling that is lucky enough to have received that rise; and a decline in wages will discourage entrants and may even cause some of the workers affected to look for other jobs. In terms of the customary parable (which does not, incidentally, support the common assumption that the donkey is a stupid animal) larger carrots will attract more donkeys and *vice versa*.

In this way the theory of wages (again in common with the theory of prices of which it is a sub-variety) neatly serves a double purpose. On the one hand it purports to explain why workers earn what they do; and on the other hand it demonstrates a mechanism for directing workers from one part of the economic system to another. This again is a matter which can, as will appear later, become very formidable in the real world—particularly in a world which is committed to extensive economic planning.

The logical conclusion of this analysis is that the wages, or at least the net rewards, of all occupations are constantly driven towards a common level. In competitive conditions 'labour tends to move into the industries which are paying the higher wages, until the wage-rate is the same in all industries'.[2] Strictly speaking, 'net rewards' or some similar expression is more accurate than 'wages', since (at least in the economic textbooks—but see below pp. 39–51) the attraction of a higher money wage may be counterbalanced by such drawbacks as long hours, or dirty or dangerous conditions of work. The attractive (or repulsive) power, to prospective employees, of two jobs carrying unequal rates of wages will, it is presumed, be identical only if the

<hr>

[1] See below, pp. 105, 158.
[2] Meade, J. E., *Economic Analysis and Policy*, 2nd ed. (London, Oxford University Press, 1937), p. 212.

higher wage in the better-paid just compensates for the more objectionable conditions of work which it involves; and it is admitted that people cannot move indiscriminately at short notice from one job to another throughout the whole length and breadth of the economic system. The equalizing process is therefore liable to be much obstructed. A particular worker may be congenitally incapable of acquiring the skills required in the better-paid jobs or unable to pay for the necessary training; ignorance and inertia must also be reckoned with. But from Adam Smith to the mid-twentieth-century textbooks, the formal presentation is with few exceptions the same. Actual wage differentials are represented as the result, so to speak, of a thwarted drive towards absolute equality.

The logic of this mode of argument cannot be gainsaid. But the result is odd. One after another the economists are at pains to explain the absence of equality to a world which (*pace* George Bernard Shaw) would have found its presence both improper and astonishing. Such an approach to the subject gives a curious air of unreality to the whole discussion. Rivers press against their banks and indeed occasionally burst them, but geographers do not on this account feel obliged to begin by explaining why all land is not perpetually flooded: the flow of water and the configuration of the river bed are both facts of experience which have an equal right to the attention of anyone who is concerned to present the whole picture. By contrast, the economists select one element in the picture, namely, the equalizing process, giving this logical priority, whilst all other elements are relegated to the secondary role of interferences. The resulting distortion must be ascribed to the method of deductive argument from simplified psychological premises which is traditional in economic theory. It would not, I think, occur to anyone whose theories were constructed on observation of the real world to write as though there would be nothing remarkable in a situation in which 'the wage rate in all industries was the same'; or to approach the study of wage determination from a presumption that bishops and road-sweepers should normally enjoy equal remuneration.

II

Traditional wage theory, like other classical economic doctrines, is essentially individualistic. At least at the initial level of abstraction it allows no place for collective bargaining. At a later stage, however, it is generally adapted in such a way as to take account also of trade union activity.

The simplest way of doing this is to treat the unions—or, on the other side, any combinations of employers—as examples of 'monopolistic organization'. A union (which must of course control the entry to the trade which it represents) is portrayed as a seller of labour enjoying a monopolistic position. The transition from individual to collective bargaining then becomes exactly parallel to the transition in general price theory from competitive to monopolistic conditions. On this basis the argument can proceed as follows. A monopolist cannot by-pass the rule that there is only one price at which demand and supply will balance: but, since he is in a position to control supply, he can weigh the relative attractions of selling a large output at a low price per unit, or a small output at a high price; and he will choose whichever he reckons likely to prove the more profitable course. Similarly a union which demands wages above the competitive level 'will not in general or for long be able to demand also that all its members shall be employed'.[1] In this case also higher prices will restrict demand.

From this point onwards, however, the parallel begins to become a little shaky; and wage theories which take account of collective bargaining lose the beautiful simplicity of the competitive classical models on to which they are grafted. The monopolist proper pursues his own economic interest with the same undeviating constancy as any other figure in the economic textbooks. But the economists never seem to have had quite the same confidence as to the line that trade unions should be presumed to follow. In consequence, from the point at which they are extended to include collective as well as individual bargaining, wage theories become both more variable and more hypothetical. Different hypotheses are featured by different authors.

One of the most elaborate versions, and one which involves an exceptionally determined effort to interpret the activities of both trade unions and employers' organizations in the strictly acquisitive terms characteristic of economic theory, is made by Professor Hicks, who abandons the assumption of a strictly competitive labour market rather more than half-way through his book. According to this theory, both union policies and employers' responses to these are determined by a nice calculation of the costs of the stoppage of work which is the presumed alternative to winning (or conceding) an advance in wages. Thus, from the employers' angle, the higher the wage demanded the greater the cost of the concession: on the other hand the longer the threatened strike, the greater the inducement to give way. On this

[1] Eastham, J. K., *An Introduction to Economic Analysis* (London, English Universities Press, 1950), p. 207.

basis it is possible to 'construct a schedule of wages and lengths of strike, setting opposite to each period of stoppage the highest wage an employer will be willing to pay rather than endure a stoppage of that period'. This is called the 'employer's concession schedule'. Meanwhile the unions are similarly engaged in balancing the cost of a strike against the loss involved in foregoing part of their claims. 'The length of time they are prepared to stand out will vary according to the prospect of gain from doing so.' The unions thus work on a 'resistance schedule' corresponding to the concession schedule on the other side of the table. These two schedules are then translated into curves and the point of intersection of these indicates the 'highest wage which skilful negotiation can extract from the employer'. To insist on more than this means embarking on a strike which will cost more than the wage advances for which it is incurred. To accept less means foregoing an additional rise which could in fact have been won without a strike.

If both parties understood all this clearly (and if, it may be added, their forecasts as to the length and cost of a stoppage were correct), there need never be any strikes at all: both parties are better off without them. Professor Hicks does, however, readily admit that negotiations are conducted in the dark, without the aid of either the telepathy or the precognition which the effective application of his analysis would require. Union leaders, in particular, are under pressure from their supporters to set their sights high, with the result that they may well get into the position of being 'forced to carry out their threat of striking, when more favourable terms could have been got without the sacrifice entailed by the strike'.

But in any event, the unions, in Professor Hicks' view, are wasting their time. The final chapters of his book lead with relentless deductive logic to the conclusion that the regulation of wages either by collective bargaining or by statutory measures is a self-defeating process. The marginal productivity theory is bound to win in the end. According to that theory, the payment of wages higher than those that would have prevailed in a competitive market leads inevitably to unemployment in the industry concerned. For a number of reasons this unemployment may be slow to make its appearance; and that makes it easier for the unions to persuade themselves that such unemployment is due to the inefficiency of employers, to labour-saving machinery or to trade depression, rather than to their own misguided wage policies.

Nor are the supposedly disastrous effects of these policies confined to the particular industry in which the wages have been forced above the competitive level. 'We can then prove conclusively that an all-round rise in wages must cause unemployment (apart, again, from reactions on the efficiency of labour) by supposing it does not, and then proving the continuance of such a situation to be impossible.' For present purposes it is perhaps not necessary to follow the highly theoretical analysis which purports to establish this dismal proposition, since this has subsequently been much discredited by the Keynesian theory of employment. It is, however, relevant to note that one of the few works on wage theory published by a leading British economist reached the conclusion that the activities of trade unions must be either futile or deleterious to their members. Certainly, as the author himself remarked in his final paragraph, 'the Theory of Wages, as elaborated in this book, has not proved a cheerful subject . . .'[1]

As Mr. J. W. R. Rowe had already pointed out four years before Professor Hicks' book appeared, a theory 'which denies any real or permanent effect to the development or influence of collective bargaining' is repugnant to common sense, though it might, of course, none the less turn out to be true. Mr. Rowe's approach to this subject is unique, and his book has a pioneering value, in that he works back from an empirical study of wage movements in five selected industries to a reconsideration of wage theories which have themselves been formulated without any reference to any empirical data at all. At the end of this journey, the central theme of the classical analysis in terms of productivity stands more or less unscathed. 'The ordinary trade unionist knows well enough that if wages are raised by more than a certain amount, there will be increased unemployment, no matter how strong his union may be.' Nevertheless, Mr. Rowe finds that 'trade unionism has been a yeast which has altered the whole shape and nature of the loaf'. In his view what is wrong with the classical analysis is that it fails to take account of the strength and multiplicity of the specific factors peculiar to each industry which emerge in great force from his own factual studies. Indeed he is led to question 'whether there can be one all-embracing theory of wages, which will sufficiently satisfy our sense of reality, and stand the test of historical experience'. 'The general theory should be relegated to its proper position as a background. At present if this is done, the stage is empty, and therefore the economist in an attempt at self-justification, too often yields to temptation, and presents marionettes cut out from this background, in place of living actors. It is now the turn of the theatre to be empty, though even marionette shows are instructive up to a point! The proper function for general wage theories is to furnish the background, and as such they perform an essential

[1] Hicks, *Theory of Wages*, pp. 141–4, 186, 232.

service and wield a vitally important influence.' In so far as he is prepared to commit himself to any general conclusions, Mr. Rowe suggests that trade unions do succeed in forcing up wages even above the equilibrium level largely because their demands are one of the best mechanisms for goading employers into using more efficient methods. In this way the unemployment, which in static conditions of production would result from an advance of wages above the competitive level, can be avoided. Mr. Rowe does not, however, claim that, in the light of his own investigations alone, this result should be treated as more than a likely hypothesis. He finds some support for it, both positively and negatively, in the history of the building, coal-mining, cotton textile, railway and engineering industries with which his story is concerned. But the fact that stands out most conspicuously from his review is the tremendous influence of custom and convention upon the wage structure of certain industries, particularly (amongst his own selection) in building and in the cotton industry. In these instances, at least, it appears not so much that the unions have succeeded in levering up both their own wages and their employers' efficiency, as that they might have done so had their attitudes been less conservative. To this question of the role of convention in wage determination we shall have occasion to recur.

It is to be observed that no direct conflict arises between the ultimate theoretical assumptions of Professor Hicks on the one hand and Mr. Rowe on the other. The difference between them is rather that which distinguishes a dynamic from a static approach to the subject. Both agree that in static conditions an increase of wages above the marginal productivity level tends to create unemployment in the industry affected. But Mr. Rowe, having looked at some at least of the relevant facts, takes the matter one stage nearer reality by observing that in practice relevant conditions are not at all likely to remain static; and that they will indeed be propelled into movement by the very fact of this disparity between wage-rates and productivity. While harmony can thus be re-established at the ultimate theoretical level, the practical morals to which the two authors are led differ widely. In contrast with the melancholy nihilism of Professor Hicks, Mr. Rowe concludes that the practice of trade unions is not to equate wages with marginal productivity, but 'to *increase* the marginal productivity of labour by reinforcing competition as a spur to progress'.[1]

Unhappily, little attempt has subesquently been made to validate Mr. Rowe's hypothesis. As has already been said, both theoretical and realistic studies of the subject have been rare indeed: Professor

[1] Rowe, *Wages in Practice & Theory*, pp. 192–9, 228. Italics original.

Lionel Robbins' comment that 'a profound unease and uncertainty dominates the work of the later Classical Economists when they are confronted with the problem of workers' combinations' is no over-statement.[1] The main shock which traditional wage theories have suffered in the past twenty years has come from another quarter, and was administered by the late Lord Keynes in the publication of his *General Theory of Employment, Interest and Money* in 1936; and this Keynesian revolution has been much more severe in its impact upon theories of the general level of wages than upon those relating to the rates paid in particular industries or occupations. In the classical models, the treatment both of the general wage level and of the for-tunes of individual industries followed exactly the same pattern. Wage-rates as a whole are determined by the demand for, and the supply of, labour as a whole; and under competitive conditions they will constantly be driven towards the figure at which this demand and supply are equated—a figure which is itself a measure of that extremely elusive conception, the marginal productivity of the whole labour force comprising everybody from the Lords of Appeal to the labourers in the gas-works. In exactly the same way each individual calling has its own equilibrium rate, which in turn equates demand and supply in that particular trade, and again reflects the marginal productivity of that particular class of workers. In the post-Keynesian era this parallel breaks down and the general theory of wages becomes circular in a new sense. It now appears that an increase in the general level of wages is as likely to be a cure as a cause of unemployment—at least in circumstances in which for some reason or other there are unused resources lying idle. Doubt is cast upon the 'simple notion of some kind of elastic-demand schedule for labour, which we have seen lay at the heart of the traditional theory of wages, with its corollary that a rise in the level of money-wages would inevitably result in a con-traction of employment'. The argument involved is in the highest degree intricate, but, as is now fairly well known, the upshot of it is that the notion, so long frowned upon by economists—that spending, even spending by wage-earners, is good for trade—has suddenly enjoyed a complete rehabilitation.

The effect of this revolution is summarized by Mr. M. H. Dobb in the 1946 revision of his textbook on *Wages* (first published in 1927) in the phrase 'the confident pessimism of early economists is gone'. What has taken the place of that pessimism is not, however, quite so clear. 'Are we left,' Mr. Dobb continues, 'only with a halting agnosticism, which can neither forecast nor understand? Can we see

[1] Robbins, L., *The Theory of Economic Policy* (London, Macmillan, 1952), p. 110.

no more pattern to the labour market than a disordered tumble of warring forces?' Mr. Dobb does not himself regard such a sceptical conclusion as unavoidable. On the contrary, he suggests that 'even when we are dealing with the general level of wages and with a long-run perspective, we know that there are definite limits within which the course of wages must lie'. This lower limit he then defines as that of 'bare physical subsistence': the 'general wage-level is unlikely to fall for long below' this level. The upper limit, is, however, rather more elusive. The total wage bill, Mr. Dobb suggests, cannot absorb more than the total product which at any moment is actually spent by property-owners; for, should it rise above this level, wages would eat into the supply of capital. This, at least, fixes the ceiling in strictly economic terms. But the practical limit is likely to be lower than this and to be 'more a matter of politics and social psychology than it is a matter for economic theory'.[1]

Mr. Rowe's doubts as to the possibility of constructing one all-embracing theory of wages have thus been reinforced from quite a new quarter. Thanks to an ironic twist of fortune, however, the Keynesian theory of general unemployment burst upon the world only a few years before the beginning of a prolonged epoch of virtually full employment in Britain and many other industrial countries. The classical economists' assumption that all resources are fully utilized, which Lord Keynes criticized as unrealistic, suddenly became more nearly true than, except for very short periods, it had ever been before. In the first instance it was the war which brought reality into line with the pre-Keynesian economic textbooks; though it may well be the practical application by governments of the lessons which Lord Keynes taught which has subsequently kept it there. So long, however, as full, or nearly full, employment continues, a general wage theory which presumes the existence of unused resources is clearly irrelevant. For any such general theory we must, therefore, revert to the pre-Keynesian classical model, thus re-establishing the analogy between the factors that fix the general level of wages (at the point of equivalence to the marginal productivity of the whole labour force) with those which similarly determine the remuneration in specific industries or occupations.

In any case, theories of *relative* wages can and do proceed virtually without regard to the Keynesian revolution. The boomerang effects of wage movements in one particular occupation upon the total purchasing power of the community, and through this upon the level of economic activity, can generally be neglected: they will not ordinarily be large enough to make any significant difference. In

[1] Dobb, M., *Wages*, revised ed. (Cambridge University Press, 1946), pp. 147–51.

the treatment of specific wage theory, therefore, the traditional mixture of the laws of demand and supply, the direct relationship between the wage-rate and the volume of employment, even the perpetual, though inhibited, drive towards equality, can be repeated as before. And that, in fact, is more or less the line of analysis that we find prescribed in the most recent economic textbooks—though mixed with a large, and perhaps increasing, dose of uncertainty as to the actual effect of collective bargaining upon the theoretical models originally designed to illustrate competitive conditions.

Mr. J. K. Eastham, for instance, follows an orthodox exposition of competitive theory with a brief discussion of the possible consequences of monopolistic organization on either the employers' or the workers' side. Thus, in the event of an employer enjoying 'some element of monopoly as a buyer of labour', it is 'not necessary that the marginal cost of labour will be equal to the wage-rate, as it is in a competitive labour market'. Such an employer will, moreover, probably employ less labour than would a 'similar-sized unit selling its product and buying its labour in competitive markets'. Conversely, a trade union may (though it does not necessarily follow that it will) 'exploit' either the employers of its members, or, more probably, the consuming public; though (thanks to the laws of demand and supply) a union will only succeed in making such policies effective if it has a strict control of entry into the occupation of its members. Mr. Eastham adds a passing reference to the contention, which plays so large a part in Mr. Rowe's discussion, that union pressure 'forces employers to keep abreast of technical developments'. His main contribution to the subject is to be found, however, in the emphasis which he lays upon the equalizing effect of union policies within any particular occupation. 'The market for labour is so sectionalized and so full of elements of monopoly that the tendency to equality of payment to workers of the same type would hardly be very strong in the absence of trade unions. Indeed, trade unions probably have the effect of introducing equality of wages where differences in marginal productivities would otherwise exist.'[1] Further, unions may break down local differentiation by insisting upon a uniform rate for a specific job throughout the country; and the equalizing effect of their activity is apparent also in their disregard of differences in the capacity of individual workers, all of whom must, without discrimination, be paid at the union rate.

Professor Alec Cairncross in a textbook planned before the war, but not published till 1944, follows much the same lines. Once more the point of departure is the need to explain both what determines the share

[1] Eastham, *Economic Analysis*, pp. 206-9.

of labour in the total national product, and 'why' (not how) 'do wages differ in different places and occupations?' Professor Cairncross's treatment of the latter topic is orthodox. Collective bargaining is left out of the picture in the first round, which follows traditional lines, postulating a theoretical trend towards equality obstructed by many practical obstacles. This author is, moreover, emphatic that it is the 'net advantages', not just the monetary remuneration, of each occupation in each place that tend to equality; and he is realistic about the difficulties which in fact prevent workers from moving from less to more advantageous occupations. Moreover, he allows for the occasional intrusion of non-economic motives into a world which is generally innocent of any but an acquisitive psychology. 'It would be a travesty of the facts to suggest that in the middle of a wage dispute employers pack their bags and go off for a round of golf by the seaside while their workers brood over an empty larder and their common wrongs.'

In Professor Cairncross's view, the introduction of collective bargaining into this picture exposes wage-rates to a new influence, namely, 'the strength of the organizations of workers and employers'. He is at pains to remind us, however, that it must not be assumed that employers will necessarily use their combined strength to depress wages to the lowest possible level. Even on grounds of self-interest, 'low-paid labour is often the dearest labour'. At the same time the 'self-interest of employers is hardly the best guarantee of high wages'. The workers therefore look to their own organizations to get them higher wages shorter hours and better factory amenities—as well as to improve their 'sense of status'. Professor Cairncross describes the unions' pursuit of these ends mainly in terms of the economic theory of monopolistic behaviour: the tendency of many trade union rules is 'plainly monopolistic', and these rules are 'generally pushed beyond the point at which they are in the social interest'. Further, 'if trade unions stick out for high wages over the whole field of industry, they may restrict the volume of employment, exactly as a monopolist restricts his output of goods, and may achieve a high standard of living for those who continue in employment, quite as much at the expense of those who fail to get employment as at the expense of employers as a class'.

It is important to notice that Professor Cairncross does not think that this fear of creating general unemployment will in practice deter a particular union from pressing for higher wages. At the same time he holds that the bargaining power of unions in any given industry is limited by three factors which are old friends to those who are familiar with economic analysis, namely, the elasticity of substitution, the elasticity of supply of alternative instruments of production, and the elasticity of demand. The combined effect of these three factors, translated into the simplest possible terms, is that, if wage claims are pushed too far, employers will dispense with labour by increased mechanization, though the rate at which this happens will depend upon the speed with which the supplies necessary for alternative methods can be obtained. The public also in its turn may find a substitute for any article the price of which is much enhanced by increased wages. In the end, Professor Cairncross concludes that unions are seldom able to squeeze their employers effectively. 'The fact is that wage disputes have comparatively little effect on the distribution of the National Income between capital and labour; they are much more likely to settle the distribution of the wage-bill between one section of labour and another, or between one industry and another. In the last analysis an increase in wages in one industry represents a levy on other industries and on the general consumer.'[1] In the hands of this author, the theory of wages certainly makes more frequent contacts with reality than are visible in the pages of Professor Hicks; but it cannot be said that it proves a conspicuously more cheerful subject.

Professor Meade, in the work already quoted, does not treat the effect of collective bargaining upon wages as a separate topic at all: his discussion of relative wage movements in a competitive market conforms closely to the standard model of economic theory. This discussion is, however, followed by a brief reference to the fact that 'the earnings of labour may vary in different occupations because of the existence of monopolistic conditions', as in the case in which a union bars the entry into a well-paid occupation. The centre of Professor Meade's particular interest lies in the relation between wages and the general level of employment, a subject which he treats mainly along Keynesian lines. The key to this relationship he finds in the distinction between real and money wage-rates, the former being the critically important factor in this context. The effect of the whole argument, which is a decidedly complex one, is substantially to maintain the equivalence between the marginal product of labour and the wage-rate, together with the inverse relationship between wages and employment, with the difference only that this marginal product must be reckoned in real, not in monetary, terms. 'Whether a reduction in the money wage-rate will cause an increase in employment depends upon whether it will cause the real wage-rate to fall.' For a number of highly technical reasons Professor Meade thinks it

[1] Cairncross, A., *Introduction to Economics* (London, Butterworth, 1944), pp. 236, 245–50.

3

'better not to rely on reducing money wage-rates' as a stimulus to employment: direct banking action of an inflationary nature is to be preferred, if only because it is likely to be quicker. At the same time we are led to the conclusion that 'Trade Unions and Trade Boards in regulating money wage-rates should not attempt to increase employment by increasing money wage-rates in the belief that this increases purchasing power. This view is fallacious.'[1]

Finally, from the other side of the Atlantic, Professor Samuelson, in a textbook that is widely used both in this country and in the USA, well illustrates the considerable dose of scepticism that the rise of collective bargaining has infused into traditional theories. Of the 600 pages to which Professor Samuelson's volume runs, two are devoted specifically to the question: 'Can Trade-Unions Raise Wages?' How to reach an understanding of the institutional forces which determine the absolute and the relative shares of labour and other factors in the national income is, as Professor Samuelson remarks, one of the most important problems of our age. 'Yet we must confess that there is no satisfactory body of economic principles that tells us a great deal about this subject. . . . The old view that artificial interferences with the order of nature cannot affect wages has long been abandoned. The opposite view that the average income of the working class depends only upon the militance and political power of trade unions is probably equally extreme and unacceptable. Within limits, real wages can be affected by the process of collective bargaining. But, although no-one can define the exact nature of these limits, they are nevertheless real.'[2] 'Limitation of space' unfortunately prevents Professor Samuelson from exploring 'this important, thorny question'; and he therefore contents himself with a few paragraphs classifying the economic policies, such as restriction of numbers and pressure for wage advances in particular numbers which are commonly employed by the unions.

From this short summary of the work of contemporary economists it would seem that no new comprehensive theory has emerged to take the place of the classical model in which wage theory is treated as a branch of the more general theory of prices. Just as price theory, originally designed to explain purely competitive conditions, has been suitably modified to take account, where necessary, of the presence of elements of monopoly, so, in exactly parallel fashion, has a competitive theory of wages been adapted in order to accommodate, also under the heading of monopoly, the new factors associated with the rise of collective bargaining. At the same time, while economists

[1] Meade, *Economic Analysis*, pp. 214, 69–73.
[2] Samuelson, *Economics*, pp. 529–30.

are still reluctant to admit that the labour market is 'only a disordered tumble of warring forces' or to deny the possibility of any all-embracing theory, 'halting agnosticism' has clearly left its mark.

In these circumstances it would seem appropriate to attempt some assessment of theory against fact. The standing of a theory which explains wage structure in terms of a continual pressure towards equality of net advantages in all occupations, obstructed only by the practical difficulties of mobility, or by monopolistic manœuvres, must in the end be judged by the measure in which these phenomena are perceptible in the real world. If some fairly close approximation to equality can be detected in broadly similar types of employment in a given area; if non-monetary advantages are found to vary inversely with pecuniary rewards; and if the degree of unionization is patently associated with superior economic advantage, such a theory will rank as at best a good starting-point. If, on the other hand, these phenomena are completely submerged by the obstructive factors or 'frictions', as the economists like to call them, it might be better to begin at the other end, and to treat those factors as the primary determinants of wage-rates rather than as tiresome accidentals blurring the outline of a theory constructed to explain conditions which are free from such disturbances.

CHAPTER II

Some Economic Curiosities of British Wage Structure

I

THE investigator who wishes to test current economic theories (or indeed any other theories) against an outline of the wage and salary structure of this country quickly runs into serious difficulty owing to lack of appropriate data. Part of this difficulty springs from the universal experience that on no subject are reliable statistics available to meet the needs of every inquirer. Part is inherent in the nature of the particular material—as, for example, in the complicated system on which many wage payments are computed, or the wide variations in earnings where workers are paid by results; and part is due, I think, to a more fundamental social factor which deserves closer examination.

In contemporary industrial society a deep reticence pervades the whole subject; and this is particularly marked at the upper end of the income scale. According to the prevailing code, a man's income is one of his private economic parts: reference to it is subject to a powerful social taboo. Many personal questions on such matters as marital status, family responsibility or voting behaviour in a secret ballot may be asked of comparative strangers, either in casual conversation or in the course of social surveys; but a conversational inquiry into even a close acquaintance's income would be extremely rude; and in surveys the subject has to be approached with special tact. Letters from banks containing statements of their clients' accounts (but not necessarily other correspondence) are marked 'private' as a matter of course, as are all communications from the Inland Revenue authorities. In some offices where interdepartmental communications are normally unsealed, it is usual to make an exception for anything relating to salaries. (In one case that came to my notice only the privacy of monthly-paid staff was thus respected, details of the incomes of the weekly wage-earners being left open to the eyes of the curious.)

There are, it is true, national variations in the strength of this taboo. In Sweden personal income-tax returns are accessible to the public and are, I am told, read with avidity. In the United States the candidates in the 1952 Presidential election made history by publishing details of their incomes for a number of previous years—but only, it would seem, in order to dispel rumours of corrupt practices. The American evangelist, Billy Graham, is reported to have said of his own salary that 'It is a personal matter, and I believe even a minister is entitled to that much privacy.'[1] In Britain members of the University of Glasgow who tried to ascertain what sort of people the local Parliamentary candidates in the 1950 General Election were, found that, though they had little difficulty in getting details about occupations, education, family circumstances or age, yet when it came to income, 'In a few cases candidates gave their actual income figures, but in most cases they gave a general classification, which tended to vary in standard according to the views of the person concerned.'[2] In this country sensitivity is indeed both widespread and widely respected. Exceptions are few. The requirement that all moneys provided by Parliament must be publicly accounted for prevents any secrecy about the salaries of even the highest grade of civil servants, or of the judiciary, while for similar reasons, the ratepayer also (though at the cost of somewhat more trouble) can discover how much is paid to officials whose salaries are chargeable to the rates; nor is the remuneration of the higher dignitaries of the Established Church hidden under any bushel. But, once one travels beyond employments that are public in the narrowest sense, a pall descends; and this thickens progressively as one moves towards the private sphere of enterprise.

Some even of the nationalized industries, for instance, which might be supposed to have a public duty to be frank, are highly sensitive, especially about the higher ranges of salaries: only the remuneration of the members of their governing boards is necessarily public knowledge, since this, even if paid out of the industry's revenues, is determined by Parliament. Thus it is 'contrary to the practice' of the Bank of England to divulge details of the salaries paid to its employees. British Railways are relatively open about salaries up to about £800, these being covered by the Railway Staff National Tribunal's decisions: the rest is silence. By contrast, the National Coal Board in its Report for 1947 disclosed salary ranges up to £4,000, but this is unusual. In both the Gas and the Electricity industries, negotiating

---

[1] Quoted by Louis Hofferbert in 'Meet Billy Graham', *The Sunday Companion* (27 March 1954). St. Paul was apparently also of the same opinion. See 1 Corinthians, ix, 11: If we have sowed you the seeds of spiritual good, is it a great matter if we reap your worldly goods?' (Moffat translation.)

[2] Chrimes, S. B., ed., *The General Election in Glasgow: February 1950* (Glasgow Jackson, 1950), pp. 39–40.

machinery for staffs with salaries above £1,000 a year has been established, and it is understood that agreements are likely to be negotiated. At least one of the unions concerned favours an open policy, but it is too early to say what will be the attitude of other unions or of the corporations themselves.

The salaries paid by the BBC were examined by the Beveridge Committee on Broadcasting. In the evidence submitted by the Corporation to that Committee salary scales reaching up to £1,950 per annum in 1949 were included, together with examples of actual posts at various grades; and these were published by the Committee.[1] During the currency of the Charter which expired at the end of 1951, the Corporation acted under instructions contained in the Government's White Paper on Broadcasting Policy, which laid down that, while the Corporation 'is not rigidly bound to relate the salaries and conditions of employment of its permanent staff to those ruling in the Civil Service, it should, in fixing such salaries and conditions, pay proper regard to those of the Civil Service and to the greater security offered by employment in a Public Corporation, as compared with employment in most business concerns'.[2] The legal status of this direction was, however, somewhat anomalous, since it was contained only in a Government statement of policy, and not in either the Charter or the Licence and Agreement with the Postmaster General, which are the two governing instruments of the BBC; nor did it impose any obligation on the Corporation to tell the world in what way this 'proper regard' for Civil Service scales was interpreted. In the 1952 White Paper, the instruction was modified to read as follows: 'In fixing the salaries and conditions of the staff the BBC should take account of the Government's general policy on wages and kindred matters.'[3] This formula, however, also found no place in either the Charter or the Licence Agreement of 1952, and its force is, therefore, moral rather than legal.

The question whether the higher salaries paid by the BBC ought to be publicly disclosed was argued by the Broadcasting Committee in the following terms: 'We discussed with the Governors of the Corporation whether there was good reason for not informing the public about these salaries' (of employees whose maxima exceeded £2,000 a year). 'After full consideration we have come to the conclusion that the desire of the Governors not to make individual salary figures in

---

[1] The Broadcasting Committee, 1949, *Appendix to Report*, Cmd. 8117 (1951), pp. 118–24.

[2] Quoted in *Report of the Broadcasting Committee, 1949*, Cmd. 8116 (1951), p. 132.

[3] *Broadcasting*, Memorandum on the Report of the Broadcasting Committee, 1949, Cmd. 8550 (1952), para. 37.

the highest grades public property is justified in the interests of the work of the Corporation. There is, indeed, no valid ground why a Director or Controller in the BBC as an individual should object to having his salary figure known, any more than the Permanent Secretary of a Government Department or a Lord of Appeal can object'; but, in the view of the Beveridge Committee, the BBC had not yet reached the stage at which rates are firmly related to jobs and not 'liable to adjustment according to the experience or standing of the holder'. The Committee concluded, however, with a hint that secrecy might not, in their view, always be in the public interest: 'It is possible that in considering information to be prescribed in future Annual Reports by the BBC . . . the appropriate Minister might consider that more detailed information as to higher salaries was necessary and justified . . .'[1]

In a number of other cases, public corporations are willing to allow responsible inquirers to see copies of the agreements made with their salaried staffs, but ask that the contents should not be published without the consent of both the corporation and the trade unions concerned. From time to time advertisements also appear in the Press for posts in the nationalized industries carrying salaries up to £2,000 p.a. or even more; though it does not of course follow that all such vacancies are advertised.

In private employment, secrecy is even stricter. A few large corporations (the Big Five banks, for instance) have no objection to divulging the salaries of their lower-paid staffs, but everything over a certain maximum (seldom above £1,000 p.a.) is generally treated as strictly confidential.[2] The business world in general is indeed a desert area for data about executive salaries, especially in the higher reaches. Even Press advertisements are apt to be very reticent, 'salary according to qualification and experience' being a much more usual formula than a definite figure. Thus out of 1,152 posts advertised in *The Times* in one week of each month in the twelve months ending 31 August 1950 (excluding public appointments, and advertisements by agencies, or for posts in domestic work or clubs, for articled clerks, or for jobs paid solely on a commission basis), only 228 or just over 19% quoted any salary figure.

To a limited extent this secrecy has been broken down by the growth of collective bargaining: but only to a limited extent. Collective

[1] Cmd. 8116, para. 449.

[2] Misrepresentation is, however, one way to break down reticence. In a letter to the *Economist* of 29 November 1952, Mr. Manning Dacey was stung into greater frankness by an alleged under-statement of bank salaries in a recently published book. 'Many branch managers' in the Big Five banks, he wrote, 'are paid £2,000 or more.'

bargaining is a step, though often a small one, in the direction of easier publicity. Undoubtedly the negotiating machinery that has been set up to settle the remuneration of auxiliary medical professions in the National Health Service has been the means both of regularizing these salaries and of bringing them into the light. Similarly, since the practice of collective bargaining in local government has crept up the social scale right up to the salaries of Town Clerks and Chief Officers, the facts about the remuneration even of the most responsible officers travel more easily than they once did from one authority to another.

The existence of a collective contract, however, is not itself incompatible with considerable reticence: that is apparent from the attitude of some of the public corporations. Indeed, the processes of negotiation are themselves often hampered by the need to respect secrecy, since this prevents publication of data which might support a decision or strengthen a case. Thus the Committee which reported in 1952 on the remuneration of professional accountants in the Civil Service expressed themselves as satisfied that the scales which they proposed were 'fairly related to those obtaining outside the Civil Service as well as in it'; but they could give no evidence in support of this view since their information about outside rates had been obtained 'often under promise of strict secrecy as regards its origin and content'.[1] The parallel Committee concerned with the pay of the Works Group of professional civil servants reported that they too had obtained information 'from Nationalized Industry, Large Scale Industry and Local Government',[2] but none of this information appeared in their report. The (Chorley) Committee on Higher Civil Service Remuneration[3] recorded that 'most of the information we have had about the rates paid to the staffs' of nationalized industries had been given in confidence, and the Committee had therefore to content themselves with quoting only figures relating to the members of the Boards of these industries, together with a few staff salaries disclosed by the National Coal Board.

A number of superficially reasonable explanations can be given for these reticences. There is, for instance, the natural desire of employers to avoid offering more than they need, or, alternatively, to pay different rates to employees engaged on substantially the same work. The latter temptation becomes particularly insistent in

[1] Committee on the Organization, Structure and Remuneration of the Professional Accountant Class in the Civil Service (1952), *Report*, para. 29.

[2] Committee on the Organization, Structure and Remuneration of the Works Group of Professional Civil Servants (1951), *Report*, para. 17.

[3] Committee on Higher Civil Service Remuneration, *Report*, Cmd. 7635 (1949), para. 23.

times of wage and salary inflation. At such times it is often possible to keep an old-established employee at a wage below the market-rate when it would be out of the question to engage a new one on those terms: many forms of inertia will keep a man in a job under conditions which he would not and need not accept once he has left or made up his mind to leave. Hence, when wages are on the move upwards, employers may have strong reasons for preventing their longer-established employees from knowing what those more lately engaged are getting.

Again, reluctance to disclose salaries in the higher reaches is often explained on the ground that these are fixed on an entirely personal basis. A bank (or for that matter almost any business) may be unwilling to quote the salary of its General Manager because this, it is suggested, depends so much upon who that General Manager is. In the more responsible employments—so the argument runs—the variation between what one man or another is worth is so great that no figure could be said to be representative.

Any fair judgement of the force of these arguments is hampered by the very secrecy which they are used to defend. Obviously so long as salaries cannot be disclosed because they are said to be personal, no one is in a position to say how personal they are. But in the light of what happens elsewhere, as well as of what can be seen on occasions when it is possible to peep behind the veil, it seems likely that the salaries paid, even at the higher levels, fall into categories, the limits of which are not less effective because they are not explicitly defined or even admitted; though in the present state of knowledge, even this is only a matter of guesswork. The fact, however, that the British Institute of Management has initiated a scheme under which business firms can exchange information, though on a confident.al basis, as to the salaries paid to their executives suggests that the notion of keeping in step is not entirely forgotten even at those levels.[1]

All in all, however, the current explanations of the prevailing reticence, no matter how good the logic behind them, hardly seem adequate to explain the strength of the resistance to frankness on this topic, nor the increase in its force as one travels up the income scale. The established social attitude to questions of personal economic status may well be a more significant sociological fact than is generally recognized. Indeed, the sociologist may be tempted to compare the secrecy which surrounds our attitude to income with that which invests matters of sexual behaviour; and to suggest that some at least of the forces at work may be much the same in the two

[1] *News Chronicle* (13 October 1952).

cases. For the customary reticence can hardly be explained away on the ground (which I have heard suggested) that income is too sordid and materialistic a matter to be a proper topic for polite conversation. Such an explanation is altogether beside the mark in a society in which the prices of goods, the fluctuations of stocks and shares, as well as betting, gambling and opportunities of money-making (realized or lost) are in fact staple subjects of general conversation. Indeed, it is often noticeable how conversations about money-making have to take circuitous routes in order to avoid explicit mention of personal income figures.

Guilt, fear and shame are, as a rule, the unexpressed forces behind taboos of secrecy: for there is no point in hiding anything if, in the popular sense, there is nothing to hide. The intimate connection of these emotions with sexual matters in societies that have inherited the traditions of Western Christianity will hardly be challenged in this age of Freud and Kinsey. Their possible association with matters of personal income, however, still awaits exploration by social psychologists and sociologists. Yet the structure of Western industrial society is such as might only too easily cause sentiments of guilt to become attached to this subject. That society is strongly acquisitive: it is characterized by an extremely unequal distribution of wealth, and by a hierarchical system of social prestige in which money plays a major role: its traditional religion blesses the meek and throws grave doubt upon the prospects of the rich in any life to come: its political philosophy is equalitarian and democratic. Here surely are conflicts enough to interest any psychologist! In a nominally Christian equalitarian culture, those who have a large share of the world's goods must inevitably feel guilty in face of those who have conspicuously less; for it is indeed difficult to square the economic and social inequalities of our culture with the Christian or the democratic doctrine that a man's worth should be measured more by what he is than by what he has.

The presence of a guilt-factor would moreover account for the fact that secrecy at the lower ranges of income is less strict than at higher levels. The lower-income groups (as they are now called in England) are also in the literal sense the under-privileged (as they are now called in the USA); and one of the privileges which these classes lack is the measure of privacy normally accorded to those more fortunately placed. Door-to-door inquiries dealing with such matters as personal saving and spending habits are more easily made in Whitechapel than in Mayfair. Since lower income implies also lesser social consequence, the taboo on income-disclosure is naturally less powerful at the lower end of the scale.

II

In terms of conventional economic theory these reticences have to be relegated to the miscellaneous category of 'frictions'—a procedure which hardly seems to do justice to their strength and persistence. But however their underlying social significances may be assessed, their total effect in restricting the available sources of information is considerable. Comparatively little is published, and private inquiries are apt to be unfruitful: data are either regretfully withheld, or are offered only on a confidential basis which precludes publication, and so inhibits their effective use.

In view of the social and economic importance of the subject, it is indeed astonishing how difficult it is to say with certainty how the rewards earned in different occupations compare with one another. Twice a year the Ministry of Labour publishes a review of earnings and hours in industry, covering the average earnings of more than 130 separate industrial groups classified into twenty main industries; while for coal-mining and railway services, which are excluded from the main series, a return is also made on closely similar lines. These earnings and hours figures (which cover workers paid by results as well as those on timework, and take account also of both overtime and short-time), are widely, if somewhat rashly, quoted as representing a sort of general working-class standard of income. They are, however, industrial, not occupational, figures: they tell us nothing about the earnings of particular categories such as shipwrights, carpet-weavers or bookbinders; and, as the Ministry repeatedly emphasizes, inter-industrial comparisons of these returns are very dangerous, owing to variations in the proportion of skilled and unskilled occupations in different industries: a high ranking in this series is as likely to mean that the industry concerned requires a large number of highly skilled workers as that the wages paid, at any given level of skill, are unusually lavish. It is, moreover, in keeping with the social distinctions of our time that although foremen as well as rank and file are included, office staffs, shop assistants, managers, clerks, commercial travellers and, in fact, black-coated workers generally, are omitted.

Alternatively, changes in *occupational* rates (in wage-earning but not as a rule in salaried jobs) which result from collective contracts, statutory orders and arbitration awards, are recorded by the Ministry in each month's issue of the *Labour Gazette*; and a selection from these forms the basis of the annual review published under the title *Time Rates of Wages and Hours of Labour*.[1] These figures relate,

---

[1] Subsequently referred to as *Time Rates*.

however, only to *rates*. From them we can learn what timeworkers in the occupations covered would earn if they worked a normal week without either overtime or short-time—which is often a very different matter from what they actually did earn in any given week or over the average of a number of weeks. All those who are paid by results (estimated in 1953 at about 29% of the adult male and 42% of the adult female workers covered by the Ministry's earnings and hours returns)[1] are necessarily omitted. Since, moreover, the material upon which these returns are based is voluntarily supplied, gaps are inevitable; nor does the Ministry include in the annual volume all the data received, especially in the case of industries in which only small numbers are employed, though it is understood that the occupations covered are chosen so as to give a selection that is in a general sense representative, and that a number of small trades are included with that object in view.

The long and the short of the position is, therefore, that we can have realistic figures averaged over a number of occupations or unrealistic ones for actual occupations; but that anyone who wants realistic figures for particular jobs or grades of skill must get them for himself; which is unfortunately an expensive process, not easily accomplished on any extensive scale. Where, however, this has been done, the results can be strikingly different from those which might be inferred from the official figures. Thus Messrs. Knowles and Robertson in their inquiry into shipbuilding earnings found that at January 1950 average weekly earnings for skilled timeworkers stood at 146s. when the rate for this grade was 109s., the corresponding figures for unskilled timeworkers being 117s. and 92s.[2] And, in illustration of the vagaries of payment by results, the same investigators found that in the engineering industry where the contract required that the worker of 'average ability' should be able to earn $27\frac{1}{2}$% over his time rate when paid by results, the *actual* excess was 46·2% for fitters and 42·6% for labourers.[3]

The only other official sources of general information deal with movements in wages, as distinct from absolute levels at a given date. In this category we have the Ministry of Labour's aggregate figures of changes in wages and hours, and the index of changes in wage-rates calculated by the Ministry from a base of 30 June 1947—both published monthly. The last-named index, being a general figure

[1] *Ministry of Labour Gazette* (April 1954), p. 113.
[2] Knowles, K. G. J. C. & Robertson, D. J., 'Earnings in Shipbuilding', *Bulletin of the Oxford University Institute of Statistics* (November–December 1951), p. 358.
[3] Knowles & Robertson, 'Earnings in Engineering, 1926–1948', *Bulletin of Statistics* (June 1951), p. 185.

weighted according to the relative share of different industries in the total wage bill cannot, of course, help in any inter-industry comparisons. Among unofficial sources, the investigations of Messrs. Knowles and Robertson, already mentioned, have made a valuable contribution; and more is promised from the same source. To these and other occasional researches must be added the index of wage changes formerly published by the London and Cambridge Economic Service and later transferred to *The Times Review of Industry*. This includes, in addition to a general figure, separate indices for a number of different occupations, or groups of occupations, calculated from a base of August 1939. The choice of occupations is, however, determined, as so often in this field, more by considerations of convenience than by any systematic attempt to get a representative picture; and in particular, the need to get regular monthly figures severely limits the possible range from which selection can be made.

As might be expected, at the higher levels, generally described as 'salaried', information is even more deficient than are data about wage payments. No official figures of salaries exist, though it is understood that the publication of an index is under consideration. The two main sources upon which the inquirer can draw are, first, private investigations such as the valuable statistics of clerical salaries now regularly published by the Office Management Association;[1] and, second (in so far as they are released from seal of secrecy), scales agreed between employing bodies and various professional associations.

Two other complications need to be mentioned. The first arises from the practice—common in the post-war period—of back-dating wage changes for long periods—even, occasionally, for as much as two or three years. Figures for any given date can therefore either be presented as those actually prevailing at the time, or as adjusted to take account of any subsequent retrospective changes. There are arguments for and against either course. Where a change is back-dated only for a short period, it seems reasonable to make the appropriate adjustment: on the other hand if all retrospective changes are taken into account (especially in the higher-paid professional classes where back-dating has sometimes been carried a very long way) figures cannot be quoted until they are two or three years old. One cannot, however, pick and choose, but must adhere to one practice or the other. On the whole since in recent years back-dating has been widely practised, the balance of advantage

[1] Office Management Association, *Clerical Salaries Analysis* (London, Management House, 1942, 1946, 1948, 1950, 1952).

seems to lie on the side of including retrospective advances, at least so far as the higher professional rates are concerned. Accordingly, in what follows, comparisons of rates confined to the higher classes are based, except where otherwise stated, on the levels of October 1951, as modified by any back-dated changes; but figures relating to lower professional classes and to industrial earnings are brought to a later date.

The second complication springs from the practice of adding many extras, in kind or in money, to formal wage or salary payments. During the war and post-war periods of wage-freezing, when explicit increases in rates were officially disapproved, these practices proliferated abundantly at all levels. Their many variations have never been fully explored, but in addition to the well-established allowances for uniforms, overalls and suchlike, or the free residential benefits long attached to certain jobs, free lunch vouchers and even occasionally free permanent waves have been used as a means of raising actual rewards without doing open violence to a 'standstill' policy. Similarly, judicious re-grading and an increasingly lavish distribution of merit-bonuses have been used to improve the pay of workers whose nominal rates remained unchanged. In the higher reaches of the income-scale, where much thought is given to what I have heard described as 'methods of meeting the Inland Revenue position', 'top-hat' superannuation schemes for senior staff under which tax-free premiums on retirement policies take the place of straight additions to taxable salaries are popular. To judge from figures quoted by Professor R. M. Titmuss[1] the total sums involved in this way are very large indeed. According to his estimates these amounted to as much as £115,000,000 in 1950.

III

With these materials to draw upon, it is certainly not possible either to validate or to disprove any general theory of wages. But some features of the rough outline which emerges from them are distinctive enough to challenge at several points any explanation in terms of traditional economic theory alone and to present, it may be added, serious problems of social and economic policy.

First, the practice of dividing the whole structure into roughly

[1] In a paper read to the 1953 Conference of the British Sociological Association. Professor Titmuss derived these figures from a paper, 'Industrial Pensions and the Welfare State', by G. W. Pingstone, read before the Insurance Institute, Newcastle-on-Tyne, October 1952, privately circulated.

defined areas indicated by such terms as 'salaried' and 'wage-earning', or 'professional', 'clerical' and 'manual' deserves notice. Some of these terms—'clerical' and 'manual', for instance—are tolerably precise descriptions of the type of work performed. Others, notably 'professional' or 'salaried', elude exact definition. A particular type of work can be classified as manual or non-manual by direct observation of the operations which it involves. 'Professional status', by contrast, arises not so much from the nature of professional work as from the prestige (accompanied often by a measure of statutory monopoly) which the professions enjoy. No one can tell merely by looking at the work of a hairdresser putting in curls or of a dentist pulling out teeth whether either or both these are professional employments. Nor is the length of the period of training a sufficient criterion. A bricklayer's apprenticeship is not so much shorter than a medical student's course, though it is true that the bricklayer can start younger and can learn on the job in a way not open to his medical counterpart; but in the last resort a profession (like a nation) can only be defined as a group of people who succeed in getting themselves recognized as such. Again, salaried workers are, in many cases, paid at longer intervals than those classified as wage-earning— by the month, instead of by the week, the day, or even the hour. Yet this definition is by no means universally observed. Many clerks are paid by the week; yet they are much more likely to be described as salaried than are railway porters.

The essential quality of these distinctions is in fact that they are *social*. They do not, of themselves, tell us anything about what people are paid; but they do indicate standing, and they have a markedly hierarchical flavour. The term 'wage-earning' is not normally applied to posts located at the upper end of the social scale; and it is exceptional (though not, perhaps, in quite the same degree) for predominantly manual occupations to be described as salaried. Traditionally, all posts that involve the exercise of much power[1] rank as salaried; and most of those in which the work is physically disagreeable or exhausting are classified as wage-earning. It would be, at the least, highly unconventional to speak of the wages of the Lord Chief Justice or of the salaries of the miners. To move from an industrial wage-earning to a salaried professional category will therefore be generally recognized as a step up, not down, the social ladder.

These distinctions play no part in economic theory; but traditionally they have had their economic accompaniments; and they

---

[1] But so long as wage-earning railwaymen are trusted with their passengers' lives, this definition cannot be widened to include responsibility.

certainly create a presumption in favour of a pattern of monetary reward which conforms to the hierarchy that they imply. Indeed so strong is this presumption that it may even lead to the paradoxical conclusion that the economic position of the 'professional' worker is actually inferior to that of the wage-earner unless he enjoys a considerably bigger income. Such a paradox seems to be not un-common in contemporary discussion of wage and salary questions. One often hears it said that the wage-earning classes are now better off than their colleagues in professional employments; though it is less usual to find cases in which holders of salaried posts have actually taken steps to transfer themselves to the wage-earning jobs of which they speak so enviously. Mr. Graham Hutton, for instance, writing in the *News Chronicle* of 21 November 1949 contrasted the lot of a university lecturer with a salary of £15 per week with that of an electrician with similar family responsibilities and a weekly income of £8, in an article headed "Who is better off?" On the face of it the question would appear quite foolish since fifteen is nearly twice as much as eight. The lecturer can only be made out to be poorer than the electrician by the strange device of treating many of the goods and services on which he chooses to spend the excess of his income over the electrician's (special training in music for his children, for instance) as items to be deducted *before* the economic position of the two parties is compared. As correspondents were not slow to point out, the lecturer, *after* paying for his flat, fares, subscriptions, children's lessons plus other items, still had as much money left as the electrician actually earned. Naturally any income, no matter how large, can be made to look small beside any other income, no matter how much lower, if that part of the former which is spent on luxuries is deducted before the balance is struck.

Actually, in the light of such evidence as is available, it would seem that as measured in simple arithmetic, the distribution of earned incomes still runs parallel to the social classification. The traditional hierarchy is still broadly maintained, even after all the upheavals of the war and post-war years, though there has been some narrowing of the gap between professional and other employments.

To consider first the picture shown by broad averages of different types of earned income, we find that Mr. Dudley Seers in his valuable study of the 'levelling of incomes' estimates the average (pre-tax) wage income per head in 1949 at £276; the corresponding figure for salary-earners being £450 and for self-employed professional workers £819. The narrowing of the gap is illustrated by the fact that the 1949 income of each of the three classes expressed as a percentage of the corresponding 1938 figures was for wage-earners

236; for salary-earners 172; and for professional people 205.[1] Similarly the pilot survey of incomes in the City of Oxford conducted by the Oxford Institute of Statistics found that in 1950–1 'the highest average income from an individual source (of those who receive some income from the source) is received by those with incomes from professional practice; they earn an average of £563'.[2] This figure, it should be explained, refers not to individual earnings, but to 'spending units', in which the incomes of husbands and wives and children under eighteen are treated as a single unit. The findings of the national survey of personal incomes, also originated by the Oxford Institute, have not been presented in a form which permits a similar comparison; but the picture there presented is broadly similar. Thus the 'average gross income of both the self-employed and managers is in the region of £1,000 a year. . . . The average income of skilled manual workers is £430, which is about £100 a year more than the average for unskilled manual workers.'[3] Clerical and sales workers, on the other hand, with an average of £393, stood a little below skilled manual workers. The inferiority of these classes, however, as the authors of the survey point out, is an effect of sex as well as of occupation; and the same factor increases also the differential between skilled and unskilled manual work, since the percentage of women employed in the unskilled group is more than three times as large as that found in skilled work.

All these figures relate to gross money income before deduction of tax. The relative gains of the wage-earning classes are of course much larger if comparisons are made in terms of post-tax incomes. Naturally those who have more money must pay more to the tax-collector. Thus Mr. Seers' figures of average per head income in 1949, if calculated after deduction of tax, are reduced in the case of wage-earners from £276 to £253; and for salary-earners from £450 to £385. (The figure for professional workers is not available.) This gives the wage-earners 218% of their 1938 income and the salary-earners only 155%: professional workers are credited with 170% of their pre-war standard. If, in addition, allowance is made for changes in the cost of living, the gap becomes narrower still, and the professional and salaried classes are found not to have maintained their pre-war standard. In terms of post-tax average income per head at 1938 prices, the wage-earners in 1949 stand at

[1] Seers, D., *The Levelling of Incomes since 1938* (Oxford, Blackwell, n.d.), p. 51.
[2] Lydall, H. F., 'A Pilot Survey of Incomes & Savings', *Bulletin of Statistics* (September 1951), p. 279.
[3] Lydall, H. F., 'National Survey of Personal Incomes & Savings', *Bulletin of Statistics* (February–March 1953), p. 47.

4

120% of the 1938 figure: the salary-earners at 82% and the profes-sional workers at 89%. Mr. Seers concludes, however, that the trend towards equality of real net income was more marked during the actual war years than in the period from 1946 to 1949 when the cost of living began to catch up on the wage-earner, and wages were still held back by the Government's official standstill policy.[1] And though gaps are narrowed, the rank order of the classes has not changed.

The present study is concerned only with pre-tax money income, or more strictly with the pre-tax net advantages of different occupa-tions. These are the values which wage theory seeks to explain, and which have to be settled at the negotiators' table. It is true that those who actually fix these values may be influenced by movements in the cost of living, and may even think in terms of post-tax as well as pre-tax results. Indeed occasionally they may go so far as to think aloud on these lines, as when in 1953 the Government proposed to award Her Majesty's Judges a tax-free addition to their pay. According to the strict canons of economic theory, however, the effect of direct taxation is not a factor that enters into the deter-mination of earned incomes. The logic of this view is simple. Everybody seeks to obtain the best price for his labour that he can; and, though after deduction of tax this will be smaller than it looks in gross figures, yet so long as the tax on any increment does not actually exceed 100%, a larger income, even after tax, is still bigger than a smaller one. Everything in the labour market, therefore, goes on just as it would if there were no income and surtax, though the amount left in everybody's pocket is, of course, greatly affected by these taxes. Certainly it requires some ingenuity to devise methods by which the (collective or individual) higgling of the market can produce a picture which counteracts in advance the effect of taxation upon that same picture: the final outcome of such a cumulative process would indeed be difficult to foresee, though it does not follow that those who are actually engaged in industrial bargaining are convinced of its impossibility. Obviously, however, the effects of direct taxation upon distribution raise issues that affect unearned as well as earned incomes and go far beyond the confines of any labour market. On that account they are neglected here, though they have of course great importance in the design of social policy as a whole.[2]

The correspondence between the social and the economic hier-archies appears even more pronounced if we now turn to consider the comparative remuneration of individual posts. The highest

[1] Seers, *The Levelling of Incomes*, pp. 53–4.   [2] See below, pp. 108 ff.

salaries of which particulars are readily disclosed stood at about £10,000 per annum (£192 6s. 3d. per week) in 1951. At the other end of the scale, the average industrial earnings of adult males in October 1951 amounted to £8 6s. 0d. a week, while some of the lowest-paid classes of labour in London, as shown in 1951 *Time Rates*, were rated at about £5 a week. Examples are the lower-paid classes in boot and shoe repairing with a statutory minimum rate of 97s. 6d. for a 45-hour week; operatives and packers in the ophthalmic optical industry at 103s. for 44 hours; general labourers in electrical cable-making at 102s. 8d. for 44 hours; and unskilled workers in glove-making at 105s. 3½d. for 47 hours.

Salaries above £10,000 were undoubtedly paid; so that the actual ratio, if all the facts were known, is without doubt appreciably higher than these figures suggest; but at these levels the taboo on publicity becomes virtually unbreakable. Amongst those to be found in the £5,000 to £10,000 a year group in 1951 are the Lord Chancellor, the Prime Minister, the Attorney-General, each with £10,000; the Archbishop of Canterbury, the Chairmen of several of the national-ized industries, the Lord Chief Justice of England and the Solicitor-General, each with something between £7,000 and £8,500; and the Judges of the High Court and the Court of Appeal, the Ministers in charge of the major departments of Government, some Deputy Chairmen and a few Chairmen and members of the Boards of nationalized industries, the Lords of Appeal, the Bishops of London and Oxford, the Permanent Secretary to the Treasury, and those consultants in the National Health Service who enjoy maximum distinction awards—all of whom received between £5,000 and £6,500. To these should probably be added the clerks to the largest municipal authorities. The salaries of county council clerks (which require ministerial approval) are not the subject of any collective agreement, but the recommendations made by the County Councils Association to the Minister suggest that they are to be found in or just below this range.

Moving down the scale to the occupations carrying salaries between £2,000 and £3,000 in 1951 we find most of the medical (and a few non-medical) professors in the Universities; under-secretaries in the Civil Service administrative class; consultants in the National Health Service; metropolitan magistrates and county court judges; the clerks and chief officers of a number of the medium-sized local authorities; the Chairman of the Prison Commission, the Chief Inspector of Fire Services in England and Wales; the Inspectors of Constabulary; the Commissioner of Police for the City of London; and the Deans of St. Pauls and of Westminster.

Round about the £1,000 a year level,[1] we find senior medical registrars at the beginning of their scale, assistant medical officers or medical officers employed by local authorities (after three years' service); the chief pharmacists in a few teaching hospitals in London (after at least six years' service and if in receipt of a 'special allowance'); the matrons of the largest general hospitals (after two years); a (male) principal probation officer in London (£1,075 after three years); prison governors (on the scale £850–£1,050 for men, in Class III, and £925–£1,100 for women in Class II, plus free quarters or rent allowance in each case); University lecturers in London (after eight years); graduate head teachers in London schools in Group V[2] in the case of men and Group X[3] in the case of women; a male Civil Service principal in the administrative class at the beginning of his scale, or a woman after three years; a senior executive officer (male) in the Civil Service (£990 after three years) and a female chief executive officer (£1,010 after two years);[4] a canon residentiary of St. Paul's Cathedral and a member of Parliament.

These examples, the selection of which is dictated primarily by the accessibility of information, may serve to illustrate the type of occupation which ranks among the more highly paid in contemporary English society. Many of the posts named carry in addition residential emoluments, expense accounts or allowances for uniforms or other special requirements. In addition, pensions are payable on retirement in some, though not in all, cases: superannuation arrangements are peculiar to each type of employment and vary very greatly.

Wage-rates[5] of levels comparable to these are not to be found in the Ministry of Labour's review of *Time Rates*: any overlap between the wages of manual and professional workers occurs only at a much more modest level. To illustrate this area of overlap, I have compared the rates at two points in the scale of teachers' salaries with those of certain other occupations. Teachers have been chosen as a yardstick for two reasons: first, because everybody has some idea of what teachers actually do, since everybody has at some time or other experienced their ministrations; and, second, because the teaching

---

[1] Nearly all the occupations in this class and a rather smaller proportion of those in the higher groups have received further advances since 1951, the date to which the figures in the text relate.

[2] That is, schools with 401–500 'unit totals': the unit total is based on a formula for weighting the number of pupils by their ages.

[3] Schools with 901–1,000 'unit totals'.

[4] These comparisons exclude the Extra Duty Allowance (of 8%) paid to certain civil servants in lieu of overtime for the extended hours worked during and since the war.

[5] The matter of earnings is discussed below, see pp. 48 ff.

profession stands at a modest level in the hierarchy of professional remuneration.

In October 1951 the male non-graduate teacher, embarking on a career after two years' professional training, was entitled in London to a salary of £411 a year (£375 in the provinces). To see this teacher in proper relation to his colleagues in professional and public employments, it may be noted that he stood on the same level (in the sense that the salary difference, in London, did not exceed 5s. a week or £13 a year in either direction) as an assistant principal just entering the Administrative Civil Service; a Civil Service executive officer at age twenty-four after six years' service or a clerical officer at age thirty after fourteen years;[1] a male staff nurse in a general hospital after seven years; a physiotherapist after two years; a newly-qualified psychiatric social worker; a probation officer at age twenty-seven after four years; a prison officer after six years; and a fireman after four years. In 1951, also, according to the Church Information Board,[2] the average parish priest in the Church of England had a net (pre-tax) income of £465 per annum, that is more than £50 a year above the London starting-rate of the non-graduate teacher, and £90 above the starting-rate for such teachers in the provinces; though it must be remembered that in the case of the clergyman, this is an average figure compounded of smaller as well as larger incomes, and that the clergyman, unlike the teacher, has no automatic incremental scale to look forward to.

Comparison with clerical rates is complicated by the fact that the material in the Office Management Association's *Clerical Salaries Analysis* relates to different dates and is arranged in a different form (in respect of age-grouping and other matters) from that relating to professional or manual working salaries; but it is perhaps worth noting that at 1 March 1952, the *median* weekly salary paid to a male clerk in the third highest of the six grades of skill and responsibility into which the subjects were divided (that is one engaged in work 'calling for the exercise of some initiative', with a 'varied daily routine' and requiring little supervision), was 159s. 10d. (or £415 11s. 4d. a year), on the average of all industries in all areas; for clerks in the West End of London the corresponding figure was 158s. 11d. (or £413 3s. 8d. a year), though in the City it was substantially higher.[3] The young teacher thus rated roughly with the clerks at this level. It may be added that apart from promotion to

[1] Excluding Extra Duty Allowance.
[2] Church Information Board, *The Work and Revenues of the Church of England* (London, C. I. B., 1951), p. 5.
[3] *Clerical Salaries Analysis* (1952), pp. 26 and 32 and (1942), p. 5.

higher grades, neither the non-graduate teacher nor any of the other classes just mentioned could anticipate ever climbing into the £1,000 a year and upwards classes of which illustrations have already been given. The teacher's eventual maximum in London was £678 per annum; and the highest maximum for any of the professions mentioned on p. 45 was the £750 figure which, in theory at least, marked the top of the Civil Service Assistant Principal's scale. Too much attention must not, however, be paid to maxima, since in some (but by no means all) of the professions quoted the great majority of entrants could normally expect to be promoted.

The modest starting salary of the non-graduate teacher, and the other professional colleagues who ranked with him compares, however, very favourably with the levels of industrial wages shown in *Time Rates*. A rate of £411 per annum is equivalent to a weekly wage of 158s. 1d.; and figures of this order are hard to find in strictly industrial time-rates: the vast majority are much lower. In a few cases, however, industrial rates do reach or even pass this level. Apart from special rates for shift and night workers, increments for experience or merit-bonuses paid by individual firms such as ICI, the following examples[1] are to be found among the rates quoted in the 1951 issue of *Time Rates*; in the cotton industry, spinning section, certain card-room operatives of whom the highest paid reached 169s. 9d.; in the cotton industry, manufacturing section, some machine operatives at 168s. 11d.; in the printing industry a number of workers at many levels, especially in newspaper work, the highest figure quoted being 233s. 8d.; in envelope and stationery manufacture, machine adjusters at 165s.; in mastic-asphalt laying charge-hands at 165s.; in electricity supply, installation inspectors at 164s. 1d.; in electricity installation, journeyman electricians at 161s. 4d.; in road transport, drivers carrying 'indivisible' loads of the enormous weight of over 45 tons—at 181s. and male gangers working in mobile gangs on tramway permanent ways at 161s. 6d.; in wallpaper manufacture, certain colour printers at 166s. 10d.; in pottery, modellers at 159s. 6d.; in coopering, men on repairs at 161s. 4d.; in catering, *chefs de cuisine* in licensed establishments at 235s. (but not mere cooks or even head cooks who had to be content with 155s.); in artificial limb-making, highly skilled craftsmen at 196s. 10½d.; in cement manufacture, boilermakers when engaged on welding at 159s. 6d.; in retail pharmacy, qualified pharmacists starting at

[1] Rates quoted in *Time Rates* on an hourly basis have been converted to weekly figures in accordance with the recognized hours for the industry concerned, without either overtime or undertime. All figures refer to the rates payable in London, except in the case of such highly localized industries as cotton textiles in which case the figures are those for the main centre of the industry.

165s.; in the fire service, sub-officers at 180s. 6d.; and in the cinema industry the top class of projectionists at 169s.

Alternatively, if for the non-graduate teacher we substitute one with a university degree (whose London starting-rate in 1951 was £507 a year or 195s. a week) only the printers, the artificial limb makers and the chefs are left in the running.

These examples may serve to give some idea of the points at which industrial time-wages reach or pass the level of such professional groups as the teacher at the outset of his career. It is evident that in 1951 those which reached the non-graduate's figure fell into four groups: in the first, we find a few workers of a very high degree of skill, or engaged in specially difficult or responsible jobs, such as the pottery modellers, the wallpaper printers or the drivers with enormous loads, in industries where rates generally run much lower. The second group consists of classes whose duties are largely supervisory, such as the chargehands in the asphalt industry, or the inspectors in electricity supply; the third which includes the *chefs de cuisine* and the cinema projectionists, falls on the fringes, if not actually outside, the field of industrial employment ordinarily so-called; and the fourth category, represented by the printers, comes from an industry in which the whole level of wages, from top to bottom, is much above what is usually found in industrial employments. Indeed all who work in the printing industry—even to the doorkeepers—are always in a class of their own.

On 1 April 1954, the date to which the latest edition of *Time Rates* available at the time of going to press refers, the teaching profession had received two further increases—one in July 1952 and one to date from 1 April 1954. At this date the trained male non-graduate teacher in London had attained a starting-rate of £486 on a scale that ran to a maximum of £773. Many of his professional colleagues had also enjoyed advances, with the result that there had been minor changes in their mutual relationships. At the 1954 rates, for instance, the psychiatric social worker needed a year's experience to reach the teacher's starting-rate, and the Civil Service assistant principal at £470 (exclusive of Extra Duty Allowance) started a little behind the fledgling teacher, but passed his rate after one year's experience. The teacher had, if anything, very slightly improved his position in relation to the professional colleagues with whom he has been compared; but the changes were not such as to create at this level a radically different picture; and the possibility of retrospective increases still being granted to those that have not yet caught up cannot be ruled out. The young teacher still represented one of the lower-paid professional groups.

If we now compare the 1954 non-graduate male teacher with the figures quoted in *Time Rates*, we find even fewer instances of time-wages that reach or pass his London starting figure of £486 a year or 186*s*. 11*d*. a week. Of those which outstripped this teacher in 1951, only the following still do so in April 1954: the artificial limb and orthopaedic appliance workers now running up to 209*s*.; many classes of printers, the maximum rate quoted being 267*s*. 4*d*.; the wallpaper craftsmen at 189*s*. 4*d*.; the chargehands in mastic-asphalt laying at 187*s*.; the installation inspectors in electricity supply at 187*s*.; the drivers of very big loads at 193*s*.; the sub-officers in the fire service now at 212*s*., together with the leading firemen who in 1951 fell below the teacher's standard; and the chefs at 255*s*. Apart from the leading firemen no new categories had appeared.

By April 1954 the *graduate* teacher had reached a starting-rate of £582 (223*s*. 10*d*. a week) raised to £612 (235*s*. 5*d*. a week) if he had a 'first-class or other good honours degree'. At these levels it will be seen, it is only the top classes of printers and the chefs who can still compete.

Judged by the standard of current time-rates, therefore, only a very small select aristocracy of the industrial world ever reaches the rate at which the professional teacher begins; and the teacher (even without promotion) will finish his career far above any figure known to *Time Rates*. In assessing these comparisons it is, moreover, pertinent to bear in mind that the London teacher cannot normally spend more than twenty-seven and a half hours a week actually teaching in school, since that is the maximum period during which the children are available to be taught. In order to reach the normal standard of an industrial worker (doing no overtime) with a 44-hour week and two weeks' paid holiday, the teacher would have to reduce his holidays from about twelve weeks to two, and do more than three hours' additional work on top of a full school day every day except Saturday and Sunday throughout all the rest of the year. In addition the teacher enjoys, though on a contributory basis, more favourable pension prospects than are usual for his industrial colleagues, as well as the incremental scale already mentioned.

For reasons already given, however, time-rates are in many ways an unrealistic index of the actual earnings of industrial workers; and the selection of rates quoted in the Ministry of Labour's annual reviews is admittedly somewhat haphazard. It may be useful, therefore, to add a comparison between our two grades of teachers and the Ministry's figures of average industrial earnings. Since, however, this latter series is averaged over the whole country, a comparison with either the London or the provincial teacher's salary would be inappropriate; and I have therefore substituted a figure midway between these two rates as the standard of comparison. It is true that the teacher who is actually paid such a salary is a mythical average who does not, in the flesh and blood sense, anywhere exist; but the same is true, no less, of the industrial earnings figures: these also represent not any individual experience, but compounds of such experiences.

On this basis the starting salary of the male non-graduate teacher in 1951 was £393 (£411 in London and £375 elsewhere) or 151s. 2d. a week. At the same date the average earnings of adult male industrial workers stood at 166s.; and for this they had worked, on the average, 47·8 hours including overtime. Of the 131 groups into which the industrial figures are classified, 107 ranked above the non-graduate teacher's starting-rate, though not one reached the maximum of his scale. The graduate teacher, on the other hand, even at his initial figure, outstripped all but nine of the 131 industrial averages. The commercial value of an academic degree (at least in this profession) is clearly demonstrated.

In October 1953 (the date of the latest available return of industrial earnings) the non-graduate teacher's salary amounted to £433 a year (mean of £415 and £451) or 166s. 6½d. a week. Average industrial earnings of adult males had by then reached 189s. 2d., for which an average of 47·9 hours had been worked. At this date 111 of the 131 classes of industrial workers stood above the non-graduate teacher's starting figure, though none of them still reached his eventual maximum of £694 (mean of £718 and £670) or 266s. 11d. a week: workers in the printing and publishing of newspapers came nearest at 233s. 7d. The graduate teacher had by this time achieved an initial salary of £529 (mean of £547 and £511) or 203s. 6d. a week; and at this figure he too was passed by rather more—twenty in all—of the 131 industrial groups that had outstripped him in 1951.

The foregoing figures all relate only to men. In the case of women, the published material is too scanty to permit any comparisons in terms of rates; but the data on earnings are as good as they are for men. The results of comparison on the above lines are, however, startlingly different. In October 1951 the female non-graduate teacher's initial salary stood at £356 per annum (mean of £374 and £338) or 136s. 11d., but at that date the average earnings of adult women in industry had reached only 90s. 1d. for 41·5 hours actually worked. Whereas the male teacher without a degree at the outset of his career was passed by 107 of the 131 industrial groups of adult male workers, his non-graduate woman colleague stood ahead of all her industrial counterparts, right from the beginning of her career:

her nearest competitors were the women employed in tramway and omnibus service at a figure of 123s. 8d. Two years later when the woman teacher's initial rate had been raised to £388 a year (mean of £406 and £370) or 149s. 3d. a week, she was still out of reach of almost all her industrial sisters. In October 1953 the average earnings of adult women workers in industry had reached 102s. 5d., for an average of forty-two hours actually worked; and only the bus and tramway workers, at 137s. 1d., passed the non-graduate teacher's initial rate. To a woman the advantage of a professional career over industrial employment (even in a profession which does not enjoy equal pay) is undoubtedly much greater even than it is for a man—a fact which reflects the inferior position of women in industry.

Taking all the evidence together it thus appears that the non-manual employments in general have on the whole retained, even after the war, their absolute superiority in financial rewards over manual-working jobs in industry, though there is a considerable overlap (especially in the case of men) in the lower reaches of the lower-paid professions. Most professional workers can expect to leave the *average* industrial worker behind well before they reach the top of their scales—though even at that point they may be passed by the highest-paid individuals in the groups to which these averages relate. It thus remains true that those who wish to demonstrate that the manual worker is now better off than his professional colleague must use Mr. Graham Hutton's sophistical type of argument; since plain arithmetic indicates an opposite conclusion.

IV

A second and an obvious characteristic of the contemporary wage and salary structure as shown by the foregoing examples is its steep grading. The distribution of earned incomes does not follow the pattern of a normal frequency curve in which most of the quantities measured are clustered about the middle, with a few extremes at each end; it is more J-shaped. While current economic theory *may* be sufficiently elastic to explain a range that extends from £10,000 a year and upwards to £5 a week or less in terms of a frustrated drive towards equality, this does seem rather an odd way in which to approach the subject. The frustrations must be so powerful that it would seem on the face of it more reasonable to treat them as primary.

Some of the explanations also seem a little lame in face of such gross inequalities. In terms of economic theory the superior rewards enjoyed by the holders of professional and administrative posts must be attributable to some kind of scarcity factor. This scarcity is generally ascribed to one or more of three distinct elements. The first is the restriction of supply arising from the high cost of the training required for these positions, which only a few are able to afford; the second is the scarcity of those who possess the necessary natural ability; and the third is deliberate control of entry to particular callings by monopolistic restrictions.

Forty years ago, in a discussion of the first of these factors Professor Cannan pointed out that, if differences in earnings are to be reckoned as the return on capital invested in the acquisition of professional skills, such investment must be quite exceptionally remunerative; and it might, indeed, well be asked why money is not 'spent in training more young people for the occupations of superior advantageousness until the competition reduces this excess of advantageousness to nil?' Professor Cannan himself found the answer in the fact that 'the conditions of human life have not hitherto allowed the spending of money in this way to become an ordinary investment to which savings can be attracted in the ordinary way by the expectation of interest. They have not done so because society has not thought fit to provide means by which money could be advanced to young people for their training on terms which would make the lenders secure of recovering their money with interest.'[1] In the forty years that have elapsed since these words were written, society has, however, experienced a considerable change of mind upon this question. Today money is not even loaned to young people for their training: it is largely provided free. If Professor Cannan and the economists have the whole truth of the matter, the destruction of the financial barriers to higher education initiated by the Education Act of 1944 should eventually reduce the 'excess advantageousness' of professional skills very nearly, if not quite, to nil. But from any such result as this we are still, clearly, a very long way off: and, as will appear in the chapters that follow, to anticipate any such outcome is to reckon without the formidable social pressures that are at work to prevent it.

The second factor contributing to this excess is the shortage of sufficiently good innate ability. Differences in natural ability have been extensively studied in recent years; and psychologists generally claim to have found *some* positive association between native intelligence and income or social standing. At the same time the distribution of income and the distribution of intelligence follow curves of very different shape—a discrepancy which Professor Sir Cyril Burt has

[1] Cannan, E., *Wealth* (London, King, 1914 ed.), p. 199.

thought sufficiently striking to deserve closer examination. The distribution of intelligence, both among children and among adults, as Professor Burt points out, follows very closely the 'so-called normal curve' corresponding to the distribution of physical characteristics such as stature. 'On the other hand, the distribution of income appeared to follow a law of the inverse square. The disparity may be illustrated by saying that, if the heights of the persons studied, instead of obeying the normal curve, had been distributed like income, the tallest giants would have been three miles high.'[1] These observations, it is true, make no distinction between earned and unearned income; and some of the highest incomes are unearned. But the distribution of earned incomes alone certainly deviates widely from the normal curve. If unearned incomes are disregarded, the 'height of the tallest giants' might be reduced from three to perhaps two miles, but it would certainly remain abnormally great.

It is true that comparisons between the distribution of intelligence and of income are necessarily bedevilled by the fact that the same meaning cannot be ascribed to the process of measurement in the two cases. An income of £10,000 a year is unmistakably twice as large as one of £5,000: it is not so clear that we are justified in describing a person with an intelligence quotient of 160 as being twice as intelligent as one who scores only eighty. Indeed it could be argued that such a statement has no meaning at all; and that very high level intelligence, functioning at a pitch with which less highly endowed minds cannot even communicate, is wholly incommensurable with that of a lower order. For present purposes, however, these philosophical subtleties can be ignored. For the economic effects of a scarcity of what economists used to call 'rare natural ability' are more easily susceptible of measurement—since the relevant quantity is not the degree of ability possessed, but the extent to which the supply of persons having whatever level of intelligence may be necessary for any given type of post matches up to the number of such posts to be filled. The critical question is, therefore, whether the distribution of different sorts of jobs differs materially in the upper reaches from the distribution of the degree of intelligence required for the performance of those jobs. Does the shortage of *innately* qualified personnel get more and more desperate as one travels up the income-scale? To answer that question, since we have not got, and with present techniques cannot hope to get, scientifically reliable evidence, we must fall back upon everyday experience. Such experience does not, I think, preclude a fair

[1] Burt, Sir Cyril, *Contributions of Psychology to Social Problems* (London, Oxford University Press, 1953), p. 18.

measure of scepticism as to the validity of an affirmative answer. Professor Burt himself argues elsewhere[1] that the high rewards of certain posts are due not to corresponding variations in intelligence, but to variations in the *output capacity* of the superior intelligence: this individual output-factor 'does not follow the normal curve, although individual ability conceivably may'. In other words a man who scores twice as high as another on an intelligence test may do work worth fifty times as much to his employer.

This line of analysis takes us into deep waters. Either the capacity to do fifty times as much work as somebody else is an innate ability or it is not. If it is itself innate, it seems odd that the psychologists should be prepared to let this important ability escape their intelligence tests altogether; and odder still that its distribution should conform to a J-shaped curve instead of following the symmetrical form common to intelligence as defined by the psychologists and to human qualities generally. If, on the other hand, the worker of outstanding output owes his achievement not to any inborn endowment, but to the exercise, in a particular fashion, of capacities which are more or less symmetrically distributed (and this appears to be Professor Burt's view)[2] then the exceptional rewards of the exceptional performers cannot be ascribed to natural scarcity. An economist would quickly point out that any one of these high level producers would be subject to the competition of his peers, and that (in the economic textbooks anyhow) their employers would be quick to take advantage of this fact.

In any case, these ingenious subtleties have more relevance to the occasional performance of the unusual individual than to the general structure of the salaries paid for particular types of work. The upper reaches of the J-shaped salary curve include such categories as those listed on p. 43, as well as the successful business man and the brilliant inventor or research worker. Even if Professor Burt's observations hold good of particular members of these classes, they can hardly be held to apply to such groups in their entirety.

The third factor to which the economists can appeal to explain the deviation of earned incomes from the equality to which these are said to be perpetually drawn, is the organized control, on monopolistic lines, of entry to a particular calling.

[1] Burt, Sir Cyril, 'Ability and Income', *British Journal of Educational Psychology* (June 1943).

[2] At least this would seem to be the right interpretation of the following passage: 'the apparent inconsistency between the two distributions [i.e. of intelligence and of income] vanishes directly we recognize that the functional relation between output (as effect) and capacities (as causes) may be of many different kinds, and indeed is more likely to be indirect and complex than immediate or simple'. (Burt, *Contributions of Psychology to Social Problems*, pp. 95–6.)

Explicit monopolization of highly-paid occupations is perhaps rare. At the same time, entry into every profession is today by no means freely open to all who can pay for their own training, or can get the State to pay for it on their behalf. It is, for instance, common knowledge that the medical schools accept only a tiny minority of the students who wish to train as doctors and have passed the required preliminary examinations. The abundant proliferation of professional organizations at many levels has indeed been a conspicuous feature of the present century; and nearly every one of these organizations seeks to restrict entry into its ranks to those whom it has itself selected. As a rule, the selection procedures adopted by such professional bodies are represented to be no more than devices for eliminating those who would otherwise have eliminated themselves for lack of the ability necessary to stay the course; and in so far as that interpretation is valid, they add no further element of monopoly beyond that which results from the scarcity of natural ability. Practical acquaintance with the actual methods employed and with their results hardly, however, supports the view that this is everywhere the whole truth of the matter; or that the rejected candidates for training in, say, the monopolistically controlled branches of social work (such as hospital almoning), or in medicine, do not include many who have sufficient native ability to reach, given the opportunity of appropriate training, the standard of competence commonly attained in the profession in question.

Such crypto-monopolistic control probably has much to do with the success of some professional groups in maintaining their standards of remuneration. It is, of course, a device which has been much used at the wage-earning level, by trade unions; and, as we shall see,[1] in recent years superior social groups have shown a new readiness to form themselves into what are virtually (and sometimes also formally) trade unions, and to copy trade union practices. But something more than vigorous trade unionism or monopolistic control of recruitment must be invoked to account for the current standards of remuneration of bishops, judges, administrators, bank managers and other highly-paid groups.

V

As we have seen, economic theory postulates that the monetary and other advantages of any occupation will tend to balance one

[1] See pp. 79 ff.

another so that jobs that involve disagreeable or dangerous work, or inconvenient or long hours, will be more highly remunerated than those that do not. Within any given occupation this kind of balancing is in fact very generally found. Shift workers and night workers, for example, are usually paid more than day workers on the same job; and builders get special rates if they have to work at great heights or at very low temperatures.

On the other hand, no one who looks at the picture as a whole, can fail to be struck by the opposite tendency; by the degree in which the incidental advantages of different employments vary positively, not inversely, with the monetary remuneration that these employments carry: the rule is that to him that hath shall be given, rather than the opposite. The security of tenure, the length of notice to be given and often also the duration of paid holidays enjoyed by professional and salaried employees are normally superior to what is customary in wage-earning employments: indeed it is only since the First World War that it has become customary to provide any paid holiday at all for manual workers in general. Again, where special allowances are paid either for service in a particular area (usually London) or for particular duties, these are normally either fixed on a flat-rate basis payable alike to all workers irrespective of grade, or so adjusted as to favour those who are in any case getting more money. Incremental scales, also, are almost a monopoly of salaried employments: to the ordinary wage-earner outside those employed in a few large corporations and public services they are unknown.

In the case of one factor in particular, that of hours of work, this absence of any positive correlation with standards of remuneration is indeed remarkable. Unlike other items that enter into the balance of 'net advantages', the length of the working week has the merit of being precisely measurable as between one occupation or one industry and another; and economic theory has always postulated that those who work shorter hours will generally get lower wages; for if you value leisure, you must expect to pay for it. Only at the highest levels, where it is understood that employees will put in as many (or as few) hours as the exigencies of the work demand, is there no such thing as a normal working week. Yet below these levels we find, first, that, in conformity with the superior social standing of clerical, as compared with manual, work, the normal office day is shorter, not longer, than that worked in the factory; and, second, that, to judge from the evidence given in the paragraphs that follow, even within industrial employments and amongst the lowest-paid and least skilled classes who might be expected most freely to compete with one another according to the rules of the textbooks, there is still no trace of such balancing.

In Table I particulars are shown of the length of the normal working week and average weekly wage payable in London (hourly rates having been converted where necessary) of the lowest-paid classes of adult males in each industry shown in the issues of *Time Rates* for 1946–51. Special rates for shift and night workers and all piece-rates or forms of payment by results have been omitted as well as rates that clearly applied only to a learner or apprentice grade. Industries located wholly, or almost wholly, outside London have also been omitted on the ground that distinct areas constitute distinct markets. On this basis eighty-six industrial groups remain, for which comparable particulars are given in each of these issues of *Time Rates*. The occupations covered are necessarily somewhat miscellaneous, the commonest descriptions being 'labourers', 'unskilled workers', 'ancillary workers', or 'other workers' in cases where the skilled classes have been separately enumerated: in one or two instances they are classified as 'porters', 'attendants', or 'cleaners'. While the degree of skill involved no doubt varies appreciably, all clearly stand at a fairly low level.

A glance at this table shows absolutely no sign of a positive relationship between normal weekly hours and weekly wage-rates in any one of these six years. Weekly hours and weekly wage-rates are in fact inversely related (though not significantly so) in every one of the six years. The correlation coefficients of hours and wage-rates in the eighty-six cases reads as follows:

1946	-0.279
1947	-0.189
1948	-0.370
1949	-0.465
1950	-0.349
1951	-0.364

It is true, of course, that the nominal and the actual working week are by no means identical, that during these immediate post-war years overtime was prevalent, and that overt wage increases were officially discouraged; but these conditions do not invalidate the theoretical presumption that a shorter normal week should mean lower pay, since, when overtime is worked, the shorter week merely lowers the threshold at which overtime rates become payable, and so increases income, if not leisure. It follows that, if a reduction of

TABLE I

Time-rates of Wages for the Lowest-Rated Grade of Adult Male Workers in eighty-six Industries 1946–51

London or National Rate

Date	Normal weekly hours	No. of Industries	Average weekly time-rate to nearest d.	
			s.	d.
1946	48	40	84	5
1 August	47¼	1	86	8
	47	26	89	9
	46	1	84	0
	45	6	83	0
	44	12	93	3
1947	48	17	89	3
1 September	47	10	95	6
	46	3	91	5
	45	18	87	0
	44	36	92	4
	43½	1	105	0
	40	1	121	6
1948	48	5	89	5
1 September	47	5	93	3
	46	5	93	10
	45	21	91	2
	44	47	97	3
	43¾	1	90	9
	43½	1	113	6
	40	1	121	6
1949	48	3	90	4
1 October	47	3	92	0
	46	6	94	8
	45⅓	1	97	0
	45	22	96	1
	44	48	100	2
	43¾	1	94	4
	43⅛	1	117	0
	40	1	129	0
1950	48	3	92	4
1 October	47	3	95	10
	46	6	98	6
	45⅓	1	98	3
	45	24	98	11
	44	46	101	2
	43¾	1	94	4
	43½	1	117	0
	40	1	129	0
1951	48	3	98	4
1 October	47	3	102	7
	46	6	108	7
	45⅓	1	113	4
	45	24	111	5
	44	46	112	0
	43¾	1	116	8
	43½	1	137	0
	40	1	138	0

nominal hours was not attractive in one way, it was in another: the prospect of getting an additional hour paid at overtime instead of normal rates must be reckoned a positive factor in the estimation of the total 'net advantages' of any job.

This evidence is hardly sufficient to justify a bold assertion that the longer you work the less you must expect to get: though, anticipating the argument that follows, I find it tempting to suggest that a prestige factor is at work here and that long hours and low pay go together because both are marks of lowly class status.[1] Admittedly, however, the rates that are included in *Time Rates* constitute neither a comprehensive collection nor a scientifically selected sample; and it may be said, accordingly, that the groups on which the figures in Table I are based are somewhat haphazardly chosen and by no means homogeneous; for the lowest-rated class in one industry may be doing work of quite a different calibre from that done by the bottom grade in another.

Table II, therefore, gives similar particulars for the statutory minimum time-rates for adult males in industries covered by Wages Regulation Orders. For the minima fixed in these industries the *Time Rates* figures are complete, and all have been included in the table except the few cases in which statutory regulation was not operative throughout the whole period. The exact scope of these orders is summarized later,[2] but here it may be said that in the industries affected by them trade union organization is generally weak; and that the general minimum rates are usually designed to be appropriate for a low grade of skill, higher rates for the more skilled classes being fixed either by further statutory orders or by collective agreements. Indeed, the general minimum time-rates fixed under these orders tend to run rather low, even by the standard of what is paid elsewhere for unskilled labour. While each of these industries has, of course, its own peculiarities, the classes to which these minima apply certainly constitute a less miscellaneous group than those covered by Table I, and may be taken to represent more definitely the state of affairs in the lower reaches of the whole labour market; and it is relevant also to note that, although every council responsible for fixing any of these rates is independent of every other, yet overlapping membership and dependence upon a common secretariat make it possible, if not for all to follow a common policy, at least for each to be in close touch with what the others are doing.

These statutory minimum wages, it will be seen, in common with the wider range of rates shown in Table I, fail to reflect any positive

[1] See pp. 68 ff.   [2] See pp. 81 ff.

TABLE II

*Minimum Time-rates for Adult Male Workers in Industries
covered by Wages Regulation Orders 1946–51*

London or National Rate

Date	Normal weekly hours	No. of Industries	Average weekly time-rate to nearest d.	
			s.	d.
1946	48	25	77	11
1 August	47	5	74	7
	45	3	79	4
	44	5	79	6
1947	48	13	81	1
1 September	47	2	83	1
	45	10	83	2
	44	13	85	6
1948	48	5	88	7
1 September	47	1	84	0
	45	17	86	9
	44	15	86	5
1949	48	3	89	0
1 October	47	2	89	0
	46	1	92	0
	45	17	90	9
	44	15	90	11
1950	48	3	89	0
1 October	47	2	93	9
	46	1	92	0
	45	17	91	2
	44	15	91	5
1951	48	3	93	8
1 October	47	2	100	3
	46	1	105	5
	45	17	101	7
	44	15	99	0

association of standard weekly wages with standard weekly hours.
The correlations, though smaller than those of the previous table, are
still negative. They read as follows:

1946	−0·073
1947	−0·228
1948	−0·099
1949	−0·115
1950	−0·072
1951	−0·125

Even in this limited group of occupations, it appears, there is still
no perceptible support for the principle that the longer you work
the more you get.

The generality of a theory which, while professing to cover the whole labour market, proves so ineffective a guide both to the whole and to the parts may well be called in question: at least its practical relevance begins to look pitifully small. Logically, it is of course a complete answer to say that even the occupations covered in Table II —and *a fortiori* those on which Table I is based—constitute distinct labour markets. But if even amongst the lowest paid, the incidentals and accidentals are so significant as to preclude any clear generalization, we seem to be getting near to the point at which the general theory of wages has no more to say than that the net rewards of any occupation are equal to the net rewards of that occupation. 'Halting agnosticism' looks like winning the day.

These results, however, though anomalous from the point of view of economic theory, are easily understood in the light of real life. In real life the inverse relationship of wages and hours of work postulated by the economists fails to emerge because the minds of those responsible for wage-fixing (by any of the methods described in the chapter that follows) simply do not work that way. During the period to which our tables relate there was, it will be noticed, a widespread reduction in the hours normally worked: more and more industries were adopting a forty-four- or forty hour week. Yet in those industries in which wages were normally fixed on an hourly basis, such reductions were regularly accompanied by a corresponding increase in the hourly rate, obviously designed to maintain for the new and shorter working week the same weekly total as before. It is in fact on this standard weekly figure that attention tends to be concentrated and it is this which by current convention, has to be maintained, irrespective of the number of hours to which it relates. It is these conventional factors which in this case, as also in the positive association at higher levels of incidental privileges and pay, override the operation of pure economics.

VI

There remain one or two other general, if familiar, features of our wage and salary structure which deserve mention on the ground that they seem to call for more than a narrowly economic interpretation. First, that structure is a thorough geographical muddle. The geographical features of the labour market were the subject of a review by the Ministry of Labour in 1949,[1] and from this it appears

[1] 'Local Variations in Wage Rates', *Ministry of Labour Gazette* (May 1949), p. 157.

that in a high proportion of collective agreements or wage-orders provision is made for some local differentiation of rates. Such differentiation may be included in the terms of national agreements, or may, alternatively, be effected through separate agreements made at a regional or district level. The significant feature of these—often very complicated—arrangements is to be found, however, in the varying degree of differentiation that prevails in different industries. Among industries covered by agreements that are nationally negotiated a few practise no differentiation at all: a single rate covers the whole country. In a considerable number of others two grades only are recognized, namely, London and the rest of the country—London being, however, very variously defined for this purpose; while other national agreements may recognize as many as ten distinct area differentials. Again, in a few cases, the areas to which each grade applies are explicitly named in what are often very elaborate specifications: in others, areas are classified on the basis of some criterion, the rates for different towns, for instance, varying in accordance with the size of the resident population. In the building industry, in which the number of grades has been gradually reduced over the past thirty years, grading is based upon a complex questionnaire which takes account not only of population, but also of such local conditions as rents, rates, prices, transport facilities, wage-rates in other local industries and the scale of the building industry of the area. But in many industries in which no national agreements are in force, any definite or intelligible relationship between the rates paid in different localities may be wholly lacking. In engineering, for instance, where there is no definite grading scheme, labourers' rates may vary even in areas in which the rates for skilled classes are the same.

According to the Ministry's summary, the local differences in weekly rates for adult male timeworkers covered by national agreements ranged from a differential of 3s. a week for one-horse road haulage drivers up to 16s. a week for roller men in the highest rated class of flour mills. Similar differences in hourly rates range from $\frac{1}{2}d.$ an hour for match-workers in London up to $4\frac{1}{2}d.$ for journeymen in the clothing trade in Scotland.

In terms of classical economic theory local differences in the wages of any given class of labour may be ascribed either to differences in the cost of living in various parts of the country, or to local peculiarities in the demand for, or the supply of, the services of the workers in question. Cost-of-living differences presumably affect all workers more or less in the same degree: London is doubtless a more expensive place to live in than is the country, but there is no obvious reason why metropolitan life should involve an extra cost of 9s. a week to domestic staffs in hospitals, 10s. to County Council roadmen and only 3s. or 4s. to railway workers, these being the London differentials shown in the Ministry of Labour's review. Clearly the mechanism for compensating each class of worker for the expense of city life in such a way as to equalize, not money wages, but net remuneration in real terms must be very much of a hit-and-miss affair. Nor is the alternative explanation that geographical differentials reflect variations in the conditions of the local market for various classes of labour easily reconciled with the constancy of these differentials. Recently there has, it is true, been a movement in several industries to reduce the number of local rates; but apart from such deliberate tidying-up, the tendency is for differentials to remain fixed over long periods. Certainly they do not fluctuate as prices fluctuate in a free market.

In the second place the differentiations commonly, though not invariably, practised on grounds both of sex and of age suggest that factors other than the laws of demand and supply play a part in shaping the outlines of our wage and salary structure. The *economic* factors that explain why women often get lower wages than men were admirably summarized by the Royal Commission on Equal Pay in October 1946. The demand for women's labour, the Commission were told, is diminished by the fact that women are inferior to men in physical strength, and are thought also to be less resourceful in dealing with unexpected situations. In general, also, women are apt to look upon paid employment as a temporary incident, likely to be terminated by marriage, and they tend to lose more time both from sickness and from other causes. Again, for purely conventional reasons, the services of women are not sought by employers in certain occupations: women are, for instance, acceptable as aeroplane ferry-pilots, but not (at least in London) as taxi-drivers; and these conventions are often reinforced by pressure from male employees anxious to keep their jobs as far as possible to their own sex. These restrictions, it was argued, lower the value of women's labour both directly in the occupations into which entry is difficult, and indirectly by increasing the supply of feminine labour in the jobs in which there are no such obstacles. Finally, the Royal Commission considered the familiar argument that women can afford to accept lower pay because they do not normally expect 'to support a married partner or a family of children out of the proceeds of their labour; on the contrary, most of them look forward to being themselves supported in the relatively near future'. On the merits of this argument, the Commissioners were clearly uneasy, since, as they remarked, family standards of living 'are not absolute things, but depend largely on what it has in fact been found possible to achieve'; and the opposite view, expressed by one of their witnesses, that wages determine the standard of living, and not *vice versa*, evidently carried much weight. On the whole, however, the Commissioners were more impressed with the fact that, whereas 'virtually all men are and always have been and always will be in the market for employment', there is a large reserve force of women liable to be drawn into or out of the market in response to both social and economic factors. While they were prepared to concede some influence to the relative weakness of trade union organization amongst women (although the 'exact nature and extent of the influence of collective bargaining on the level of wages is a large and difficult subject, of which . . . we can only scratch the surface'),[1] the Commission were on the whole disposed to believe that factors affecting the supply of women's labour were secondary to those on the side of demand.

These arguments have been recapitulated many times, and they are admittedly very broad generalizations. In real life some women are more resourceful, some are even stronger physically and have lower rates of absenteeism than some of their male colleagues. Some do not marry and are as ambitious and career-minded as any man: some have families to support, and some even have the backing of powerful trade unions. The point which the purely economic explanations miss is why the economic system has successfully managed to ascribe to *all* women but to *no* men certain attributes which have a (sometimes rather shaky) statistical predominance in women—or more correctly, why it has ascribed these attributes to all the women but to none of the men in some but not all occupations, since in some callings no differentiation is made on account of sex and all these supposedly economic factors are ignored. The nice logic of economic theory on the equivalence of wage-rate and marginal net product is indeed reduced to a sadly clumsy affair, if the determining factor turns out to be not the actual net product, but what that product would have been if the worker concerned had happened to resemble the majority of his or her sex in certain particulars. It would seem that a great many women must get less and a great many men more than their marginal net product.

Somewhat similar considerations apply also, though with more qualifications, to the practice of paying young people less than their elders. On the one hand, it can be argued that the young are always worth less than their elders because they are inexperienced; and on the other hand, that they are unlikely to carry heavy family

[1] Royal Commission on Equal Pay, *Report*. Cmd. 6937 (1946), pp. 107–21.

responsibilities, and may even themselves, like many wives, be partially supported by somebody else. These arguments again are generalizations, though it is true that every employee is inexperienced in his first job, whereas every woman is not, for instance, more liable to absenteeism than every man. But again it is significant that the discriminations are extremely rough-and-ready. In manual employments in industry the maximum adult rate is generally reached at twenty-one or a year or two later. Even if we continue to deal in broad generalizations and we ignore the very considerable difference between one man's life-history and another's, this means that the maximum wage must anticipate by some years, in the average case, the period when family expense is heaviest: nothing further is forthcoming to increase the family income at the age when there are most likely to be young children to be supported. In the professions and in salaried employments, on the other hand, where regular increments are customary, the length of scales varies very greatly from one occupation to another. Thus a teacher (if he does not become a headmaster) takes seventeen years to climb to the top of his scale, as compared with five years for the physiotherapist and twenty years for the prison officer. In part these differences may be explained by the fact that some scales are not intended, so to speak, for life tenure but are designed on the assumption that most of those who receive them will be promoted in due course to a higher grade. Even so, however, not everybody will in fact achieve such promotion, and the fact remains that if any of the scales are correctly adjusted so that maxima coincide—in the average case—with maximum family responsibility, others must miss this mark by a considerable margin on one side or the other.

A third feature of our wage structure in which social rather than economic factors appear to be operative is the principle that, within any one group of employees, those who give orders should normally be better paid than those to whom such orders are given. In practice a fair number of exceptions to this rule may be found, as for instance when operatives paid by results earn more than the foremen, paid by time, under whom they work; or where incremental scales overlap, so that a newly recruited official at the beginning of a higher grade receives less than an old-established employee who has reached the top of the grade below. In the former case, however, piecework earnings are not publicly disclosed and any disturbance of the recognized hierarchy is, therefore, not generally known; and in cases where there is overlapping of incremental scales, the inversion is necessarily temporary: viewed as wholes, such scales conform to the normal pattern. But the significant feature of these exceptions is the measure in which they are generally regarded as anomalous: when they come to light, they become the subjects of explanations, if not, indeed, of apologies.

That the hierarchy of pay should correspond with the hierarchy of authority is explicable in terms of classical wage theory on the ground that the qualities necessary for filling positions of responsibility are naturally scarce, or expensive to acquire, or both. On the other hand, power has its sweets as well as its burdens; although some fear responsibility, others seek it greedily; nor is it altogether certain that the qualifications which count in the race for promotion are as scarce and costly as those ideally desirable. All these are factors which should *lower* the price that responsible jobs can command; indeed on psychological grounds the opportunity to exercise authority ought perhaps to figure as much on the credit as on the debit side of the balance of net advantages.

Finally, we have to reckon, here and there, with features of individual industries, which in addition to the more widespread anomalies already mentioned are difficult to reconcile with the doctrine that every wage tends to be equal to the 'marginal net product' of the labour for which it is paid. In the case of professional footballers, for instance, this principle appears to be quite flagrantly disregarded. In 1952 a Committee appointed under the Conciliation Act of 1896 reported on the wages of association football players. At that time a player's maximum wage could not exceed £14 per week during the playing season, and £10 per week during the summer—to which must be added a number of quite modest benefits, payable at the absolute discretion of the employing club, such as match bonus varying from £1 for a draw in a League match up to £20 for a win in an FA cup match. Yet at this date transfer fees ranging up to as much as £34,000 might be paid for a star player.

There are two strange anomalies here. The first is the fact that professional footballers, unlike practically all other employed persons, operate under agreements expressly providing for *maximum* wages: economic textbooks have never heard of such maxima. The second anomaly is the enormous discrepancy between the wages paid and the player's true market value as reflected in the transfer fee. As the Conciliation Committee pointed out, a fee of £34,000 amounts to 'nearly twice what the player could get in a full playing life of fifteen years'; that is to say, a player for whom such a fee is paid must himself be getting barely one-third of the net product of his labour, measured in strictly economic terms. Very naturally, the players' unions expressed a sense of grievance about this. Nevertheless, the Conciliation Committee recommended that no major change should be made in the existing form of contract, though they did suggest that match benefits should be 'substantially increased'; that these and similar bonuses should be made obligatory, instead of optional; and that the clubs should consider raising the figures for maximum wages. The Committee justified their approval of the wage ceiling and of the system of transfer fees on the ground that 'the right of a player to insist on the payment of a premium . . . and to a wage without ceiling, would give an undoubted advantage to the rich as against the poorer League clubs', and that 'large individual payments to transferred players . . . would encourage an urge for constant transfer'.[1] Such differences and such transfers are, however, part of the very essence of economic theory. Superior skill, being in keen demand, ought to command a high price; and classical wage theory only comes out right if every worker betakes himself to the most remunerative employment that he can find.

VII

Classical wage theory thus appears insufficient by itself to explain a number of the characteristic features of our wage and salary structure. The actual picture is very different from what the textbooks would lead us to expect, in the sense that its most striking features are just those which this theory dismisses as incidentals. Wages and salaries are extremely unequal; and the spread from top to bottom far exceeds the range of differences that can credibly be ascribed to variations in inborn aptitudes. It is also greater than can be accounted for by the cost of acquiring the necessary training. Nor is it possible to discover any sign at all of an inverse relationship between the monetary and the non-monetary attractions of different jobs. If the entire structure of earned incomes is treated as a single whole, it is apparent that the more agreeable and more responsible posts win on every count. They are generally better paid than those that carry less responsibility, though less so than formerly, and with some exceptions. If, on the other hand, attention is concentrated on a relatively narrow section of the labour market, the picture is still confused, and there is no sign whatever of any positive relationship between the length of the normal working week and the standard time-rate of wages. Geographical differences, again, conform to no constant pattern; and it is difficult to accept an economic explanation of sex differentiation, while this is rigidly observed in one industry and disregarded in others. Even the superior rewards conferred by seniority or authority

[1] Committee of Investigation into a Difference Regarding the Terms and Conditions of Association Football Players, *Report* (1952), pp. 7, 13, 15.

are not easily reconciled with the postulates of economic theory; and finally, the case of the football players shows that some workers at least can be paid demonstrably less than they are in the most literal sense worth. In fact almost the only consistent feature of the whole picture is the principle that those who give orders expect (though even this rule is occasionally broken in practice) to be paid more than those to whom such orders are given.

The significance of these facts, and, in particular, their social implications are discussed at length below. Here it is important to stress that nothing that has been said must be construed as evidence that classical wage theory, within the limits of its own carefully defined assumptions, is actually wrong. Indeed, it is characteristic of this and other economic theories that they are cast in a shape in which it is impossible to prove them wrong. Where laboratory experiment is not practicable, no one can prove or disprove the reality of tendencies constantly obstructed by forces more powerful than themselves. Wherever the facts are in apparent conflict with the results theoretically to be anticipated, some explanation, as I have tried to show, is in every case possible. What is significant is not that these explanations are inaccurate, or even that they are hard to find, so much as the fact that they have to be invoked at all: there would seem indeed to be almost as many labour markets as there are jobs. The economic theory of wages leaves as much to be explained away as it explains. It fails, in Mr. Rowe's words, 'to satisfy our sense of reality and stand the test of historical experience'. To say this is not to deny the reality of the part played by economic forces in the determination of wage incomes, but to suggest, rather, that other factors also are involved which deserve analysis in their own right, since they so patently distort the simple picture presented by the economists.

CHAPTER III

Modern Methods of Wage Determination

I

NEARLY all the features of the wage and salary structure sketched in the preceding chapter which are anomalies from the angle of economic theory become intelligible in a broader frame of reference. It is the social factors which are missed in the economist's interpretation; and what is anomalous to the economist may make perfectly good sense to the sociologist. In a hierarchical society such as ours, large issues of social status are involved in wage and salary scales. Pay and prestige are closely linked; and (in spite of some exceptions) it is the rule that the high-prestige person should be also the highly-paid person; and *vice versa*. Once this rule is admitted as a factor in its own right, it is remarkable how effectively it explains much that, on a purely economic hypothesis, has to be explained away. On this principle the fact that the highest salary classes are monopolized by the first of the five social classes (professional, intermediate, skilled, partly skilled, unskilled) into which the Registrar-General classifies all occupations, is socially just as it should be; and the same principle explains the importance attached to the rule that those who give orders should be paid more than those to whom their orders are given. Where prestige depends on pay, one cannot be expected to obey, or even, perhaps, to respect, one's economic inferiors. Again, the positive relationship between monetary and non-monetary remuneration, which appears so persistently from top to bottom of our wage and salary structure and squares so badly with the economist's 'balance of net advantages', is just what one would expect in a society in which the dirty and disagreeable jobs are left to people whose pay is appropriate to their humble social position; nor is there anything to cause surprise in the fact that one may search in vain for signs of the supposed compensation of longer working hours by higher rates of wages. Similarly, the failure of the professional footballer to obtain for himself anything like the demonstrable economic value of his skill may be largely explained in social terms. The social distinctions that run through the world of sport would indeed be a fascinating study in themselves. Owing, perhaps, to the traditional emphasis on the distinction between amateur and professional status (ladies and gentlemen play games for fun, not for a livelihood),[1] those who earn their livings in professional sport enjoy lower social esteem than many other popular entertainers; and, in the subtle social hierarchy of the sporting world, association seems to rank below rugby football. These silent social forces must take some responsibility for the discrepancy between the remuneration of the soccer player and his potential market value.

The differentiation between the rates paid to men and to women in the same employment lends itself also to a comparable interpretation. The attitude of our society to women is highly ambivalent. On the one hand, a tradition of chivalry and a convention about their frailty make women objects of formal respect: conventionally well-mannered men do not sit when women are standing, or walk through doorways in front of their wives. On the other hand, in industry and in the world of affairs the assumption that women should normally occupy the humbler positions is still strongly entrenched. Rare indeed is the calling in which the proportion of women who attain the highest positions is comparable to the proportion of potential recruits of their sex to be found at lower levels. Those who do rise above these levels are nearly[2] always made aware of subtle differentiations or of tacit assumptions of masculine predominance. Indeed, an interesting parallel could be drawn, in the recent history of this country, between the position of women and that of the manual working classes. As members of two groups conspicuously ranked as socially inferior, both must have had many of the same experiences—including, on occasion, that of being (as it has been aptly called) 'elaborately treated as the equals' of more favoured social categories. Both also tend to be paid as befits their modest station. And both, in the present century, have succeeded in pushing themselves noticeably upwards, significantly improving their relative economic position in the process.

[1] They also sing and act for fun, though for some reason which it would be interesting to explore, no fuss is made about the distinction between amateur and professional in music and drama comparable to the rigid rules which determine amateur status in sport.

[2] Nearly, but not quite. In the course of my life I have myself had a hand in a good many jobs (paid and unpaid) in which members of both sexes were engaged. In perhaps two of these absolutely no discrimination on grounds of sex was detectable, and in one other the women appeared to suffer only a very slight disadvantage. These were, however, exceptions: as a rule the women were seriously handicapped chiefly by the tacit assumption that positions of higher responsibility would be (if with certain recognized exceptions) normally filled by men. For a fuller discussion of the bearing of the social position of women on the 'equal pay' issue, see my evidence to the *Royal Commission on Equal Pay* (*Appendices IX and X to Minutes of Evidence Taken Before the Royal Commission on Equal Pay*, London, H.M.S.O., 1946, pp. 114–15).

This presumed relationship between pay and prestige must account also for the curious arithmetic of arguments such as those used by Mr. Graham Hutton in his article referred to on p. 40. Explicit acknowledgement of class privilege is not in keeping with the conventions of this ostensibly democratic age: to say that a university lecturer ought, regardless of the laws of supply and demand, to enjoy a standard of living superior, in some specified degree, to that of an electrician would today be neither good taste nor good economics. The point can therefore only be made by the dubious device of attempting to prove that the lecturer at fifteen pounds a week is actually worse off than the electrician at eight.

It is of course easy to argue that high pay itself confers high prestige. That is no doubt true; but there is nothing in that to invalidate the converse proposition. Circular relationships are in fact everyday occurrences in social life: hens are constantly laying eggs and eggs growing into hens. In an acquisitive society those who enjoy large salaries are also, as a rule, accorded high social prestige; and the prestige of these callings in turn requires that their standard of pay should be correspondingly generous.

II

The broad similarity between the social and the wage hierarchy needs no elaborate demonstration. It could hardly be missed after even a most casual glance at the facts contained in the preceding chapter. Neither considerations of prestige, however, nor the laws of supply and demand can directly alter the size of anybody's wage-packet: prestige and economic calculation alike exist only in the minds of men. In order, therefore, fully to understand the forces that shape our wage structure, account must be taken of the human processes by which wage and salary rates are actually determined. Today these determinations are commonly the result of conscious and explicit decisions made, not by the phantoms that people the unimotivational fantasy world of the economic textbooks, but by men and women of real flesh and blood, whose business it is to fix wages in one or other of the ways described later in this chapter, and who must in so doing act according to their lights. Both the mental processes of these men and women and the social environment in which they move leave their mark upon the final picture. To the study of those processes and of that environment we may now turn.

Among the many social revolutions that have taken place in this country in the present century, not the least is the revolution in the institutional machinery for settling rates of wages and salaries. Today three main instruments are used for this purpose—collective bargaining, statutory regulation and quasi-judicial settlement by arbitration tribunals; and the part played by each is altogether different from what it was even fifty years ago.

At the beginning of the present century the practice of collective bargaining had already been established in some industries (as in engineering, iron and steel manufacture, and in textiles), often after a hard struggle on the part of the trade unions; but the unions were still fighting battles for recognition on many fronts; and, even where wage agreements were jointly made with employers, these were often only on a local basis even in such great industries as coal-mining. Comprehensive national bargaining was quite exceptional. Some idea of the change which has occurred in the prevailing mental climate may be gained by recalling that fifty years ago no trade union leader had ever been knighted or made a peer, and that even on the railways collective bargaining was not fully established until the second decade of this century. Comparisons of attitude are always dangerous when no precise measures are available, but it can safely be said that at the turn of the century employers were at best disposed to look upon the negotiation of wages with trade union representatives as an unwelcome concession to the growing power of the unions: fear and suspicion were the dominant themes in the conventional attitude to trade unionism. Today arrangements for collective bargaining are part of the ordinary constitutional machinery of industry, and few indeed are the manual jobs (other than those governed by statutory regulations or arbitration awards) for which a rate has not been jointly agreed (even if it is not universally observed) between employers' and workers' organizations. Miners, chemical and metal workers, engineers, shipbuilders, all branches of textile workers, leather workers, wood workers, builders, paper workers and printers, brewers, transport workers on the roads and railways, in ships and aeroplanes, shop assistants and other distributive workers—all can now quote a recognized union rate for their jobs embodied in a formal collective agreement. Private domestic service and some fields of clerical employment must be almost the only remaining fields of substantial employment on which collective bargaining has made no perceptible impact. Meanwhile trade unions have become pillars of society, and governments of every political complexion go out of their way to stress the honourable place which these bodies occupy in the structure of the community. The entrance hall of the headquarters of the Trades Union Congress at Transport House, with its directory of titled or decorated names, epitomizes an astonishing social change.

Nor is it only in industry that collective bargaining has become respectable. Hardly less remarkable has been the spread of the practice amongst clerical and professional workers. The professional civil servants, the dental mechanics, the chief officers of local authority departments, the psychiatric social workers, the journalists, the remedial gymnasts, the hospital engineers—as well as doctors, actors, musicians and staffs engaged in broadcasting—all have their own professional organizations, every one of which is at least partly concerned in looking after the financial interests of its members. Even in the universities, where no formal arrangements for joint negotiation of salaries have yet been made, the Association of University Teachers and in extra-mural education the Tutors' Association act as collective spokesmen on orthodox trade union lines for the staffs from whom their membership is drawn.

These dramatic developments can hardly be dismissed without further inquiry, as just examples of the 'imperfect competition' described in the economic textbooks. Indeed, any attempt to explain trade union activity in terms of models based on monopolistic selling involves an important fallacy. For a trade union is not a monopolistic seller of labour: it is not a seller of labour at all, but a representative of individual sellers—which is something quite different. The manufacturer who enjoys a monopoly in the production of some article can weigh the probable rewards of a high-price-restricted-output policy against those of large output and low prices, choosing whichever he thinks will yield the highest return. Which of these two courses he decides to follow will affect the size of the resultant profit, but not its destination. If he is the sole owner of the business, he will obviously be the sole beneficiary (or sole loser) irrespective of whether a restrictive or an expansionist policy is pursued. Similarly, even if a monopolist is in fact a board of directors acting on behalf of a company, each shareholder's slice of the distributed profits (large or small) will be determined by the amount of his holding, and not by the type of price policy by which those profits were made. In the case of a union, however, this is not so. Even if we assume that a monopolistic labour market works in the same way as the market for any article the sale of which is monopolistically controlled, the parallel breaks down, when it comes to the distribution of the proceeds. Just as the model monopolist might in some circumstances anticipate a larger total profit from limited sales at high prices than from larger sales at low prices, so the union leaders might argue that the total wage bill would be greater if a small number of men are employed at a high wage rather than a larger number at lower rates. But the effect of these two policies upon the whole body of their members is entirely different. In the former case the whole benefit is appropriated by those individuals who are lucky enough to get employment: the rest get nothing. In the alternative case, whatever the size of the wage bill, a larger number will enjoy a share of it.

No simple analogy can, therefore, be drawn between the capitalist who prefers to hoard or to destroy goods rather than risk his spoiling his own market by selling them at possibly unfavourable prices, and the union which, by the same logic, might be expected to choose good wages for a few and unemployment for the rest in preference to lower rates all round. Unsold goods will cost a firm money, and any loss on that account must be deducted from the possible gain in keeping them off the market. Since both credit and debit items fall within the same business, that is a straightforward (if speculative) calculation; but the loss of income due to unemployment and the gain from higher wages accrue to *different* people. Furthermore, people and things are different in kind. A bag of coffee does not, presumably, care whether it is sold or whether, alternatively, it is burnt in order to keep up the price of the rest of the crop. An unemployed man is likely to take a different view of any policy that prices him out of the market.

Again, trade union leaders who negotiate collective contracts, unlike businessmen, are not out to make money for themselves. Their job is to get the best possible terms for their members. When contracts are made between agents on both sides—the union official on the one hand and the officer of the employers' association on the other—the relation of each party to his constituents is in principle the same; though even in this case the position of a representative acting for perhaps a score of firms is different from that of a union leader representing perhaps tens of thousands of workpeople. But when (as sometimes happens—more often perhaps in the United States than in this country) wage agreements are made between union officials on one side and the directors or owners of firms directly concerned on the other, the personal interest of the two parties in the outcome is of a quite different order. The one has to think of his own pocket, the other of the temper of the members to whom he will have to justify his action: the former is clearly much nearer than the latter to the ideal monopolist pictured by the economic theorists. The economic theory which postulates that the one party is simply concerned to minimize, and the other to maximize, the wage bill overlooks this distinction. An *individual* applicant for a post may say to himself, 'If I make my

6

terms too stiff, I won't get the job.' To that, in collective negotiation, there is no true parallel.

The representative nature of collective contracts indeed distinguishes them in more ways than one from the bargains struck by individuals. The private individual has to convince an employer that he is worth the money that he is asking: the union has to persuade the employers or their representatives that the rate which it demands is appropriate for the job. Theoretically that can, of course, be done in strictly economic terms, on the lines of 'you can afford to pay what we are asking and you won't get the men you want until you do'. But in practice the argument is unlikely to stick at the economic level: the very fact of formal, representative discussion tends to push it on to a different plane. With the advent of collective bargaining, diplomatic negotiation takes the place of commercial haggling; and there are subtle differences between diplomacy and business. A case now has to be made, not just a bargain struck. That is why the role of the union, as not itself a seller, but as the spokesman of those who have labour to sell, becomes significant. Spokesmen and salesmen think in different patterns and use different language; and they may even come to different conclusions.

The formalization of discussion is thus itself a factor in the development of the handling of wage questions in ethical terms which is such a notable feature of our time and is discussed at length below.[1] Although most collective bargaining takes place behind closed doors, in the more important cases progress reports are issued to the Press, and there is certainly much public interest in the outcome. If no agreement is reached, and the issue is referred to arbitration, hearings are sometimes held in public. A collective agreement demands a degree of social justification which a private bargain can ignore. Negotiators and diplomatists, despite their reputation for cynicism, are incurably ethical in their choice of arguments.

The trade union leader, moreover (whether elected or appointed), functions as the representative of a society which is organized for specific purposes under a democratic constitution. Like other representatives he is, therefore, necessarily concerned with what are essentially political issues—domestic issues affecting his own position *vis-à-vis* the membership, and external issues affecting the standing of the union in relation, not only to the employers, but also to any rival organizations catering for the same group of workers. Even if he is himself apprised of all the niceties of the economic situation, and reacts appropriately, his members cannot be expected to have attained an equal degree of sophistication. They look to the union to deliver

[1] See Chapter V.

the goods: to give them something tangible in return for their subscriptions and for the loyalty which is often a real force in the trade union world.

There are, moreover, but few unions whose membership is so completely homogeneous that no possibility arises of a conflict of interest within the membership between different grades or different geographical areas; whilst large national organizations covering many industries and occupations (the Transport and General Workers' Union is the outstanding example) consist of an extremely complex web of potentially divergent interests which have to be most delicately handled. Mishandling is not only damaging to the negotiating officers' comfort and prestige (though not to their pockets unless they actually get fired): it is damaging, no less, to the status of the union as an institution, and so enhances the risk of a breakaway. The modern union leader must shape his wage policy with due regard to the balance of interests within his own organization. In this country, where the Trades Union Congress keeps a tolerably firm hold upon empire-building activities by rival unions, the danger of actual disruption is indeed nothing like as menacing today as it was thirty or forty years ago. But the fact that it has not entirely disappeared is illustrated by the Engineering Officers (Telecommunications) Association's recent breakaway from the Post Office Engineering Union; or the relations between the Colliery Winders' Federation and the National Union of Mineworkers which were the subject of protracted negotiation ending in the absorption of the winders into the National Union of Mineworkers in 1951. The annual reports of the Trades Union Congress General Council regularly include accounts of inter-union disputes in which the Council has been called upon to intervene—as, to take a few examples from recent years, between the National Union of Printing, Bookbinding and Paper Workers and the National Union of General and Municipal Workers; or between the Confederation of Health Service Employees and the National Union of Public Employees; or between the latter and the Transport and General Workers' Union.

In his work on *Trade Union Wage Policy*, Professor Ross gives a number of examples of how these political issues affect the trade union leaders' attitudes in wage negotiations in the United States, where inter-union rivalry is still quite formidable; and in particular of how such issues may lead to decisions which by the standard of economic analysis must be judged quite irrational. Strikes, for instance, may be called when only the narrowest margin divides the parties, in gross defiance of the principles adduced by Professor Hicks to explain industrial disputes.[1] Thus in the General Motors strike of 1945–6, 'the President's fact-finding board proposed a 19½ cent settlement in January; the company offered 17½ cents in February; and the parties finally settled for 18½ cents in March. Why,' asks Professor Ross, 'was the extra penny so important to the Union? It will take the workers ten years to make up the loss of one month's pay, at the rate of a penny an hour. And why was the penny so important to the company?' Again, 'in the bargaining process, . . . the size of the wage adjustment [is] often more crucial than the amount of the wage which results. . . . The trade union leader must achieve a 15 per cent increase for his group because most of the other locals affiliated with his international union have done so.'

Equally irrational is the insistence of many unions on both sides of the Atlantic upon a uniform wage throughout their jurisdiction—a principle to which great importance is attached. By this policy unions throw away all the advantages known to the economist as the rewards of 'discriminating monopoly'. To quote Professor Ross again, 'There is little doubt that a union could achieve a higher average wage-rate, and a greater total wage income for its members, if it were to extract from each employer the most that he could be made to pay.' And why do unions constantly press for the area of the bargaining unit to be extended and for 'multi-union' and 'multi-employer' bargaining structures? 'The assumption seems to be that the union's bargaining power varies directly with the size of the unit. . . . A craft union representing only a minority of workers may have more bargaining power than a trades council representing all the workers. If the craft is indispensable and the workers are irreplaceable, the union can achieve the effect of a complete walk-out by withdrawing its own members.'[2]

In this country Mr. H. A. Turner has recently traced in somewhat similar fashion the effect of internal political considerations upon the contemporary wage policy of a number of our own unions.

Mr. Turner's article deserves to be consulted at first hand, since it is too full of information to be readily summarized. Among the points which he makes, however, the following are of special interest in the present context. In recent years—indeed on and off ever since the First World War—there has been a persistent tendency in many industries for the wage differentials between skilled and unskilled workers to become narrower—largely as the result of the practice of awarding increases in the form of equal flat-rate additions to all grades. Alternatively, in other industries increases have taken the form of equal percentage advances all round. Both these methods contrast

[1] See p. 17.   [2] Ross, *Trade Union Wage Policy*, pp. 46, 48–9.

with the older practice of separate negotiation, usually on a local basis, for different classes of workers: they are in fact a characteristic of collective bargaining on a national scale. Indeed, it commonly happens that national agreements in the first instance simply result in the crystallization of existing differentials, both for locality and for skill. Some such arrangement, as Mr. Turner points out, is in fact practically a pre-condition of the establishment of national bargaining machinery involving separate groups of workers; for organizations which have previously looked after their own interests will only be induced to join with others, if by merging their separate identities they see a prospect of '*general* improvements in wages and conditions superior to those which the separate groups could achieve alone'. Amalgamations 'in any case always involved lengthy and difficult inter-union negotiations and diplomatic interchanges. It was clearly advisable for their leaders to confirm them by some success, and equally politic for them to accept the existing relation *between* rates as the line from which to launch their campaign. Some minor standardization may have been envisaged on occasion, if only to facilitate central negotiation. But any great discussion of the relativities between the allied groups might not only have diverted their energies from the main ends of their co-operation but even endangered its continuance. . . . Certainly no united strategy could have been based on the assumption that disproportionate concessions might be given by one class of workers.'

Once joint bargaining machinery has been established the 'need of union negotiators to secure the widest possible consent of the workers they represent compels them so to formulate their claim as to avoid any appearance of discrimination against a substantial section of their constituents. . . . In such cases any settlement which appears to place the membership of one of the associated unions at a disadvantage as compared with the other groups puts a great strain upon the alliance and may lead to the withdrawal of the offended party.'

When to these considerations we add the fact that an overall advance for everybody has the merit of simple convenience, it is easy to appreciate why it has become quite unusual for unions to ask for an increase in any form other than that of straight flat-rate or per-centage additions for all the workers involved. What then determines the choice as between these two systems, between, that is, a method which reduces proportionate differences but stabilizes differentials measured in absolute amounts of money, and one which maintains relativities? Again Mr. Turner shows how the internal politics and structure of the unions concerned lead them to prefer one or other method. Individual unions show definite and consistent leanings to one side or the other, which reflect the balance of power between the different classes of worker included in their membership. Thus flat-rate claims tend to be preferred 'where the lower-paid sections of workers are powerfully organized, and particularly so in industries where the skilled and the unskilled belong to separate trade unions which negotiate jointly with employers'. The cotton textile workers are a case in point. Again the 'same sort of "balance of power" situation is also often seen within industrial unions where the lower grades of worker are strongly represented'—as in the National Union of Railwaymen. In some unions, too, constitutional forms, the block vote in particular, give a weight to the views of unskilled workers which if proportionate to their numbers does not nevertheless reflect what Mr. Turner calls 'the quality of their organization'. The consti-tutional structure of the unions in the building industry, for instance, favours the labourers whose 'attachment to both the industry and their unions is rather unstable'.

In those occupations, on the other hand, in which percentage, not flat-rate, claims are the rule, as amongst the miners, the mule-spinners in the cotton industry, and the steel workers, three factors, as Mr. Turner reminds us, are important. First, none of the unions concerned has any rival to fear in its own field. Second, none of them has any membership outside its principal industrial interest. 'They organize occupations which are confined to the industries in which these unions operate.' Third, each of them operates a system of re-cruitment (either as the result of technical requirements, or thanks to rigid conventions which protect them from risk of dilution), in which vacancies in each grade are automatically filled from the ranks of those immediately below. These unions are thus relieved of the fear, which is a real factor in, say, the building or the engineering industry, that, if the skilled craftsman's rate is pushed too high, his job will be stolen by a professionally unqualified competitor.

Mr. Turner draws the moral that wage relativities are increasingly set 'by neither the accident of the labour market (a dubious term) nor the conscious will of those involved. They derive rather from the interplay of forces in the present structure of trades [sic] unionism, collective bargaining, and relations between people at work.'[1] That structure, we may add, is itself the result of a history of struggles for power (both between the unions themselves and in their conflicts with employers) and of a thousand and one events in the lives of both individuals and institutions, which from the angle of economic theory

---

[1] Turner, H. A., 'Trade Unions, Differentials and the Levelling of Wages', *The Manchester School of Economic and Social Studies* (September 1952), pp. 244, 246, 259, 280.

must be judged wholly accidental. The appearance of two unions where only one grew before may be due to the clash of incompatible personalities: giant amalgamations may bear witness to the dominance of a single ambitious leader. The aristocratic attitude of one union, the political colour of another, the general intransigence of a third, reflect the interaction of individual personalities with the traditions and the economic and social environment of the organizations which they serve; and the resulting picture is as complex as the character of the men and women who move across it. These complexities, unknown to the psychology of economic theory, are the familiar stuff of political life in any of its forms. They certainly leave their mark at the conference table where wage agreements are concluded.

The influence of the shape of trade union organization upon wage policy has, moreover, a potential importance in connection with the modern tendency, already mentioned, for more and more non-manual occupations to engage in collective bargaining. Now that collective bargaining has travelled far up the social scale, its influence upon our wage and salary structure has been revolutionized. The professions mentioned upon p. 72 include some that, as we have seen, rank among the most highly paid in the country. In consequence it is no longer true that trade union action or collective bargaining is primarily an instrument for levelling up the incomes of the lower-paid workers. Although his freedom of action may be restricted by sensitivity to public opinion, the trade union or professional representative in wage negotiation at *every* level has a duty to get the best bargain that he can for his members in all the circumstances of the moment (amongst which the prevailing mental climate must be included). And his concern is with his own members and nobody else: that is what he is paid for. Should he permit the interests of some other group to take priority over the claims of those whom he represents, he would, in fact, be open to just criticism for failure to fulfil the terms of his employment. It makes no difference that his own members may already have attained the £1,000 or £2,000 a year class: his vigour as their champion must not be tempered by any regard for equalitarian policies.

These developments really amount to a revolution within a revolution—both inside the trade union world, specifically so-called, and even more strikingly beyond its limits. At the end of the nineteenth century, the trade union movement consisted on the one hand of organizations catering for skilled craftsmen, and on the other hand of general labour unions. The professions and the blackcoats were hardly in the picture at all. While there were, without doubt, material differences in the rates earned by different groups within this field, all alike could fairly be said, on grounds of both income and social prestige, to fall within the category of the 'working-class'. To take a simple test, fifty years ago it would have been most unlikely that anybody holding the card of a union affiliated to the Trades Union Congress would have been found dining in the house of, say, an architect or other representative of the professional middle-class. The Trades Union Congress could therefore fairly claim to speak for a group of which all the members had *something* substantial in common over and above the mere fact of working under a contract of employment. All trade unionists stood to benefit, though, in varying degrees, from equalitarian policies. This simple fact explains, no doubt, much both in the unions' own attitude and in the view of their activities taken by the members of other social classes.

Today, Equity representing the stage, the Medical Practitioners' Union representing doctors (though only a small minority of the whole profession), as well as the Association of Scientific Workers, with a membership drawn from all ranks of scientists, and the Association of Supervisory Staffs Executives and Technicians, representing managerial grades in engineering, are all affiliated to the Trades Union Congress. The Congress now has the benefit of advice from a Non-Manual Workers' Advisory Council (on which the National Federation of Professional Workers is in turn represented); and in 1950 its General Council was instructed to examine the constitution and general effectiveness of this body with a view to giving it 'greater freedom and encouragement to participate more widely in matters of concern to non-manual workers'. In consequence of this resolution the representation of non-manual unions on the advisory council was increased, and the number of delegates who attended its annual meeting was nearly doubled; though the number of resolutions moved at Congress primarily in the interests of the non-manual and higher-paid workers remains only a small proportion of the whole. (The Congress is in fact largely occupied with general topics, such as the development of hydro-electric power, the control of atomic weapons or the method of repayment of income tax credits.) At the 1951 Congress, however, a resolution was carried calling on the Minister of Health 'to take those steps which are urgently required to improve the working conditions of general practitioners'; and at the Margate Congress of 1952 the representatives of British Actors' Equity Association carried a demand for stricter quota legislation to protect British films and for discriminating tax relief in favour of British producers. These are indeed signs of the times.

The essence of the trade union attitude remains today as much as ever respect for the principle of the rate for the job; and the blackleg is still the man who accepts a post below the union rate. The difference between today and yesterday is that these principles are now applied at every level; and at every level the good trade unionist is expected (often to his own manifest disadvantage) to support them. Neither the significance of this revolution, which spells the end of the identification of trade unionism with the interests of the lower-paid manual working class, nor the possible range of its effects, is yet perhaps fully appreciated. Indeed it may not be fanciful to suggest that some link can be traced between these happenings and the somewhat similar changes that are noticeable in political life—particularly in the attitude of the Labour Party, which owes so much both of its income and of its ideology to the trade union world. Certainly the period which has seen the trade union umbrella extended to cover those who represent clerical and professional workers is also the period which has seen the gradual disappearance from Labour Party programmes of frankly equalitarian proposals. But to pursue this aspect of the matter further would not be relevant to the theme of the present study.

The traditional association of the Trades Union Congress with the manual workers (and with Labour politics) no doubt slows down the rate at which organizations of non-manual workers seek actual affiliation with the Congress. No such legacy, however, inhibits these bodies from copying the distinctive trade union practice of collective bargaining at more and more exalted levels. In consequence, this practice has been transformed, in little more than half a century, from a principal weapon of class struggle into a mechanism for the protection of vested interests that extends almost from top to bottom of the employed community.[1]

III

The machinery for statutory regulation of wages has often been described: only a broad outline need be repeated here. This machinery now (1954) covers agricultural workers; catering workers; and those engaged in over fifty miscellaneous trades covered by the Wages Councils Acts, including, since 1948, transport workers employed on vehicles used in the carriage of goods 'either wholly or partly for reward', who were previously covered by a separate Act. In addition, an Act of 1934 made provision for statutory effect to be given, subject to certain safeguards, to rates of wages agreed by employers'

[1] This statement must not be held necessarily to imply criticism. Vested interests are generally less dangerous when they are acknowledged; and frank discussion of their claims at least opens the door for justice to be done.

and workers' organizations in the weaving section of the cotton industry; while, in the event of complaint that the existing remuneration in any particular case is 'unfair', a statutory rate can be fixed for such workers engaged in the transport of goods by road as are not covered by the Wages Council Acts. The two last-named provisions are, however, little used today (no wage orders are now in force in the cotton industry) and they are neglected in the discussion that follows.

The basic machinery in all other cases follows an identical pattern with only minor variants. In each case a Wages Board or Council is established, appointed by the Minister of Labour (for agricultural workers the Minister of Agriculture) and consisting of equal numbers of representatives of employers and workers in the trade or industry concerned, together with a smaller number of 'impartial' or 'independent' members, one of whom is designated as chairman. All the members of these bodies are directly appointed by the Minister, who is however specifically required under the Wages Councils Acts to consult the appropriate organizations of workers and employers before choosing the representative members of the Councils. In practice this consultation means that the organizations are normally successful in getting their own nominees appointed; and there is in fact a considerable overlap of membership between different councils. The geographical as well as industrial range of these wage-fixing bodies varies considerably. Under the Wages Councils Acts there may be a single Council for the whole of Great Britain or one for England and Wales and another for Scotland; under the Catering Wages Act five separate Boards deal with distinct sections of the industry. In agriculture, in addition to the Central Wages Boards for England and for Scotland, Committees are also established in every county. Originally, the initiative in fixing rates lay with these committees; but during the war this was transferred to the two Central Boards, though the Committees still have a legal right to make representation about proposed rates.

In all cases except that of agriculture, the rates proposed by wage-fixing bodies must be referred to the Minister before they come into effect. The Minister does not, however, enjoy any powers of amendment: he can only refer back proposals which he does not like, for reconsideration by the Councils concerned; and the Councils can (and do), if they are so minded, decline to modify their original proposals. Provision is also made for the establishment of committees to co-ordinate any two or more Wages Councils, and to recommend to those Councils how they should exercise their powers. Only one such co-ordinating committee has in fact been appointed, but the

Councils are linked by a common secretariat based on the Ministry of Labour. Under the Catering Wages Act, a permanent Commission is established in addition to the Wages Boards; and this may inquire, with wide terms of reference, into the remuneration and conditions of workers covered by the Act, as well as into the means of meeting the requirements of the public, including visitors from overseas and the tourist traffic generally. This Commission has power to report directly to any Government department and the departments concerned are required to consider what the Commissioners have to say.

All these wage-fixing bodies, which together cover something like three million workers, and were responsible in 1953 for over one-third of the total of wage advances granted throughout industry,[1] have a duty to fix minimum rates of wages to which in due course force of law is given; and they mostly do fix elaborate scales for different grades of worker, including overtime and other special rates as well as in many cases piecework standards. How then do they set about the job? Parliament, which created them, has certainly given them very little guidance. The statutory formula varies a little from one case to another. Wages Councils under the Act of that name are simply instructed to 'fix' rates: the matter is left at that. The declared purpose of the Catering Wages Act is to make provision for regulating the 'remuneration and conditions of employment of catering and other workers and, in connection therewith, for their health and welfare and the general improvement and development of the industries in which they are employed'. The Wages Boards in this industry presumably, therefore, have a duty, in framing their wage policies, not to neglect the 'improvement and development of the industries' in which the workers concerned are engaged; but, apart from this not very specific instruction, their job, like that of Wage Councils, is simply defined as a matter of 'fixing' rates. Nor are they likely to get help, at any fundamental level, from the Catering Wages Commission. In practice the Commission has concerned itself either with matters affecting the establishment and scope of the various boards, or with special topics, some of which, such as those discussed in the Commission's report on the *Development of the Catering, Holiday and Tourist Services*, are primarily of interest to the industry as a whole, while others, such as an inquiry into the problems affecting the remuneration of catering workers that result from the practice of giving tips, bear more closely upon wage problems. The activities of the Commission must certainly be of value to the Wages Boards in helping them to appreciate in a more informed way the

[1] *Ministry of Labour Gazette* (January 1954), p. 3.

complexities of the situations by which they are faced, and the probable consequences of alternative courses of action; but they do not extend to indicating which of those courses should be followed.Wide though the Commission's terms of reference are, they could hardly be stretched to include the right to tell the Wages Boards how to conduct their statutory business.

Only in the regulation of agricultural wages has an explicit objective been prescribed. The Act of 1924, which first gave the power to fix statutory wages to county wage committees, laid down that each committee should fix such minimum rates in its own area as would 'so far as practicable secure for able-bodied men such wages as in the opinion of the committee are adequate to promote efficiency and to enable a man in an ordinary case to maintain himself and his family in accordance with such standard of comfort as may be reasonable in relation to the nature of his occupation'. This rubric certainly embodies a brave attempt to grapple with a problem which on other occasions has been consistently evaded. But it cannot, I think, have given much concrete help to the committees or to the Central Wages Boards which later took over their functions. At least in the attempt to answer one question it provokes a long string of others. In what circumstances must it be reckoned frankly 'impracticable' to award a wage that is adequate for efficiency? What is an 'ordinary case'? What size of family is supposed to be dependent upon this able-bodied worker in this 'ordinary case'? Six children? Two children? No children? And—most elusive (and question-begging) of all—what is a 'reasonable standard of comfort' and how is this related to the 'nature of a man's occupation'?

These are far from being frivolous questions. The agricultural wages formula puts into words the kind of considerations that must lurk at the back of the mind of everybody who has a hand in statutory wage determination: indeed, one of the many possible sets of practical answers to the questions which it raises is necessarily implied in every rate actually fixed. But the real difficulty lies in the fact that the range of possible answers is so large that the formula does nothing to ease what are in practice the critical problems of choice.

In these conditions some influence may perhaps be ascribed to the circumstances in which statutory wage authorities came into being and the fields in which they have been given power to operate. Parliament may not have disclosed just what these bodies were intended to do, but it must have had its reasons for inventing them, and for establishing them in some industries, and not in others: some guidance can presumably be derived from these. Certainly a broad hint was implied in the Act of 1909, which restricted the establishment of the first

Wages Councils (or Trade Boards as they were then called) to industries in which the rate of wages was 'unduly low'. Such a require-ment was indeed natural enough in an Act which followed directly upon a great public outcry against 'sweated labour'; and each Board must have felt bound to interpret it as a mandate for fixing statutory rates in the first instance somewhere above the then prevailing level. The Boards were, however, left to fend entirely for themselves in determining both how large an increase would be appropriate in any particular case; and how they ought to shape their policy as the years went by, and (thanks to their efforts) wages in their industries ceased to be 'unduly low'.

Nine years later the scope of statutory wage regulation was extended by a second Act, which, in place of the restriction of Trade Boards to industries having 'unduly low' wages, substituted a new formula, which, with only minor changes, is still in force today. In its modern version, as incorporated in the Wages Councils Act of 1945, this formula allows the Minister to make an order establishing a Wages Council in cases where he is of opinion that 'no adequate machinery exists for the effective regulation of the remuneration of the workers described in the order and that, having regard to the remuneration existing amongst those workers or any of them, it is expedient that such a council should be established'. Applications for a Wages Council can be addressed to the Minister by joint repre-sentative bodies in any industry on the ground that the existing machinery for collective bargaining is likely to cease to be adequate or to come to an end altogether. In such cases (as indeed sometimes also on his own initiative) the Minister appoints a Commission of Inquiry to advise him as to whether a Wages Council should be established. This Commission then reviews the bargaining machinery available in the industry concerned, and may make suggestions for improving this. Alternatively, should the Commissioners take a pessimistic view of the present and possible future state of such machinery, and also form the opinion that 'a reasonable standard of remuneration is not being or will not be maintained', they may draft a 'Wages Council recommendation' to which the Minister can, if he thinks fit, give statutory effect.

These provisions may reasonably be read to imply a radical change from the attitudes of 1909. The original purpose of statutory wage regulation was, avowedly, to raise wages where they were lower than (judged by some unspecified standard) they ought to have been. Today the ostensible object is to make good any gaps left in the voluntary arrangements for collective bargaining. Logically, such a transformation of Wages Councils into a kind of statutory substitute for spontaneous collective bargaining would seem to imply that the Councils should behave as nearly as possible as, in similar circumstances, voluntary negotiating bodies would have behaved; that they should envisage their role as that of bargaining instruments, rather than as the means of putting into effect high principles of social policy such as those to which the Agricultural Wages Act gave expression. Certainly the new formula reflects both the increased influence of the trade unions, who naturally have no wish to see their own functions transferred to statutory authorities, and the growing public acceptance of collective bargaining as the *normal* method of wage determination.

Actually, this change in terms of reference probably exaggerates any corresponding change in practical policy. The structure of Wages Councils (and of the earlier Trade Boards), with their representative members recruited from employers and workers in the industry affected by their decisions,[1] encourages the view that they are more or less a sub-species of collective bargaining; and some points in their procedure facilitate this interpretation still further—as, for instance, the regulation which allows employers and workers' representatives to vote by sides, and not as individuals, the majority on each side determining the vote of that side as a whole. The role of the independent members can be harmonized with this interpretation if it is conceived as a matter of bridging gaps and effecting compromises between the parties directly concerned, rather than of importing *a priori* principles. Statutory wage-fixing boards all meet in private and are under no obligation to disclose to anybody the lines along which their minds travel: one may, however, conjecture that even the earlier Trade Boards may well have found that the formula 'unduly low' was most easily translated to mean 'lower than would have resulted from voluntary bargaining'. Nevertheless, the concept of inherently 'just' or 'reasonable' rates is not easily banished. Even today a Wages Council cannot be established under existing legislation *merely* because employers and workers have failed to develop the practice of collective bargaining. The law requires that regard should also be paid to the remuneration of the workers in the trades in which such Councils are proposed; and the Minister must ask himself, or the Commission of Inquiry must advise him, whether or no this remuneration is, and is likely to continue to be, 'reasonable'.

Statutory wage regulation operates, therefore, more or less in a vacuum: or perhaps one should say in a haze of vague suggestions, never explicitly formulated or reconciled with one another. The

[1] In contrast to arbitration tribunals. See below, pp. 88 ff.

historical background of statutory wage regulation in this country suggests that its primary purpose was to secure 'living' or at least 'subsistence' wages. On the face of it a wage must surely be reckoned unduly low if it is too small to live upon. Any attempt to establish a criterion on these lines must, however, inevitably founder on the difficulties implicit in the agricultural wages formula. Apart from the problem of emptying out the large conventional element that enters into even the most severely scientific calculation of the cost of subsistence at physiologically minimum levels, there remains the insuperable difficulty that what is enough for one person is not enough for six, while bare subsistence for six is more than enough for one. The point is as obvious as it is important. The common way out of the difficulty is, of course, to calculate the subsistence wage in terms of an 'average family'. In an uncharted sea this formula may be as good a sailing direction as any other—so long as we recognize that its avowed destination is in fairyland. At any one moment the average family (usually reckoned at two adults and two or three children) is sure to be the exceptional family. According to the sample census returns of 1951, out of just under $14\frac{1}{2}$ million households in Great Britain, just under 2 million have two children, while just over a million more have three or four children. More than 8 million have no children at all. In these conditions (family allowances at their present level notwithstanding) there can be no meaning in the concept of a 'living wage'. It is, therefore, perhaps not surprising that for more than thirty years the agricultural wages formula has stood alone: no attempt has been made to repeat or to improve upon it.

IV

The third method by which wages are settled is by reference to some kind of arbitration tribunal or independent investigation. This is also, practically speaking, a twentieth-century invention, and it is one which now plays a considerable part. In 1953 the proportion of all wage increases reported by the Ministry of Labour as effected by 'arbitration and mediation' was 20·0%: the corresponding figure for the previous year was 12·8%; and for 1951 4·8%. Unlike wages boards with statutory powers, industrial arbitration came into existence not to raise scandalously low wages, but to prevent breaches of the peace in industry. Formal machinery dates back to the Industrial Conciliation Act of 1896, but for present purposes the more important bodies are the Industrial Court set up under the Industrial Courts Act of 1919 and the Industrial Disputes Tribunal.

These are both standing bodies, the IDT being the post-war version of the National Arbitration Tribunal established in 1940 to prevent war-time disputes: the change of title, together with certain changes in powers and procedure, occurred in 1951 when strikes, forbidden during the war, again became lawful. The detailed differences between these various bodies are somewhat complex and need not trouble us here; but it should perhaps be noted that whereas reference to the Industrial Court normally involves the consent of both parties to a dispute (sometimes embodied in advance in an undertaking to refer all differences arising out of a particular agreement), a complaint from one side alone can bring a dispute before the Industrial Disputes Tribunal, as was also the case with its predecessor the National Arbitration Tribunal.

In addition to these standing bodies, *ad hoc* Boards of Arbitration, or single arbitrators, may also be appointed by the Minister to deal with disputes as they arise; and a number of the larger industries (as, for instance, the Civil Service, the coal-mining industry and the railways) have arbitration machinery of their own. Mention must also be made of the Courts of Inquiry which the Minister has power to appoint under Part II of the Industrial Courts Act. The function of these courts is to get at the facts in any dispute and to make these known to Parliament and to the public. They are not, therefore, arbitral tribunals properly so called and do not issue any award, though they can, and do, make recommendations for a settlement. In practice, the problems which these courts have to face in the search for principles of wage settlement are closely similar to those that occupy arbitrators proper; and much of what follows applies equally to both types of body.

Both arbitration tribunals and courts of inquiry share—with one important difference—the tripartite structure of statutory wage councils: they are composed of equal numbers of representatives of employers and of workers, under an independent chairman, together with (in some cases) additional independent members. The essential difference between their structure and that of statutory wage authorities is that the representative members of the latter are chosen from within the industry concerned, whereas employers and workers on arbitration tribunals come from outside the industry whose disputes they have to resolve: if in any case technical knowledge of a particular industry is required, this is normally supplied by the help of assessors who take no part in the final award. This difference between the constitution of wages boards and that of arbitration tribunals clearly implies a corresponding distinction between the legislative function of the former and the judicial function of the latter. The wages board drafts laws for its own industry, whereas the arbitration court gives judgment on matters submitted by others. The choice of industrial arbitrators unconnected with the industries the merits of whose claims they must judge, is evidently intended as a guarantee that they, like other judges, will be free from bias arising from personal interest.

At the same time conformity with judicial models is not quite complete. A court of arbitration normally includes persons chosen to represent employers and workers generally, though not for their connection with a particular industry; and this raises a rather curious ambiguity which has not, I think, attracted the attention that it deserves. The question arises whether it is the duty of these representative members to act, in the course of the court's deliberations, as advocates of the interests of the employing or the employed community which they respectively represent, or whether every member is bound only to serve the public interest as he sees it. Either interpretation is possible; but the difference between them is real. On the one hand, the employer and worker members may feel that, just because they *are* chosen as representatives, it is their first duty to see that full weight is given to the arguments of the side whom they represent, and that they should look for the weak rather than the strong points in the case of the opposite side. On this view, the primary role of the representative members is, between them, to make sure that their independent colleagues have seen the case of both the parties in the best possible light before coming to a decision. In support of this view may be quoted the fact that, when the members of an arbitration tribunal cannot agree, it is not usual for the issue to be decided by majority vote: instead, the award is made in the name of the chairman alone. This rule certainly emphasizes the representative position of the employer and worker members. If the court were deemed to consist wholly of independent persons (however chosen) looking at the issue judicially, there might be a case for insisting (as with a jury) on unanimity; or, alternatively, for permitting (as with a bench of magistrates) a majority decision; but it would be illogical to relieve the rank and file members of responsibility for the finding of their chairman.

On the other hand, the fact of representative choice does not preclude the alternative interpretation that all members of arbitration tribunals should ignore their representative standing and strive to fill the role of wholly unbiased guardians of the public interest. The parallel of the lay justices of the peace who staff most of our magistrates' courts is evidence of that. Though justices are not chosen on any formally representative basis, it is recognized that they should

7

be drawn from different social classes and should represent different types of opinion. Once appointed to the bench, however, they must forget their origins: any tendency to favour defendants of their own way of thinking would be scandalously unjudicial behaviour. In the case of magistrates the issue is thus unequivocally settled: representative selection must not affect judicial detachment. In the case of wage tribunals the parallel issue has never been clearly determined; indeed I do not think that it has even been explicitly raised. Certainly the representative members of these bodies do not receive clear guidance on the point (the question is one of high policy which ought to be settled at parliamentary level, and could not be appropriately dealt with by an administrative ruling on the part of the Ministry of Labour); and yet the answer must profoundly affect the frame of mind in which they approach their duties. I write as one who (as in the circumstances described in the Introduction to this book) has experienced real doubt in practice as to which is the right attitude to adopt.

Much of the time of arbitration tribunals is occupied with disputes that arise in the interpretation of existing agreements or awards. In these cases (many of which affect only a handful of workers or perhaps a single firm) no fundamental questions of principle are involved: the issues can be dealt with in purely legalistic fashion. For the purposes of the present argument, only those cases are relevant in which, the parties having failed to come to terms, an arbitration award affects a change in the prevailing wage structure by the introduction of new rates.

In dealing with these, arbitration tribunals, like statutory wage boards, have to rely upon their own wits. In this country they do not have the benefit of any formal instructions as to the principles on which they should proceed—apart from the general (and somewhat confused) pronouncements on government wage policy which are described in the following chapter. Indeed governments may be said to fall over backwards in their determination to refrain from offering any guidance to arbitrators, as the following parliamentary incident shows: 'Mr. Isaacs asked the Minister of Labour whether he will state the policy of his Department as regards the issue of instructions or guidance to the various arbitration tribunals regarding the level of wage increases which they should award. *Sir W. Monkton*: "Yes, Sir. The policy of my Department, and, indeed, of Her Majesty's Government, has been and remains not to issue instructions or guidance of any sort to these bodies. On the contrary, the Government have scrupulously respected their independence." *Mr. Isaacs*: "I am sure that the House and the community will be very pleased to have that information. May I ask the right hon. and learned Gentleman if he is aware that the slightest hint of a suspicion among the workers that arbitration is being tampered with will kill it? I hope that his answer will satisfy them." *Sir W. Monckton*: "There will be no tampering with arbitration as long as I hold my office." '[1]

It will be noticed that Mr. Isaacs, a former Minister of Labour in a Labour Government, as well as Sir Walter Monckton, used the word 'tampering' to describe the issue of official instructions or guidance to arbitration tribunals; and that Sir Walter, at least, appears to regard such an attitude as a necessary mark of respect for the independence of these bodies.

In their freedom from explicit direction arbitration tribunals resemble, at least superficially, the courts of justice which administer —and have in fact created—the common law. Indeed, the first President of the Industrial Court, after ten years' experience in that capacity, was led to suggest a close parallel between this court and the courts of common law. 'The Common Law,' he writes, 'is organic; it undergoes change, and at any time bears a relationship to current moral and ethical opinion. . . . The early Courts endeavoured on the particular facts of a case to give a decision which would be regarded by men in general as a right one—not right according to "law" which was embryonic and unfounded, but right according to prevailing ideas. Much depended on custom because custom or established practice was regarded as embodying what may be called the good sense of mankind, and was a safer guide than abstract notions of right and wrong. Notwithstanding the appeal to custom and later to precedent, however, the principles of the Common law were in fact rules devised by the judges themselves as conducive to a proper adjustment of men's relationships in the various affairs of life. It is hardly open to doubt that should the Industrial Court or any other industrial tribunal of authority continue to indicate the principles or considerations upon which its decisions are based there would develop in course of time a body of "law" governing industrial relationships, recognition of which would not only facilitate the settlement of disputes which had, in fact, occurred, but would tend to prevent their occurrence; for the rights of the parties in any matter of difference would thus be indicated from the outset.'[2]

The analogy is attractive; but it has not stood the test of time. Unlike courts of law proper, industrial arbitration tribunals in the

---

[1] 19 January 1954, 522 H.C. Deb. 5 s., 821–2.
[2] Amulree, Lord, *Industrial Arbitration in Great Britain* (London, Oxford University Press, 1929), pp. 186, 191–2.

United Kingdom have refrained from establishing, or even from making any serious attempt to establish, any case law. In their awards, references to earlier decisions are fairly frequent, since the natural human urge for consistency does not allow industrial arbitrators, any more than any other body of men engaged in continuous decision-making, ever wholly to ignore everything that they have ever done before. But precedent in any formally binding sense has no place in wage awards; and the reasons for a decision are seldom given. Actual practice varies a little as between one tribunal and another, or one period or another. The Industrial Court, in its early days, was inclined to be comparatively frank, as its President clearly intended that it should continue to be. Thus a famous decision of 1920 (No. 521) discussed in several paragraphs the degree in which increases in the cost of living were justifiable grounds for wage advances. The Court at that date expressed the view that 'some compromise is necessary between the mechanical regulation of wages on the basis of the cost of living and the regulation of wages solely by reference to the state of the market in the particular industry which might be under consideration. Increases in the cost of living must be allowed due weight as a factor in the situation, but it would be against the interests of the workers and of the whole community that claims for increases in wages on this ground alone should be pressed or conceded to the full extent that might be proper if normal economic processes had not again begun to operate.'[1] Again, two years later, in adjudicating on a claim on behalf of railway shopmen, the Court had to consider the vexed question of the relation between craftsmen employed in railway service, and those in engineering or building operations in other industries. After debating this issue at length, the Court reached a decision explicitly based on the following principles: 'So long as the railway service is regarded as a separate industry, subject to its own conditions of prosperity and depression, it appears to be undesirable that alterations in rates of wages brought about in other industries, by the conditions of those industries, should automatically result in exactly similar changes on the railways. At the same time, the effect of demand and supply in the case of particular kinds of labour cannot be ignored, and general movements of wages in outside trades, or in those akin to railways in their manufacturing aspect, must probably be reflected in some degree in the rates of the railway shopmen. The mechanical regulation of wages by reference to a cost of living sliding scale does not, therefore, appear to the Court to be

[1] *The Industrial Court, Decision No. 521, Textile Workers—Hillfoots* (HMSO, 8 November 1920).

very appropriate to the circumstances.'[1] By 1939, however, when a claim on behalf of the railway shopmen was once again before the Court, the climate had begun to change. Award No. 1732, dated June 1939, follows a pattern which has since become very familiar. First, a fairly full summary is given of the arguments put forward by the two contestants; then follows the formula that 'the Court have given careful consideration to the evidence and submissions of the parties'; after which the first and third items of a threefold claim are dismissed, the one as simply 'not established', and the other merely with the observation that the 'grounds advanced' in support of it 'were not such as in the view of the Court to warrant the concession' of the claim. The reasons for rejection of the second item were only a little more fully elaborated—with a reference to the fact that its concession would involve a departure from the principles of the award of 1922 and would also 'affect the basis upon which piecework prices are fixed and would render inevitable a review of the rates of wages of other classes of workpeople whose rates of wages had been fixed in relation to those affected by the present claim'.[2]

A fairly full résumé of evidence submitted, followed by a bald announcement of the Court's decision, is now the standard practice of the Industrial Court, subject to occasional exceptions in which reference is made either to previous awards or to voluntary agreements that have been, or might be, made between the parties. A similar formula, often with the summary of evidence more severely compressed, has been used also from the beginning by the National Arbitration Tribunal, the Industrial Disputes Tribunal and the Civil Service Arbitration Tribunal.

Remarkable violence was indeed done to the English language by these bodies in their earlier attempts to confine themselves to a coldly neutral epitome of the evidence before them. The National Arbitration Tribunal early in its career initiated a practice of presenting these summaries under the formula 'statements were submitted as to', followed by a list of topics separated by semi-colons. On occasion this practice resulted in a single sentence occupying as much as two whole pages of print. In and after Award No. 1222, however, the Tribunal adopted a less unusual narrative form of summarization. The effect of this change was more than linguistic, for the new mode of presentation makes it considerably easier to see the shape of the argument put before the tribunal; and this later practice has been continued,

---

[1] *The Industrial Court, Decision No. 728, Railway Shopmen—England and Wales* (HMSO, 8 July 1922).
[2] *The Industrial Court, Award No. 1732, Railway Shopmen* (HMSO, 29 June 1939).

in its turn, by the Industrial Disputes Tribunal. But, like its prede-cessor, this tribunal regularly refers to the 'careful consideration' which it gives to the arguments put before it, without betraying any hint of the link between that consideration and the decision ultimately reached.

Specialized and *ad hoc* Boards of Arbitration also make it a rule to publish summaries—often rather fuller than those given by the National Arbitration Tribunal or the Industrial Disputes Tribunal—of the evidence laid before them; but they too are hardly less chary of disclosing the grounds for their decisions. Courts of Inquiry, ap-pointed under the Industrial Courts Act, on the other hand, are in a different position. As already mentioned, these courts are not, in the strict sense, arbitration tribunals at all. Their business is to tell the world the rights and wrongs of a dispute; and, if they are so minded, to suggest a possible way out—not to impose a formal judgement upon the disputants. Accordingly, these courts have con-tributed some of the most illuminating material available to illustrate the principles currently invoked in wage determinations: their sig-nificance in this context is discussed more fully in Chapter V.

Industrial arbitrators are thus bound to move in their own mysterious ways. Like statutory wage boards, however, they are to some extent conditioned by the circumstances of their origin. In this connection it is significant that in Britain arbitration has traditionally been a voluntary affair, and so remained until the Second World War. Its voluntary character is twofold. On the one hand, before the establishment of the National Arbitration Tribunal in 1940 arbi-trators could only function by consent of both sides to a dispute; and, on the other hand, apart from war emergency regulations, awards are not binding on the parties in the sense that criminal penalties attach to their infringement: at most they are deemed to be implied terms in the contracts of employment of the workers to whom they apply, and subject, therefore, to enforcement only by civil process. These facts alone put arbitration tribunals into a posi-tion entirely different from that of the ordinary courts of law in which a prosecutor does not have to wait upon the defendant's consent to his action, and in which defiance of the court's judgement is punishable as a criminal offence.

In this country arbitration has, moreover, consistently been treated as a last resort to be invoked only in cases where collective bargaining fails. This condition has been emphasized in every piece of legislation on the subject. The Industrial Courts Act lays down that if any trade or industry has its own arrangements for conciliation or arbitration the Minister shall not, unless with the consent of both parties, refer a dispute to arbitration, except where the industry's own attempts to obtain a settlement have failed. As Lord Amulree has pointed out, so long as the consent of both parties was anyhow necessary for arbitration, this provision was apparently superfluous; but it certainly does rub in the need to try everything else first. Similarly, the Order which established the National Arbitration Tribunal required the Minister in the first instance to refer any dispute reported to him to collective joint machinery in the trade or industry concerned, if such were available. Only if no such machinery existed, or if a settlement was unduly delayed, could he hand the matter on to the Arbitration Tribunal. The Industrial Disputes Tribunal operates under similar provisions.

In these conditions it would be logical, if slightly cynical, to ascribe to the arbitrator the role, not of dispensing justice, but of preventing strikes. His job is to search for some solution which it would be to the advantage of both sides to accept; which in fact they might have found for themselves, if they had kept their tempers, and remained as sweetly reasonable as their models in the economic textbooks. At least, so long as arbitration remains voluntary, a tribunal can, in fact, only hope to keep in business if it does succeed in pleasing both sides. Contestants on either side who are annoyed by a court's decisions, will refuse to submit further disputes to it; or they will flout decisions that are not legally binding.

Professor Hicks, in the work already quoted, forcefully upholds this view. Indeed, he castigates severely any arbitrators, who under a voluntary system allow themselves to be seduced by the 'fatal attractions' of an alternative line. 'It is difficult,' he writes, 'to get out of the minds of arbitrators the notion that their function is in some way judicial—and this in its turn induces a legalistic approach, which has remarkable consequences in the field of industrial relations. . . . It cannot be too clearly recognized that in an arbitrator, legalism is a bias; the arbitrator's job is to find a settlement that the disputants can with advantage accept, not to impose a solution that seems to him fair and just. If he is influenced by considerations of justice (based nearly always on very limited conceptions of where justice lies) he cannot expect that party, whose procedure he is inclined to consider unrighteous, to be very ready to bring disputes for his decision.'[1] The implications of this passage are curious. To his logical conviction that considerations of justice are out of place in wage arbitrations, Professor Hicks appears to have joined a nervous fear that those who nevertheless pursue justice will in fact necessarily be guilty of injustice: the would-be just arbitrator must be

[1] Hicks, *Theory of Wages*, pp. 149–50.

expected to show (for what reason is not apparent) unjust favour to the unions. Nor, in Professor Hicks's view, can we rely on this bias being balanced by the class prejudice of arbitrators, most of whom are middle-class persons. In this case two blacks will not make a white because, whereas class prejudice is so obvious as to be deliberately discounted, the 'bias of legalism is less easily recognized, and so more insidious'.

Writing a year or so before Professor Hicks, Miss M. T. Rankin criticized the policy of the Industrial Court from an opposite point of view. According to her thesis, developed in an analysis of the decisions promulgated by the Court, in the first ten years of its life, arbitrators ought to apply principles: they go wrong only when they invent principles of their own instead of applying those that are already available. 'The discredit [of arbitration] is not due, as is usually represented, to the *absence* of accepted principles, but primarily to the failure on the part of such Courts to recognize that there are principles, and secondly, that their own province is not therefore to lay down other principles but to interpret principles already laid down for them, either by law or resolution, or such principles not being involved, laid down by the parties themselves.' The brief discussion that follows, however, leaves the reader in some doubt as to this distinction between accepted and unaccepted principles, as no criterion of acceptability is defined by the author. To the former class Miss Rankin assigns the two concepts of the subsistence wage (which we have seen to be inherently illusory), and the fair wage as defined in the Fair Wages Clause in Government contracts, which requires contractors to observe the rates paid by reputable employers. On the other hand, she takes the Court to task for following the policy, during the first five years of its life, that 'there were certain new standards of life that had been established, and *must* be maintained and also *should* be raised if possible'. This may indeed have been a foolish policy (indeed in Chapter VI of the present book it is argued that a similar policy today is producing deplorable results); but it can hardly on that account be dismissed as being based on principles less firmly accepted in any objective sense than those of which Miss Rankin herself happens to approve. Nor is it clear just what course, on this view, the Court ought to follow in circumstances in which neither the subsistence wage nor the Fair Wages Clause is relevant. Miss Rankin's own prescription reads as follows: 'In the case of wages which are above the standards of subsistence . . . the principle to be applied . . . lies in the hands of the parties concerned. The Court's province is therefore to interpret to the parties the principle on which they would seem to be proceeding and also (possibly) alternative principles, and the nature of the wage that would corre-spondingly result, i.e. whether the wage is to be the result of the economic forces of demand and supply both particular and general —the market value of the labour—or whether they are to be on a profit-sharing principle or on what might be called a profit-absorbing principle, the utmost the firm or industry can bear. If, as is very improbable, it be left entirely to the Court to make the contract for the parties, then there being no principle laid down in this connexion the Court must be guided by the principles which under the circum-stances and for the parties in question, is most consistent with the unavoidable principles of subsistence and fairness.'[1] The principles of 'subsistence and fairness' seem in fact to be definable only, by a circular process, in terms of 'unavoidable principles of subsistence and fairness'—which can hardly be much help in practice to the puzzled arbitrator.

In the twenty years which have elapsed since Professor Hicks and Miss Rankin published their studies, the practice of wage arbitra-tion has increased much faster than any discussion of its principles. A detailed factual study of the whole subject of conciliation and arbitration in this country, published in 1950 by Dr. Ian Sharp, has only a very few words to say about the fundamental issues of policy. The author does, however, make the comment that the Industrial Court 'has in fact proceeded in wage as in other matters along lines of conciliation and opportunism rather than of strict adherence to pre-conceived principles', and he supports this with a reference to the large proportion of cases in which the decision has amounted to a compromise between the parties. 'It is difficult to see,' Dr. Sharp adds, 'how else the court could have operated with equal success. Despite its name the Industrial Court is not in any real sense a court. It is but an arbitration tribunal with no powers beyond those bestowed by the consent of the disputing parties. In this position a strict judicial stand is impossible.'[2]

Much the same conclusion is reached by Mr. H. A. Turner in the course of a penetrating discussion published by the Fabian Society. Mr. Turner has studied in some detail the actual behaviour of arbitration tribunals during and since the Second World War, and finds evidence that during the period 1949–50 some attempt was made to impose principles derived from the Government's national wage policy.[3] In his view this 'amounted to a breach of that implied

[1] Rankin, M. T., *Arbitration Principles and the Industrial Court* (London, King, 1931), pp. 169–72.

[2] Sharp, I. G., *Industrial Conciliation and Arbitration in Great Britain* (London, Allen & Unwin, 1950), p. 359.

[3] This is discussed further below: see Chapter IV.

agreement on which the working of arbitration itself depended', and provoked trade unionists to the criticism that 'tribunals had ceased to judge cases "on their merits"'. Mr. Turner has himself no doubt at all that 'arbitration must continue mainly in the role in which it has been historically successful—that of an auxiliary to collective bargaining'. Indeed, for that very reason he has a word of comfort to offer to those trade unionists who are apt to be suspicious of the impartiality of arbitrators. This suspicion Mr. Turner finds to be 'beside the point. If impartiality means to make judgements in the light of some objective principle independent of the interests involved, then arbitrators cannot be impartial because no such universal principle has yet been revealed by their experience. The concern of arbitrators (again, saving the "wage freeze") is to make the decision which is least likely to provoke resistance by either side. In effect, this means that arbitration awards—like ordinary collective agreements—will be most favourable to workers when the unions generally are strong and determined, and to employers when *they* are strongest. Arbitration awards reflect, on the whole, the industrial situation, not the personal prejudice of arbitrators.'[1]

The two opinions last quoted thus reinforce the negative view of industrial arbitration advanced by Professor Hicks twenty years ago. The advice of all these authorities to an arbitrator in search of a principle is that he should desist from the quest; and if he thinks that he has caught one, he is urged to let it go.

This advice, however, is not quite so easy to follow in practice. Though the formal laws of evidence are not observed, arbitration proceedings are conducted in an ostensibly judicial atmosphere, obviously influenced by the parallel of the courts proper, and by the lawyer's concept of 'natural justice'. There is statement and counter-statement by each party of his case: each has also an opportunity, amounting virtually to a right of cross-examination, to comment upon the submissions of the other; and, in some cases, the parties are legally represented. Moreover—and this in the long run may prove to be the critical point—the (often very elaborate) arguments submitted by the parties are apt to be couched in terms which presuppose a view of the tribunal's functions entirely different from that voiced by the authorities quoted above. As is apparent from the analysis undertaken in Chapter V of this book, claims are normally based on implicit acceptance of *principles*, and on ethical principles at that. The claimants do not say: 'Concede this demand because we are a powerful union with a near-monopoly, and therefore in a

[1] Turner, H. A., *Arbitration: A Study of Industrial Experience* (London, Fabian Publications), pp. 20–4.

position to get what we want anyway'; nor do employers respond by reference to the strength of their own economic position. The unions quote the failure of wages to keep pace with the cost of living, or the injustice of one calling getting left behind in a general advance; the employers respond with homilies on the danger to the public welfare inherent in an inflationary spiral.

Any arbitration tribunal, therefore, which sought faithfully to abide by the rule that it is only 'an auxiliary to collective bargaining', would have to dismiss nearly all the argumentation to which it has to listen as irrelevant. Almost from beginning to end, the formal proceedings in the courtroom would have to be treated as a gigantic façade—not to mention a great waste of time and money. Such an attitude contains perhaps an element of realism; but it would be a very difficult one to sustain, since indeed it would make all arbitration proceedings tedious, if not ludicrous. Conversely, the judicial setting of an arbitrator's job cannot but encourage him to take a judicial view of his functions; and the implications of this alternative interpretation, which are more fully explored in the next chapter, appear to be more in keeping with the trend of the times.

CHAPTER IV

Wage Policy in a Vacuum: Attitudes of Government and Trades Union Congress

I

ALL the three instruments—collective bargaining, statutory regulations and arbitration awards—which have taken over so much of the business of wage determination in the present century, have one thing in common. They may all be said to reflect the modern tendency to deal in ethical currency. Whether or no wage-fixing remains fundamentally a matter of smash and grab, it is clear from the picture presented in the preceding chapter that those who are actually engaged in the business like to dress it up as something more respectable. The presence of this ethical element does not indeed imply that wage decisions have suddenly become moral: the true implication is not that the decisions themselves are in any sense morally good, but that those who make them recognize the need for their justification in ethical terms. In the economic textbooks wage bargains, like other price determinations, lie outside the jurisdiction of any moral law at all: justification is not called for. That is no longer true in real life.

In the case of collective bargaining the ethical approach to wage negotiations springs, as has already been suggested, from the role of the union as not itself the seller, but as the spokesman of potential sellers of labour; and from the need to use explicit argument, particularly argument that will appeal to the widest possible public. For the public is always better at ethics, which are warm and real, than at economics, which are cold and abstract. When the Industrial Courts Act of 1919 provided machinery not only for the settlement of disputes by arbitration, but also for their investigation by Courts of Inquiry, it did so in the hope that public opinion would support the rights and denounce the wrongs of the cases to be thus laid bare. When the late Mr. Ernest Bevin exhibited before one of the earliest of these courts a minute portion of bacon on a plate, explaining that this was all the breakfast that a docker's wage would stretch to, his intention was not to instruct the public in the economics of the dock industry, but to create moral indignation; and he succeeded.

The presence of this ethical element is, moreover, quite compatible with the role of the union as the protector, at any level, of the interest of whatever occupational or industrial group it represents, and with the negotiator's need to give due weight to all the—possibly conflicting—interests for whom he speaks. These factors condition only the choice of premises which must be made so that, explicitly or implicitly, argument from them can be used to justify the claims advanced. If this sounds unduly cynical, the same proposition can, more reputably, be put the other way round, revised to read as follows: claims on behalf of interest-groups can only be advanced when, and in so far as, they can be squared with given moral premises. Those who speak for vested interests must, in fact, as much as anybody else, use the moral currency of the community which permits the growth of these interests; and unions must 'seek justice' or 'fair treatment' for their members—not 'preferential advantage' or the right of the strong to exploit the weak.

If the growth of collective bargaining encourages the transfer of wage discussions from purely economic to social and ethical categories, the same is even more clearly true of statutory wage regulation or of arbitration awards. The genealogy of the original Trade Boards is plain enough: they were got by public agitation out of moral indignation. In the case of arbitration tribunals, as we have seen, the use of judicial forms cannot but encourage the belief that justice is, or ought to be, dispensed by their proceedings. The doctrine, favoured by Professor Hicks and Mr. Turner, that the arbitrator's only function is to keep the peace, is highly sophisticated: it would hardly bear stating in the naked form that the arbitrator's function is to keep the peace at any price, just or unjust. Whatever the principles upon which the members of wages councils and of arbitration tribunals actually base their findings, the very existence of these bodies both reflects and fosters a mental climate in which 'just' or 'fair' or 'reasonable' decisions are expected. It is indeed significant that Mr. Turner finds it necessary to deal with the question of the impartiality of arbitrators. Though he dismisses this issue as 'beside the point', it is a matter that is bound to be raised. Impartiality is a virtue; and the public holds that we have a right to expect it from our arbitrators.

This modern habit of discussing wage questions in ethical terms would remain a socially important fact, even on the improbable hypothesis that, in the end, every wage was actually fixed at exactly the level which it would reach in an unregulated competitive market. To the sociologically-minded it is not only what people do which is important: what they think they do, or what they pretend to do, has hardly less significance; and this in turn can hardly fail to react upon what they do. Certainly the gulf between the ethical frame of reference of the contemporary wage claim and the private, ethically neutral, commercial bargaining of employer and employee postulated by classical economic theory is wide indeed; and hardly less remarkable is the contrast between contemporary practice and that of even fifty years ago. The moral approach to wage problems may indeed be reckoned as yet another of the minor social revolutions of our time.

In the course of its growth this moralizing trend has itself also undergone significant development. Two distinct phases can be traced. In the first, the emphasis lies upon the need for a just bargain between employer and worker. The transaction is still essentially a two-party affair; the community at large is interested only to see that justice is done between the parties, and that the stronger does not exploit the weaker. It was this attitude which justified the positive action involved in statutory regulation of trades with 'unduly low' wages; and it was this attitude which, along with other strains of early twentieth-century idealism, found formal expression in the triumphant optimism that marked the end of the First World War. 'In right and in fact,' wrote the Commission on International Labour Legislation of the Peace Conference at Versailles, 'the labour of a human being should not be treated as merchandise or an article of commerce'—a declaration surely worthy of King Canute in its defiance of the tides of economic theory; and in the Treaty itself this formula (though in a less uncompromising version)[1] appears as a 'general principle' of 'special and urgent importance'. In the three decades that have since elapsed, little specific reference has been made to this principle: I know of no case in which the clause has been quoted in wage negotiations. Yet silently the doctrine which it proclaims has slipped into the implicit assumptions of contemporary argument.

In the second phase, the duration of which coincides roughly with the period of the Second World War, the wage bargain is no longer regarded as the private concern of the parties directly involved and of the organizations acting on their behalf, in which the community is concerned only to enforce fair play on both sides. It now becomes a three-cornered transaction, in which the public at large has its own interest, no less deserving of consideration than the interests of the employers and the workers directly concerned.

[1] viz.: 'Labour should not be regarded merely as a commodity or article of commerce.'

Justice must now be done as much to those who are not parties to the immediate bargain as to those who are.

This new development again involves quite astonishing changes. It has, in particular, profoundly modified—and for a time at least it virtually turned upside down—the role of the union leader, who must now address his argument to two other parties instead of only to one. It has even produced the almost unbelievable spectacle of trade union leaders devoting their main energies to holding back the militant demands of their members. During the Second World War, and for five years afterwards, as described below,[1] while the Trades Union Congress was openly committed to a policy of wage restraint, the influence of leading British trade unionists was constantly used to discourage applications for advances: the trade union leadership achieved 'a "new sense of responsibility" (described by its critics as conservatism)'.[2] Strikes were persistently discouraged by the official leadership—and not only because during, and for six years after, the war they were illegal; such unofficial strikes as occurred from time to time, notably in the mines and at the docks, were a constant source of embarrassment to the union chiefs. Indeed, the unofficial dockers' strikes of 1945, classified by the Ministry of Labour as arising from a dispute over wages, soon developed into what was virtually a strike by the rank and file against their own leaders.

As a result of this new attitude many prominent trade unionists received both titles and less formal bouquets; though the new orientation has brought its own difficulties. Union leaders, particularly in the nationalized industries, found themselves, as one miner put it, 'in the unenviable position, after years of "boss-bashing", in which the miner was always right, of having to prove to their members that the boss can be, and now almost always is, right'.[3] Even the speakers who, as described below,[4] persuaded the Trades Union Congress (against the advice of its own General Council) to abandon support for a policy of wage restraint, felt it necessary to rest their case upon figures purporting to show that substantial increases could be wrung out of profits, and need not involve any material increase in the cost of living. They would have had no chance of success, if they had failed to show sensitivity to the effect of their proposals upon the public at large.

The whole-hearted Marxist will, of course, deny the reality of any third-party interest in wage bargains, or at least its independence of

[1] See pp. 113 ff.
[2] Knowles, K. G. J. C., *Strikes* (Oxford, Blackwell, 1952), p. 95.
[3] Yorkshire miner's opinion, quoted in *Daily Express* (17 September 1947), quoted in Knowles, *op. cit.*, p. 94.
[4] See p. 115.

the interest of employers. According to the Marxian analysis, public policy is dictated by the ruling class, and any alleged public interest is merely the interest of that class masquerading in a more appealing dress. In the particular case of wage policy, at least in the economic circumstances of immediate post-war Britain, this thesis can be made to look very plausible. For with full employment and a seller's market, the community is chiefly concerned to avoid a wage-price spiral—an attitude which suits employers very nicely in their natural opposition to wage increases. It cannot, however, be assumed that this identification of employers' interests with those of the public at large would always hold good. In the event of a slump, the arguments from general economic welfare would be entirely on the side of wage advances. Moreover, even if the conception of a third-party public interest in wage bargains should be entirely illusory, once again it must be remembered that an illusion is important in its own right—for its demonstrable effect upon the behaviour of those who fall victims to it. Even if we suppose the trade unions to have been lured by the clever wiles of the ruling class into an entirely false belief that a wage advance in one trade may be detrimental to the economic health of the whole community (in which is included the welfare of other groups of workers), it would still be true that their behaviour in this deluded state will be different from what it would have been had they refused to be thus taken in. Certainly the union leader of today, oppressed by the need to meet arguments based ostensibly on the public interest, is farther away than ever from the hypothetical figure of Professor Hicks's analysis,[1] responsive only to the readings of his 'resistance schedule'. Whether or no he is mistaken in his admission that wage bargains are more than the private concern of the employers and workers immediately concerned, the behaviour of a trade union leader who acts upon that assumption cannot be explained in terms of the hedonistic calculus of economic theory.

The very phrase 'wage policy' is itself indicative of the modern view that wage questions concern a wider public than those who make these bargains or on whose behalf they are made. Seldom heard before the war, this expression has crept into a recognized, indeed a popular, place in our vocabularies—even though, as will appear, it remains little more than a formal expression. To the whole change of climate of which this new terminology is symptomatic, more than one factor has contributed. A long spell of near-full employment, conditions of extreme stringency and a strong trend towards economic planning have all combined to highlight the social effects

[1] See pp. 17 ff.

of wage agreements. In these conditions the risk of a wage-price-inflationary spiral needs no emphasis. Similarly, the dependence of Britain upon overseas markets, and the risk that wage increases may react unfavourably upon the export trade, are themes that have been worn threadbare: no one concerned in wage decisions can possibly overlook them.

Not less relevant to the new conception of a third-party interest in wage bargains (but as a rule less prominently featured) is the link between wage policy and general economic planning. In classical economic theory, it will be recalled, wage movements are assigned chief responsibility for directing the flow of labour to different parts of the economic system. The relevant argument runs as follows. If the demand for any article increases, the price of that article will tend to rise, and increased profits will be made from its production. Sellers will therefore be in a position to offer higher wages, higher wages will attract an increased labour force, the increased labour force will produce a larger output, and so the rising demand will be met—and, one is tempted to add, everyone will live happily ever afterwards.

With the introduction of economic planning, the invisible hand which was supposed to operate this mechanism is stricken with paralysis. The familiar sequence—higher prices, higher profits, higher wages, more labour, increased output—is irrevocably broken. The planned economy, no longer content that output should follow market demand, sets its own production targets for particular industries; and the industries in which expansion is planned are by no means necessarily those which make the greatest profits or are most likely, of their own volition, to offer wages that will attract the desired labour supply—as the perpetual call for increased production of coal and increased recruitment of miners only too plainly demonstrates. It cannot, therefore, be taken for granted that wages will automatically move in conformity with production plans. Yet such plans are liable to be wrecked, if control of the direction of labour is left to relative wage movements and these movements are themselves entirely unplanned. Once the invisible hand is reduced to impotence, only a visible substitute can avert chaos. Certainly no very profound analysis is necessary to demonstrate the link between wage policy and economic planning.

Finally, the social element in wage bargains is thrown into still greater prominence by the growing weight in the British economy of the nationalized industries and other public services, most of which have a monopoly of their respective spheres. These services now employ more than one-fifth of the whole labour force engaged in civil employment:[1] the combined impact of their wage policy on the living standards of the community is, therefore, far from negligible. Unlike privately-owned monopolies, however, the nationalized industries are under no obligation to maximize profits. On the contrary, their prescribed objective is to break even, taking one year with another—though none of the Nationalization Acts specifies the period within which gains and losses are expected to balance. The nationalized industries cannot, therefore, in any circumstances, meet increased wage bills out of superabundant profits. Apart from economies of operation, they can only pay their workers more by charging more to consumers—a fact which can hardly fail to sharpen both their own need of a wage policy and the public's interest in their decisions.

Both inside and outside the fold of the nationalized industries, however, the hungry sheep look up and are not fed: at least not very substantially. Recognition of the need for a wage policy is one thing; discovery of the right policy is another. During and since the war a series of official pronouncements has dealt with the subject of wage policy. All of these, as might be expected in the special circumstances of the war and immediate post-war situation, have been chiefly concerned to emphasize the undesirable consequences of any general rise in the wage bill. Even in war time, however, an absolute veto on all change is hardly a possible policy, and in fact no such veto has ever been imposed or even publicly recommended. Every pronouncement has left a loophole for some exceptions to a general standstill; and indeed the facts that throughout the war and all the post-war economic crises unions have been left free to negotiate, and that tribunals have been required to arbitrate, are evidence that such exceptions are always contemplated. Under a complete stand-still these bodies would simply have to put up their shutters indefinitely.

The critical questions, therefore, relate to the choice, the handling and the number of these exceptions; for the advice: 'when in doubt, don't give it' is little help, unless one knows when it is, and when it is not, permissible to doubt. On these problems, however, little clear guidance has been given. It is now (1954) fully twelve years since the public interest in wage bargains has been explicitly acknowledged; but the successive official pronouncements of those years have brought us little nearer to any interpretation of that interest in concrete terms. The issue is critical, and the story is worth following in some detail.

[1] Mr. G. A. Isaacs, in reply to a parliamentary question, put the total number of such public servants at 5,025,000 in 1950: at that date the total number of persons in civil employment stood at 22,354,000. 14 December 1950, 482 H.C. Deb. 5 s. 200.

II

The series begins with the Chancellor of the Exchequer's budget statement of 1941 and the White Paper on *Price Stabilization and Industrial Policy* published in the summer of that year. In the former the Chancellor announced his intention of stabilizing the cost of living round about the then level of 125%–130% of the pre-war figure, emphasizing that this policy was necessarily contingent upon 'the wages situation' being 'held about where it now is'. Apparently, however, this policy was 'not generally understood': the White Paper, therefore, opened with a fresh exposition of the futility, and indeed the danger, of wage increases in circumstances in which fewer goods were available for purchase. There followed an appeal in terms that the addressees must long since have learned by heart to 'both sides in industry to consider together all possible means of preventing the rise of costs of production and so to obviate rise of prices which is the initial step in the inflationary process'. 'The use of the experience and knowledge of workpeople,' the paper continues, 'is not less necessary than the application of managerial training and experience, and the maintenance of wages and employers' remuneration at a reasonable level should be achieved as far as possible by improvement in the efficiency of production by the joint efforts of employers and workpeople. At the same time there may, consistently with these considerations, be proper grounds for adjustment of wages in certain cases, particularly among comparatively low paid grades and categories of workers, or for adjustment owing to changes in the form, method or volume of production.' Finally, it is admitted that if 'there were to be further increases in the cost of living this would need to be taken properly into account', but the hope is reiterated that the Government's stabilization policy in conjunction with a restrained attitude on the part of both employers and employed will 'prevent such increases from arising'.[1]

This paper remained the governing document on the subject throughout the war. The exceptions which it contemplates are, it will be noticed, primarily those due to improved efficiency, and, in the second place, cases of 'comparatively low' wages. No explicit reference is made to the function of wage movements in directing the supply of labour—an omission which was logical enough in view of the imposition of conscription, both military and industrial; and it will also be observed that 'reasonable' remuneration for both parties in industry is only to be maintained 'as far as possible' by the

[1] See *Ministry of Labour Gazette* (August 1941), p. 154.

methods suggested. The standards by which reasonableness is to be judged, or the steps to be taken when it becomes impossible to maintain these standards without going outside the prescribed methods, are not specified. A high degree of precision cannot, indeed, be expected of documents drafted in the grim summer of 1941; but vagueness has, it will be seen, become a precedent.

The 1941 White Paper was followed, seven years later, by what has proved to be probably the most widely quoted of any document on wage policy. This was the *Statement on Personal Incomes, Costs and Prices* of 1948. After a renewed exposition of the dangers of a wage-price spiral, this paper boldly asserted that 'the last hundred years have seen the growth of certain traditional or customary relationships between personal incomes—including wages and salaries—in different occupations. These have no necessary relevance to modern conditions. The relation which different personal incomes bear to one another must no longer be determined by this historical development of the past, but by the urgent needs of the present. In the changed world of today and with our present economic difficulties these old relationships of income must, where necessary, be adapted to conform to the national interest. Relative income levels must be such as to encourage the movement of labour to those industries where it is most needed, and should not, as in some cases they still do, tempt it in a contrary direction.'

The 1948 White Paper is exceptional in its exclusive emphasis upon what may be called old-fashioned economic criteria. Changes in the wage structure are evaluated solely from the point of view of their effect upon the distribution of labour. Traditional relationships, as will be seen from the passage just quoted, suffer a direct and rude assault; and the attack is repeated in a list of guiding considerations, set out for the benefit of all those who are concerned in the determination of personal incomes, of which the final clause reads as follows: 'It does not follow that it would be right to stabilize all incomes as they stand today. There may well be cases in which increases in wages or salaries would be justified from a national point of view, for example where it is essential in the national interest to man up a particular undermanned industry and it is clear that only an increase in wages will attract the necessary labour. It does, however, follow that each claim for an increase in wages or salaries must be considered on its national merits and not on the basis of maintaining a former relativity between different occupations and industries.' No reference at all is made to the claims of the lowly-paid; only in the event of some hypothetical (and much to be deprecated) future marked increase in the cost of living would 'the level of those personal incomes which as a result became inadequate'[1] need reconsideration. On the introduction of this White Paper to the House of Commons, a Member of Parliament inquired whether 'this statement means that the Government will now try to work out in conjunction with the trade unions a scientific, differential wages policy as a means of attracting labour into the most essential and undermanned industries'? The Prime Minister's reply was tentative: 'We are trying to work out a general policy with regard to this matter. I do not know whether there is an exact scientific method of dealing with it.'[2] But on paper, at any rate, the 1948 White Paper represents a remarkable victory of economics over ethics.

Such an attitude was, however, out of harmony with the mood of the times. Little over a year later the question of wage policy became still more pressing in consequence of the devaluation of the pound. In the course of the devaluation debate on 27 September 1949, Sir Stafford Cripps, then Chancellor of the Exchequer, re-emphasized the need to observe most strictly the general restraint advocated by the 1948 White Paper, while in the same breath he admitted a category of exceptions which the White Paper had itself ignored. 'It is only,' said Sir Stafford, 'in the exceptional and genuine cases where some wage survives which, together with all the subsidies and social services, is insufficient to provide a family with a minimum reasonable standard of living, that there can be any possible excuse for going forward with a claim for an increase.' Even if 'such an increase is given to those at the bottom', the Chancellor continued, 'we cannot accept the maintenance of differentials or relativities as any argument for present increases to those who are receiving higher rates. Especially and specifically there can, in our view, be no justification for any section of workers trying to recoup themselves for any increase in the cost of living due to the altered exchange rate.'[3] The emphasis is thus shifted back from the undermanned industry (to whose problems the Chancellor made no reference in the context of wage policy) to the underpaid worker; while in the two sentences last quoted, the Chancellor denounced two of the arguments which have subsequently been most widely used in support of wage claims.

Only six months later came the first hint of impending relaxation. In his 1950 budget speech, Sir Stafford admitted that the policy of restraint in the matter of personal incomes 'which was first put

---

[1] *Statement on Personal Incomes, Costs and Prices*, Cmd. 7321 (February 1948).
[2] 4 February 1948, 446 H.C. Deb. 5 s., 1835–6.
[3] 27 September 1949, 468 H.C. Deb. 5 s., 26.

forward rather more than two years ago', and had been loyally appreciated by the union leaders, must understandably have become 'difficult to carry through', and 'the longer the time that passes the more difficult it must become to apply it fully'. The Chancellor was, however, still troubled about the bottom dog. 'The real difficulty,' he observed, 'is that there are still some cases of low earnings which are very difficult to correct without upsetting the relative wage levels that have been established within each industry for the different grades and classes of workpeople employed in it. This,' Sir Stafford remarked, though not perhaps very constructively, 'is an immensely difficult problem to solve.'[1] It certainly is: indeed, to raise the lowest level without upsetting differentials is a mathematical impossibility. Sir Stafford had no solution to offer, but passed forthwith to the discussion of other topics.

On 3 July 1950, this speech was interpreted by its author as an indication that 'it was not possible to continue indefinitely the rigidity of the policy in regard to personal incomes which was initiated immediately after the devaluation of sterling last autumn and that some degree of relaxation would be called for'. In a statement which must be reckoned as a masterly demonstration of the strategy of indirect approach, Sir Stafford then proceeded to convey the impression that the moment for such relaxation had arrived, without either explicitly stating this, or giving any indication as to which claims should have priority. 'We cannot,' he said, 'at present afford anything but a limited degree of relaxation of the very rigid standards laid down after devaluation, and I therefore hope that all those concerned with the fixing or negotiation of personal incomes will bear in mind the principles set out in the White Paper and the continued need for a large measure of restraint so that we may not lose the benefits earned by our efforts during and since the war, and particularly since devaluation.' Asked by subsequent questioners in the House whether he proposed to issue a further White Paper 'in view of the changed circumstances', Sir Stafford replied that he did not, but that 'the original White Paper stands in its full force, but not as reinforced after devaluation'. Pressed to say whether there was now 'a hope of the amount available for wage increases being given in the first instance to the lower paid workers',[2] the Chancellor indicated that his interlocutor would find the answer in the White Paper itself. The White Paper, it will be recalled (in contrast with the Chancellor's own speeches), had made no mention of the claims of the lower paid.

[1] 18 April 1950, 474 H.C. Deb. 5 s., 64–6.
[2] 3 July 1950, 476 H.C. Deb. 5 s., 35–6.

During the past two or three years the flow of ministerial pronouncements dealing specifically with wage policy has noticeably diminished. In May 1952 Mr. R. A. Butler as Chancellor of the Exchequer approached the General Council of the Trades Union Congress with renewed concern as to the risks of a general increase in wages. Mr. Butler proposed that a joint committee of the National Joint Advisory Council (which represents the General Council, the British Employers' Confederation and the nationalized industries) might be set up to consider the possibility of devising methods of relating wages more closely to productivity by modifying the existing wages structure in many of our industries. This proposal to play with fire received a cool reception. The Economic Committee of the Trades Union Congress turned down the idea of a joint committee as 'impracticable' and incompatible with voluntary collective bargaining, and contented themselves with producing their own statement on *The Trade Unions and the Economic Situation*,[1] which, for all practical purposes, by-passed the central problems of wage policy.

The recent tendency[2] of Ministers to leave wage policy severely alone may be in part ascribed to political changes, and in particular to the general distaste of Conservative governments for all forms of economic planning. This has left its mark also on the annual Economic Surveys in which, every spring, the Government reviews the economic fortunes of the country in the preceding year and takes a look into the future. Since the fall of the Labour Government, the 'targets' that used to be boldly described as such in the surveys have changed into 'forecasts' or 'prospects'. Significantly also in the present context, no detailed estimates are included after 1950 of the distribution of man-power between different industries which it is hoped to realize at the end of the current year. Governments which do not like economic planning in any shape or form can hardly be expected to show much zeal for experiments in planning of which even the most socialistically-minded are demonstrably afraid.

At the same time, the change in the political colour of the government probably has only a transient importance in this connection. The Conservative bias against all forms of planning may serve as a good pretext for letting things rip—at any rate for a time; and a Conservative government has to reckon with the fact that the unions are less likely than they would be under a Labour administration to

[1] Trades Union Congress, *Report of Proceedings at the 84th Annual Trades Union Congress*, 1952 (London, TUC), p. 284.
[2] By 1954, however, there were signs of renewed governmental interest. See below, p. 167.

co-operate cheerfully in a policy of restraint. Such differences are, however, quite superficial in comparison with the deep-seated reluctance of any government, no matter how plan-conscious, to face the problems of wage policy. It is this reluctance which, right from the beginning, has torn a large rent in every economic plan ever framed for this country.

Some uneasy consciousness of the fundamental absurdity of elaborating production plans while leaving wages to take care of themselves appears here and there to peep through the tentative statements on wage policy already quoted. Every one of these reiterates with monotonous insistence the need to retain voluntary collective bargaining as the normal method of wage settlement. Thus the 1941 White Paper referred to the 'traditional and well-tried practice of the principal industries to regulate wages through their joint voluntary machinery for wage negotiation'; praised the restraint already shown, and declared it to be the policy of the Government 'to avoid modification of the machinery for wage negotiations and to continue to leave the various voluntary organizations and wage tribunals free to reach their decisions in accordance with their estimate of the relevant facts'.[1] The 1948 White Paper proclaimed categorically (on behalf of a government which had at least a socialist ancestry) that 'it is not desirable for the Government to interfere directly with the income of individuals otherwise than by taxation. To go further would mean that the Government would be forced itself to assess and regulate all personal incomes according to some scale which would have to be determined. This would be an incursion by the Government into what has hitherto been regarded as a field of free contract between individuals and organizations.' To this argument is joined the more practical consideration that collective bargaining, so long as it is faithfully observed, prevents individual employers from initiating inflation by competitive bidding, and 'tends to ensure that wage and salary movements take place in an orderly manner and with due regard to the general as distinct from the individual interest'.[2]

Such repeated tributes to voluntary negotiation, side by side with recommendations (however hesitant and confused), as to policy seem at times to have the ring of a rearguard action. One wonders whether perhaps their authors do not protest too much, conscious of the fundamental absurdity of planning everything except wage movements. It is as though we were told that in the modern idiom it is right that employers and workers should settle their own wage

[1] *Ministry of Labour Gazette* (August 1941), p. 154.
[2] *Statement on Personal Incomes, Costs and Prices*, Cmd. 7321 (February 1948).

questions; but would they please be careful to settle them properly? The insecurity of such an attitude needs no comment.

Nor is the Trades Union Congress, on its side, prepared to commit itself to a more definite policy. Indeed, the Congress seems to have become, if anything, progressively less and less inclined to give any definite lead on wage priorities. The 1941 White Paper was not well received by the General Council which read into it an 'attempt to control the movement of wages', and complained that 'nowhere . . . is it made clear that provision would be made for comparatively low paid grades and categories of workers to have their earnings improved'; and in presenting the Council's report on the subject the then General Secretary, Sir Walter (now Lord) Citrine expressed himself very forcibly in a speech in which echoes of the once-traditional equalitarianism of the trade union movement could still be heard. 'If,' he said 'we were within a society where every section of the community had approximately the same standard of life, the case would be watertight, perhaps, for a common sacrifice by everybody. But nobody can argue, despite the shortcomings War has brought, that the richer classes of the community, aye, even the comfortable sections of the community who are not really rich in the sense of this world's goods but have an assured income, are not infinitely better off than the working-class people, and have not felt the burden infinitely less. Let us recognize that this claim has no social justice behind it which seeks to stabilize wages in present conditions. It is basically inequitable.'[1]

In 1948, however, we find no such exclusive emphasis on the claims of the lower paid. By this time the Congress was more ready to accept a policy of restraint; and union leaders generally were already practised in their new function of discouraging applications for higher pay. The terms on which consent to this policy was given deserve, however, to be quoted in full as the classic statement of the prevailing reluctance to face the realities of a coherent wage policy. In a statement approved on 18 February 1948, the General Council declared the principles of the 1948 White Paper to be 'acceptable to the Trade Union Movement to the extent that they:

(a) recognize the necessity of retaining unimpaired the system of collective bargaining and free negotiation;

(b) admit the justification for claims for increased wages where those claims are based upon the fact of increased output;

(c) admit the necessity of adjusting the wages of workers whose incomes are below a reasonable standard of subsistence;

[1] Trades Union Congress, *Report of Proceedings at the 73rd Annual Trades Union Congress, 1941* (London, TUC), pp. 198–9 and 364.

(d) affirm that it is in the national interest to establish standards of wages and conditions in undermanned essential industries in order to attract sufficient manpower; and

(e) recognize the need to safeguard those wage differentials which are an essential element in the wages structure of many important industries and are required to sustain those standards of craftsmanship, training and experience that contribute directly to industrial efficiency and higher productivity.'[1]

No hint was given as to how the conflict that might be expected to arise from these mutually inconsistent conditions was to be resolved.

A further statement on wage policy by the Congress General Council was accepted by a special conference of trade union executives in January 1950. This again gave cautious support to the policy of restraint. The Council expressed themselves as not yet satisfied that 'the requisite degree of equality of sacrifice' had been secured: they noted 'increases of higher salaries in industry, in the professions, and in the academic world', and expressed disapproval of 'extravagant payments' to directors in the motor manufacturing industry. They promised, accordingly, to 'take such steps as seem appropriate to secure a more equal sharing of burdens'.

The programme that followed was perhaps more concrete (and more conservative) than any to which the union leaders have committed themselves before or since. Any possible conflict between the claims of the low-paid worker and those of the undermanned industry was dismissed with the observation that 'changes in wage differentials are not the only form of incentive'. Special attention was given to the problem created by industries in which agreements provided that wages should automatically follow upward movements of the cost-of-living index: unions were definitely recommended to suspend such agreements, provided that changes in the index occurring in the next twelve months did not exceed certain prescribed (and narrow) limits. For low-paid workers the Council recommended assistance 'by the establishment of incentive schemes'.[2]

This programme, the ostensible purpose of which was to promote equality of sacrifice, amounted, in effect, to an exceptionally rigid standstill. It lasted, however, little more than six months. At the end of June 1950, a few days before the Chancellor of the

[1] Trades Union Congress, *Report of Proceedings at the 80th Annual Trades Union Congress, 1948* (London, TUC), p. 290.
[2] Trades Union Congress, *Trade Unions and Wages Policy:* Report of the Special Conference of Trade Union Executive Committees, January 1950 (London, TUC), paras. 41, 46 and 49.

Exchequer's 'relaxation' statement in the House of Commons, the General Council of the Trades Union Congress issued a fresh statement on wage policy. This heralded a move away from the 'rigorous' restraint advised in the preceding November and upheld at the January conference of trade union executives, to simple restraint, not reinforced by any adjective. Indeed, it now appeared that the proposed suspension of sliding-scale agreements had proved impracticable within a matter of weeks. Further, while special reference had been made in the earlier pronouncement to the case of low-paid workers, the General Council now recorded that 'there has certainly been a growth of discontent felt by skilled and semi-skilled workers at the steady narrowing of differentials which has taken place in recent years and which has all along been a real and complicating factor in the General Council's consideration of wages policy'. The Council, however, were no better able than was Sir Stafford Cripps to explain how the claims of the low-paid were to be reconciled with the maintenance of differentials. They had to be content with merely advocating 'greater flexibility' than had been envisaged in January; though they remained 'firmly convinced that there is no formula which can be devised as to how this flexibility can operate'.[1]

At the 1950 Congress, the whole policy of wage restraint was defeated from the floor in defiance of the recommendations of the General Council. A resolution moved by Mr. W. C. Stevens of the Electrical Trades Union declared that, 'Congress is of the opinion that until such time as there is a reasonable limitation of profits, a positive planning of our British economy, and prices are subject to such control as will maintain the purchasing power of wages at a level affording to every worker a reasonable standard of living, there can be no basis for a restraint on wage applications.'[2] This was carried by card vote against the wishes of the platform. Even after this change in the official attitude of their constituents, the General Council have, however, continued to issue gentle reminders of the possibly disagreeable consequences of a 'free for all'. In 1951, while admitting that some favourably-placed unions might be able to achieve maintenance of their members' real incomes by wage advances, they emphasized that this was not likely to be possible for workers as a whole; and expressed grave concern as to whether 'now that the relative wage-price dividend stability of the last few years has broken down' it would be possible 'to prevent wage

[1] Trades Union Congress, *TUC and Wages Policy*, June 1950 (London, TUC).

[2] Trades Union Congress, *Report of Proceedings at the 82nd Annual Trades Union Congress*, 1950 (London, TUC), p. 467.

increases from being at the least fully offset by price increases'.[1]
Having lost the mandate for a policy of wage restraint, the Council
proceeded, in a passage which clearly reflects their uneasiness at
the possible consequences of uncontrolled wage advances, to draw
the moral that wage increases ought to be accompanied by more
effective stabilization of prices. Again in the following year, in a
report on the economic situation, they developed an elaborate
argument as to the impact of wage increases upon the demand for
goods in the home market and upon costs, including the cost of
exports. 'As regards the effect on industrial costs, it is clear that in
the absence of a rise in productivity, which cannot be expected to
occur quickly, substantial wage increases are bound to raise costs.
Moreover it is likely that the largest wage increases would be secured
in the industries whose products are most in demand at home and
abroad; this likelihood is increased by the fact that broadly speaking
it is in these industries that profits are highest. In other words,
industrial costs are likely to increase most in precisely those industries
on which we are most dependent for exports at the present time.'
This passage (which is printed in italics) is followed by several
further paragraphs on the need for increased production and exports,
culminating in yet another italicized warning that, 'We face the
danger today that higher costs may so force up the prices of our
exports as to make them unsaleable.' But at the same time the
Council explicitly rejected any inference that when the prices of the
necessities of life are rising, 'wage-earners and particularly those
whose incomes are not high enough to enable them to make ends
meet, are not justified in seeking wage increases'.[2] Wage claims, in
fact, are still admissible; but not—most emphatically not—without
reference to their consequences for the community as a whole.

Since then the Trades Union Congress has steadily refused to
adopt any more specific wage policy. Dissentient voices have indeed
been heard in more Congresses than one; but they have failed to
move either the rank and file or the official leadership. Thus at the
1951 Congress, Mr. J. H. Williams moved on behalf of the Association of Supervisory Staffs, Executives and Technicians a resolution
in the following terms: 'This Congress, recognizing the inconsistency
of supporting a planned economy on the one hand and insisting on
an unplanned wages sector on the other, calls upon the General
Council to examine the possibilities of formulating a planned wages
policy and to place its findings before the 1952 Congress.' In the

[1] Trades Union Congress, *Report of Proceedings at the 83rd Annual Trades
Union Congress*, 1951 (London, TUC), p. 283.
[2] Trades Union Congress, *Report of Proceedings at the 84th Annual Trades
Union Congress*, 1952 (London, TUC), pp. 289 and 291.

course of his speech Mr. Williams referred to the 'great responsibility' which lay upon the Congress, and asked, 'Are we in the future to be a body consisting of sections, each of which is only concerned with concentrating its energies on improving the interests of its own members? Or are we to be one brotherhood making certain that we advance in unison? Should we behave like a pack of wolves, striving to grab by fair means or foul the largest or sweetest piece of the carcase, or should we act as civilized human beings seeing that everyone has his fair share of necessities and luxuries according to his needs and his services, whether he be doctor or docker, miner or mimic, dentist or dough mixer, railwayman or road sweeper?'[1] Mr. Williams' resolution was defeated without recourse to the card vote.

In the following year Mr. Douglas Houghton, M.P., tried again, on behalf of the Inland Revenue Staff Federation. His resolution instructed the General Council 'to review the existing machinery for wage fixing and negotiations; covering collective bargaining, Wages Councils and other statutory and non-statutory wage fixing bodies, the facilities for arbitration for the settlement of disputes and to report upon the operation and effectiveness of this varied machinery: and to consider and report whether greater co-ordination is desirable with a view to providing greater equity and fairer relativities in the rewards for labour in all branches of private and public employment'. Mr. Houghton referred to 'big differences in rewards' that have in many cases 'nothing whatever to do with the social or economic value of the job done'. He laid emphasis also on the growing importance of the socialized industries in the total economy, arguing that wages generally would come to be more and more dominated by the rates paid in these industries, and that this made it even more important that 'we should get our minds clear on this important question of relative values and rewards and the principles of fixing wages'. 'What,' he asked, 'will "fair shares" mean in a socialist society? . . . Are all our present differentials written into the Ten Commandments and sacrosanct?' Mr. Houghton's resolution also was, in the words of the official report, 'overwhelmingly defeated'.[2]

In 1953 the Report of the General Council contained no reference to wage policy at all. At the Congress of that year, however, the indefatigable Mr. Stevens of the Electrical Trades Union moved a resolution in terms considerably more vigorous than those of its

[1] Trades Union Congress, *Report of Proceedings at the 83rd Annual Trades Union Congress*, 1951 (London, TUC), pp. 526–7.
[2] Trades Union Congress, *Report of Proceedings at the 84th Annual Trades Union Congress*, 1952 (London, TUC), pp. 505–6.

predecessor which was responsible, three years earlier, for the defeat of the General Council's policy of restraint. This new resolution read as follows, 'Congress declares its complete opposition to wage restraint and agrees that it is the responsibility and, in fact, the fundamental concept of the Trade Union Movement to uphold and improve the living standards of the working people, and will actively support the efforts of unions to defend the living standards of their members by vigorous campaigning in favour of higher wages. Congress further declares that increased productivity should be reflected in improved living standards for the working people.' In seconding this motion, Mr. Doughty of the Association of Engineering and Shipbuilding Draughtsmen referred to the 'fact that the employers and the general public may still believe that this Congress supports the remnants of a wage restraint policy'. The resolution, which was defeated on a card vote by a majority of nearly $2\frac{1}{2}$ million, provoked from Mr. Deakin, representing the General Council, the comment that Mr. Stevens' suggestions could 'be regarded only as the economics of bedlam'—a comment intended, apparently, to refer particularly to the mover's confidence that higher wages could be extracted from profits without any consequent increase in the cost of living.

At a later stage in the same Congress Mr. Bryn Roberts moved, on behalf of the National Union of Public Employees, a lengthy resolution on wage standards, the final clause of which instructed the General Council to 'examine and report upon the possibility of a long term wage policy, with particular reference to whether some form of national regulation and/or control of wages can be devised which will ensure higher, more stable and more equitable wage standards to all sections of the Movement, and to advise upon the changes, if any, which may be necessary in the practice and organization of the trade unions in order to give effect to such policy'. On behalf of the General Council Mr. W. L. Heywood contended that if the issue of wage policy was to be discussed, it should have been raised as a specific issue, 'as Congress has discussed the subject over and over again and has made declarations of policy on it'. This motion again was defeated.[1]

The reluctance of the Trades Union Congress to formulate any policy of its own is no doubt a consequence of its role as primarily the mouthpiece of organizations professionally interested in collective bargaining: as such it must naturally champion the right of employers and workers to make their own wage bargains. On this point the

[1] Trades Union Congress, *Report of Proceedings at the 85th Annual Trades Union Congress*, 1953 (London, TUC), pp. 442, 444, 452 and 454.

sentiments of the Trades Union Congress and those contained in the successive governmental statements already quoted are completely harmonious. But it is remarkable how persistently the Congress is at pains to underline the limitation of its own powers. Indeed just as governments reiterate, and indeed applaud, their own impotence in the face of the autonomy of employers' and workers' organizations, so the Trades Union Congress in its turn passes responsibility to its constituent unions. 'In matters of wage determination,' reads the General Council's (1949) statement on Trade Union Policy and the Economic Situation, 'the powers of the Trades Union Congress are limited. The General Council do, indeed, survey the general economic position and make recommendations for the guidance of Unions. But within each industry it is the responsibility of the Unions concerned to assess the position and to take appropriate action.'[1] 'The T.U.C. itself cannot, by its constitution,' repeats the statement presented to the Conference of Executives in January 1950, 'impose a wages policy on affiliated unions. The T.U.C. does, however, give expression to the collective experience of the Movement and has the right to expect affiliated unions to conform to policies and recommendations democratically agreed as being in the best interests of the Movement as a whole.'[2] Yet again, six months later, in the statement of June 1950, the General Council reiterated that they 'cannot impose a wages policy'. The Trade Union movement was 'a democratic movement'. The application of the new policy of flexibility then recommended must be left 'to the good sense and reasonableness' of which the unions had already, at least in the Council's view, shown themselves capable.[3]

[1] Trades Union Congress, *Report of Proceedings at the 81st Annual Trades Union Congress*, 1949 (London, TUC), p. 548.
[2] Trades Union Congress, *Trade Unions and Wage Policy*: Report of the Special Conference of Trade Union Executive Committees, January 1950 (London, TUC), p. 49.
[3] Trades Union Congress, *TUC and Wages Policy*, June 1950 (London, TUC).

CHAPTER V

Wage Policy in a Vacuum: Attitudes of Trade Unions, Employers and Arbitrators

I

THE story of government and trade union pronouncements upon wage policy as told in the preceding chapter is long and perhaps tedious; and it is singularly inconclusive. The picture which emerges is, however, highly significant. It is the picture of a community determined, on the one hand, to fix standards of remuneration that are fair and just as well as economically defensible; and no less determined, on the other hand, to abdicate from all responsibility either for the definition of general policy or for the actual decisions made—a community, in fact, which is engaged in the impossible task of attempting to do justice in an ethical vacuum. Yet without acknowledged standards of reference, no one can distinguish a good wage claim from a bad one, or determine the limits of reasonable remuneration for any particular occupation. As we have already seen, the rates of pay deliberately fixed (by people who presumably consider themselves to be acting reasonably) range from figures in the region of over £10,000 a year down to a mere five or six pounds a week. These variations cannot in the nature of the case be self-explanatory or self-justifying: they must be explained and justified in terms of *something*. Custom (the rule that whatever is is right), scarcity of labour supply in relation to planned requirements or to market demand, the title of superior skill or heavier responsibility to higher pay in its own right, or, conversely, the intrinsic virtues of equalitarianism—all these are *possible* principles in terms of which the merits of a total wage and salary structure could be judged, or a rational decision reached in a particular case. But without any such principles to refer to, either explicitly or by implication, judgements can be neither intelligent nor defensible.

An official pretence that this vacuum does not exist can be more or less firmly maintained so long as the case is heavily loaded against all increases. So long as changes are neither very frequent nor very large, the fact that they conform to no considered policy can be overlooked. A permanent standstill is, however, obviously impossible.

Unless the wage and salary structure of 1949, or 1950 or 1953 is to be standardized for all time, there must in due course be changes; and these changes in an age in which they are consciously made by negotiators, arbitrators and members of statutory wage-fixing bodies, must be defensible—morally as well as economically. Moreover, since, as we have seen, no standstill has ever been complete, and since from 1950 up to at least the end of 1953, the brakes have pressed comparatively lightly on the wheels of wage advances, in practice decisions are constantly being reached by one means or another; and these decisions, whatever the processes by which they are actually determined, are always presented as the outcome of argument and counter-argument in socially responsible terms. Whatever the factors that may lead them to press their demands, claimants never openly ask for a wage increase on the grounds that they hold an impregnable monopoly and that it will be dangerous to refuse them. Instead, they produce facts and figures purporting to prove that they are, by some standard, 'underpaid'. Similarly, employers do not explicitly reject claims or demand reductions on the ground that they do not mean to miss an opportunity of exploiting workers who are poorly organized: they speak, rather, of the dangers of inflation, or, in their turn, adduce facts and figures to show that their employees are, by some standard, adequately, if not excessively, paid. Even arbitrators, on the rare occasions when they show their hands and confess to the grounds of their own decisions, never admit that they have split the difference between the parties because they could not think of anything else to do; they, too, defend their judgements as being 'fair' or 'reasonable'. Where no principles are explicitly formulated, implicit standards must, in fact, take their place; and these must be read between the lines of the arguments used in support of, and in opposition to, claims; or extracted from the unspoken assumptions which are common to both sides.

What, then, are the standards and the assumptions to which by implication we commit ourselves?

Some light may be thrown on this question by the terms in which applications to Courts of Arbitration are presented and rebutted. In order to utilize this, I have selected from the cases submitted to the National Arbitration Tribunal during the first nine years of its life and to the Industrial Court during the same period those which might be described as 'cases of substance'; and have asked the employers and unions concerned if they would be good enough to let me see the documents relevant to these cases. The definition of 'cases of substance' was unavoidably subjective; but the aim was to

9

include only those in which the tribunal or court was asked to fix a new rate, as distinct from determining the status of particular workers under existing agreements; and to exclude all which were of purely local interest or involved only small numbers of workers. Such cases of substance constitute only a small proportion of the total number of awards (since many deal with matters of interpretation) made by these tribunals in the period under review; nor was it possible to obtain documents in more than a modest proportion of the cases selected. In the end I was successful in getting more or less complete documentation from the unions in fifty-seven and from the employers in forty-four cases: in twenty-two cases a *verbatim* report of proceedings was made available. The bias of this sample presumably favours those unions and employers' associations which are particularly confident and experienced in the presentation of arbitration cases; but a study of the published summaries of evidence in those cases in which documents were not forthcoming does not suggest that the arguments used in these differ conspicuously from those in the sample. For the period subsequent to 1949, the fuller and more lucid form in which evidence given before arbitration tribunals is summarized in the published awards makes it less necessary to refer to the original documents.

Unfortunately, the use made of this material (for which I am greatly indebted to the unions and employers' associations in many industries) must be restricted by the fact that those who supplied it were not as a rule willing that it should be quoted in any form which would make it possible to identify the organization responsible: the prevailing taboo of secrecy could not lightly be disregarded. It is, therefore, seldom possible to give specific references for the statements quoted in support of the conclusions that follow. This omission is, however, the less serious inasmuch as the argumentation to be found in these documents can be supplemented from the published reports of the considerable number of Courts of Inquiry set up under the Industrial Courts Act, and from those tribunals, such as the Railway Staff National Tribunal and the Civil Service Arbitration Tribunal, which sit in public or publish relatively full reports, as well as from the annual reports of nationalized industries, the authors of which have occasionally allowed themselves to think aloud on the subject of wage policy. Comparable information is available also in some professional occupations (notably medicine) in which the whole question of remuneration has been the subject of a special inquiry; while in others (notably teaching and nursing), salaries are periodically reviewed by standing committees appointed for that purpose, or (as in the case of Her Majesty's judges) there has been considerable public discussion of the issues involved.

From these various sources it is possible to get some idea of contemporary attitudes towards wage questions, and of the arguments, on both sides, which are apparently thought to carry weight. Before, however, we proceed to an analysis of these arguments, it is desirable to remind ourselves of certain obvious, but important, peculiarities in the economic climate of the whole post-war epoch in this country. In the first place, this epoch has been one of very nearly full employment. Though local temporary depressions have hit particular industries and areas from time to time, the monthly average percentage figures of unemployment in Great Britain have seldom exceeded 2%. Secondly, and no doubt as a result of this conquest of unemployment, this has been a period in which wages and salaries, with negligible exceptions, have been moving only in an upward direction. And, thirdly, ever since the outbreak of the Second World War, official policy has always leaned—sometimes more, sometimes less, heavily—on the side of wage restraint. As we have seen, in Chapter IV, even when the extreme stringency of the post-devaluation period was relaxed, only cautious and limited advances were countenanced at ministerial level—no matter what government was in power.

These conditions (since they have lasted for some fifteen years it is perhaps wrong to call them 'peculiarities') naturally have a great influence upon the course of wage discussions. So long as they persist, the initiative must lie exclusively with applicants for advances. We do not find employers stating a positive case for reductions: theirs is the opposition's task of finding fault with whatever is proposed by the other side; and this task is still further simplified by the official presumption that the onus of proof lies with the applicants, and that increases are in general contrary to the public interest. For the past fifteen years an employer has only had to show that applicants for wage increases have failed to establish that their case is entitled to special treatment—that it is a legitimate exception to a general policy of restraint. Apart from this, the general propositions that in a full-employment situation all wage increases tend to be inflationary, and that all inflation is bad, have been sufficient in themselves.

The significance of this situation, for the future course of policy, should not be overlooked. It is something new. Except for a much shorter period of wage inflation after the First World War, it has normally happened that every year some occupations have enjoyed an advance while others have suffered a decline in wages. With the ups and downs of trade there have, of course, been years in which increases greatly outweighed reductions, or *vice versa*. But apart from the exception just mentioned, the initiative has never before been so completely and persistently in the hands of one party. In the Ministry of Labour's annual summaries of aggregate wage changes in nine of the fourteen years from 1940 to 1953 inclusive, there were no reductions at all; and in the remaining five years, the total of decreases recorded is in every case very small, the largest figure being £2,900 a week in 1943, for which year the total of wage increases involved an addition of £1,630,900 to the weekly bill.

Memories are short, and that which has lasted for fifteen years is readily believed to be part of an eternal order of nature. If an unwelcome fall in the economic temperature of sufficient violence should occur, this particular belief may no doubt be rudely shattered; and employers may set themselves to preparing the kind of arguments in support of wage reductions that they think will look good in the second half of the twentieth century. But not only will they be seriously out of practice in the appropriate skills; the long period in which reductions have been unknown will itself constitute a formidable obstacle to their efforts under modern methods of wage determination. For precedent has itself become a factor to be reckoned with in wage discussions; and precedents for reductions will soon be far to seek.

In present conditions it is indeed more or less standard practice for a wage claim to open with a historical introduction, covering not only the course of the negotiations in progress or leading up to an arbitration case, but the movements of wages over a much longer period; and precedents are often explicitly invoked—sometimes, as will be seen in what follows,[1] from quite remote periods of history. Such reliance on the past is a symptom of the shift of wage negotiations from the economic to the ethical plane. Thirty years ago when I used myself to assist in the preparation of wage claims on behalf of a variety of trade unions, I do not recollect that we ever thought it worth while to bother very much about the past. Reference to established practice is natural enough in any issue that is to be decided upon ethical or social grounds—particularly so, in cases where no guiding principle other than precedent is generally recognized. But in terms of economic theory, precedent is altogether irrelevant: it is the present and the anticipated future state of the market which alone can determine the price of a man's labour or of anything else. What has happened in the past may explain how things came to be the way they are; but economic theory does not

[1] See pp. 133 ff.

allow that it should be invoked as an independent factor in its own right capable of modifying the conclusions to be drawn from the conditions since established. If the demand for a particular kind of skill has fallen, so must its value also fall; and it is beside the point to argue that such skill was once more highly rated—as the British miners had cause to recognize in the nineteen-thirties.

In one other respect, also, the fact that, in the period under review, wage negotiations were concerned only with claims for advances affects the discussion that follows. Inevitably, in these conditions, it is the arguments used by the unions much more than the employers' replies which disclose the standards by which the proper remuneration of any given calling is implicitly held to be determined. The party that carries the onus of proof is bound always to be the more informative; and employers, in the war and post-war climate, have, as we have seen, been under no pressure to produce any specific arguments at all for rejecting particular wage claims. It is for this reason that in the following analysis, material supplied by the unions bulks so much larger than that contributed on behalf of employers.

II

In the whole post-war epoch probably the most popular of all arguments for wage advances is the failure of wages to keep pace with the cost of living. In principle, this is too familiar to call for much elaboration here, but it may be useful to note some of the many ways in which room for manœuvre in the use of this weapon is obtained. Opportunism plainly dictates the choice of date on which comparisons are based. Present standards may be compared with pre-war figures; or with the levels prevailing at the date of the last advance; or indeed at any date that looks favourable and does not appear to have been too obviously chosen for that purpose. Alternatively, if the composite official index of retail prices does not lend sufficient support to a claim resting on this ground, attention may be directed to the disproportionate rise of particular prices, e.g. those of foodstuffs; or criticism may be directed against the index itself, or against its relevance to the case under review. One wage claim quotes newspaper reports of the prices of various articles in everyday use in an attempt to show that the index underestimates the rise that has actually occurred: another boldly declares that 'a wide volume of public opinion laughs' the retail price index 'to scorn'. And so on.

The significant feature of this argumentation is not the factual question whether in any given case wages and salaries have actually kept pace with rising costs, but the implied ethical assumption that they ought to do so. This principle is invariably taken for granted by claimants—never argued on merits. On the other side, the employers' attitude towards it varies. From their point of view the simplest, and during the period of extreme stringency perhaps the commonest, course is to shelter behind the 1948 White Paper, and so, by implication, to deny the validity of the whole assumption, without involving themselves in the dangerous business of explicit argument. In the phase of moderate relaxation, however, reference to the White Paper becomes less frequent, and cost of living arguments tend to be simply ignored by employers—presumably on the ground that, since the original postulate on which they are based is not admitted, the arguments themselves are just irrelevant. Occasionally, however, replies are made in detail, e.g. to criticisms of the retail price index—a procedure which logically involves the admission that an increase in the cost of living is, on the face of it, proper ground for a wage claim. But at no time is there any sign that employers are prepared to come into the open and frankly challenge the ultimate presumption which underlies every cost of living argument.

The cumulative effect of the practice of simply taking for granted at the conference table, in the Press and before courts of arbitration that everybody's pay ought normally to keep pace with the cost of living is not to be underestimated. In a period in which wage increases are continually being granted, this assumption at least *appears* to work. Obviously, the unions believe that it works: otherwise they would hardly spend so much time and energy on assembling evidence which is relevant only if this postulate is accepted. Moreover, the belief that an argument works goes a long way to make it work: Biblical authority notwithstanding, repetitions in a complex modern community are not vain. And whether it works or not, the public is now deeply imbued with a sense that it is just. Indeed it must rank as one of the unspoken major premises of contemporary thinking on social questions.

For the cost of living argument is not only popular: it is also, of all the arguments used on wage questions, the most completely innocent of economic considerations. Its colour is ethical through and through. In terms of this principle the maintenance of their standards of living is conceived as a moral obligation which the community owes to its members: it is to be justified on that ground and on that ground alone. But to squeeze this doctrine into the framework of classical economic theory, or indeed into the teaching of the contemporary textbooks reviewed in Chapter I of this book, would require remarkable ingenuity. One would need to argue either that the rise in living costs is due wholly to monetary inflation, and never to any change in the quantity of goods available for people to buy (an assumption which, whatever may be the case later, certainly does not hold for the actual war period); or, alternatively, that all workers who find their standard of living depressed by rising costs somehow succeed in reducing the supply of their labour so as to raise its price to the level previously obtaining. Intellectual gymnastics of this order may be possible; but they are not very helpful. It is simpler, as well as more realistic, to admit that the determination to maintain standards is a social fact of the first importance; and that, as such, it has a *direct* major influence on wage-levels.

At the same time, social facts, no matter how uncomfortably they may be housed in classical economic theory, have to live in the same world as economic realities; and, if that necessity is ignored, their economic consequences may be disastrous. In the prediction of those consequences orthodox economic theory is, in the present instance, much more successful. Indeed common sense alone might be able to foresee what is likely to happen. No great sophistication or technical economic training is necessary for the discovery that the determination to adjust wages to a rising cost of living involves a circular process; or that it is an inflationary device of consummate efficiency.

Equally obvious is its conservative influence. If everybody keeps neatly in step with the cost of living, everybody will also keep in step with everybody else: by running as fast as we can, we shall, in fact, all manage to stay in the same place. In that case a dynamic economy with a changing pattern of demand and supply can no longer look to wage movements to direct workers into those jobs in which their labour is most urgently needed. A wage policy which is socially acceptable may thus prove economically futile, perhaps even intolerable. To that contradiction we shall return.[1]

An alternative and less frequently used, form of the cost of living argument involves an attempt to deal in absolute standards: to show that, quite apart from any reference to the past, or any comparison with other occupations, it is not possible to live upon a given wage. For this purpose hypothetical, or even actual, family budgets are sometimes produced, relating to what is said to be an 'average' family. During the period of general rationing, some claimants sought by such figures to show that, on the prevailing wage, workers must be unable to purchase even their full rations.

[1] See pp. 178 ff.

This line of attack is open, of course, to the objection, already mentioned, that lies against all attempts to define a living wage irrespective of the number of people who have to live on it. The average family is at any one time actually the exceptional family; and it follows that any wage which is appropriately adjusted to the needs of the average family will be inappropriate to the needs of the majority of those to whom it is paid. The habit of dealing in averages involves here, as elsewhere, enormous and glaring absurdities. At the same time it seems to be a well-established habit: and, paradoxically, the inherent absurdities might perhaps attract more attention if they were a little less large. Extraordinary though it is that so grossly unrealistic a formula should have been swallowed both by the economic theorists and by the practical policy-makers, we cannot, I think, entirely discount the social acceptability of the idea that wages should be adjusted to the needs of the 'average' recipient.

More significant socially are the issues raised in cost of living claims by the fact that attempts to measure absolute standards of living are inevitably conditioned by the whole gamut of conventions implied in our social hierarchy: their absolutism is indeed quite specious. Occasionally these conventions are explicitly acknowledged, and the cost of living is frankly defined as the cost of maintaining an appropriate social position. As the spokesman of one set of claimants put it, 'No matter what way of life one has to live one gets used to that way of life.' In another case a wage advance was asked for—in order to enable the recipients 'to dress in a manner befitting their vocation'. The terms of reference of the Spens Committee, which was appointed to make recommendations as to the remuneration of the various branches of the medical and dental professions, included an instruction to have 'due regard to . . . the desirability of maintaining the proper *social and economic status*'[1] of the professions concerned; and in the public discussion of the Government's proposal early in 1953 to increase the salaries of Her Majesty's judges, the same argument was freely used. After pointing out that the puisne judges had enjoyed no increase of salary at all since 1832, a leading article in *The Times* went on to remark that 'there are practically no rich men nowadays—as the subjects of King William IV understood riches—and it is far beyond the capacity of public funds to endow the present Judges with the opulence that their predecessors enjoyed a century ago. *But it is of first-rate public importance that they should continue to be men of substance and security. The vast moral authority of the law in this country is bound up in the public mind with the visible dignity of*

[1] Inter-Departmental Committee on the Remuneration of Consultants and Specialists, *Report*. Cmd. 7420 (1948). Italics mine—B.W.

the men who dispense the Queen's justice.'[1] Ten days later *The Times* returned to the topic in a second leading article. By this time a good deal of public outcry against the Government's original proposal to make any advance free of tax had made its impression, and *The Times* was disposed to prefer a method, if such could be found, which did not involve gross increases ranging from £5,000 to £30,000 a year, according to the rank of the judge in question; but the argument that, 'The dignity of the Bench must be upheld by a certain way of living, which must extend as much to the judges' home lives as, for example, to the manner in which they travel to and from the courts'[2] remained. Justice, it seems, must be rich as well as blind: travel by bus would threaten her—but not by Rolls-Royce. Commenting on the same proposal a few days later, Sir Hartley Shawcross (who occupies a seat in Parliament on the Labour front benches) observed that 'we do not live in an egalitarian society'.[3] Evidently not; but in the present ostensibly democratic age it is unusual to say so quite so candidly.

The admissibilty of such arguments turns, of course, entirely on the degree of sanctity attached to the present social hierarchy, the significance of which in our present wage structure was emphasized on pp. 68–70. It is perhaps a fair summary of present attitudes to say that frank challenge of conventional standards is today about as unusual as are the unabashed acknowledgments just quoted. For the most part, established standards are accepted, so to speak, by default;[4] and the common phenomenon of inability to live on salaries of widely differing size is explained by the fact that the verb 'to live' is tacitly redefined at every level.

This strictly social element in wage and salary claims easily becomes confused with certain economic lines of argument which are discussed at length below.[5] But they are distinct. Differentiation can be defended, in economic terms, as being necessary to attract sufficient recruits to a particular occupation, or as compensation for the heavy cost of training which this perhaps entails. At least in theory these are measurable factors: the test of adequacy is the extent to which the required recruits are in fact forthcoming. The social conventions relating to pay are, by contrast, immeasurable: in the last resort they rest on nothing but themselves; and an 'appropriate' style of living for any profession can only be defined as the style of living that the profession happens to have established for itself.

Partly for this reason, the purely social element in wage and salary

---

[1] *The Times*, 14 March 1953. Italics mine.—B.W.
[2] *The Times*, 24 March 1953.   [3] In a letter to *The Times*, 30 March 1953.
[4] Attempts to relate standards of remuneration scientifically to the nature of the work done are discussed below. See pp. 143 ff.
[5] See pp. 153 ff.

differentiation cannot easily be explicitly pleaded in wage negotiations: there are no arguments—that can be used in support of it—except the circular one that highly-paid jobs carry high prestige, and that high prestige demands high pay. And partly, also, explicit recognition of a prestige hierarchy is precluded, as being too difficult to square with the temper of the age. Sir Hartley Shawcross was right—we do not live in an egalitarian society; but we do like to pretend that we do.

Occasionally, however, the insecurity of the standards, which are said to be the minima on which it is possible to live, is ruthlessly exposed from the other side. Thus a Board of Conciliation appointed to consider railway wage problems in 1949 found themselves unable to accept the contention that the then minimum rate of 92s. 6d. a week was below 'the figure necessary to maintain the minimum standard of human needs'. 'It is clear,' the Board continued, 'from the information before us that there are other industries in which by negotiation between employers and unions concerned minimum rates have been fixed below 92s. 6d. Judged upon a human need standard the needs of a railwayman are no different from the needs of any other member of the community. If, therefore, we were to decide, as we are invited to do, that the human need standard of a railwayman should be assessed at a minimum figure of 102s. 6d. we would of necessity be cutting across the negotiated agreements in other industries which provide a minimum below that figure, and we would in essence be establishing a principle, namely, that a national minimum rate for unskilled labour should be set at 102s. 6d.'[1] In other words, a minimum is a minimum: there cannot be several minima, each representing the lowest figure at which it is possible to live. The logic is unanswerable but it cuts at the root of the claims for a minimum living wage which are commonly advanced at many different levels.

On another occasion one group of employers even went so far as boldly to defend the view that the whole question of standards of living is irrelevant to wage determinations. 'It is no part of the Tribunal's duty to assume,' runs their submission, 'a position of authority in relation to the level at which standards of life must be maintained. Their duty is to assess, in the absence of agreement between employer and employee, the remuneration appropriate to services rendered and, if they were to conclude that such remuneration was in fact inadequate to maintain a proper standard of life,

---

[1] Ministry of Labour and National Service, *Report* of a Board of Conciliation appointed by the Minister of Labour and National Service to assist in the consideration and settlement of certain problems relating to salaries, wages and conditions of service of the Conciliation and Salaried grades on the Railways (1949), p. 31.

such conclusion must not be permitted to influence the sum which is considered to be a just reward for services rendered. The employers, in making this submission, do not, of course, suggest that the present wage is inadequate either in relation to the value of the work or in relation to the maintenance of a reasonable standard of life. They are, however, concerned to point out that it is the first of these considerations which is relevant to the issue before the Tribunal. The second consideration is of national concern and can be, and is being, achieved without interference with the principles upon which employment and remuneration are based.' The statement then proceeds to enumerate the various benefits, such as free meals, free milk and children's allowances by which the standard of living is supported independently of wages. This passage, however, with its old-fashioned insistence on the economic rather than the social or ethical aspects of wage-rates, is quite out of harmony with the prevailing trend even of the statements submitted on behalf of employers.

III

Almost as popular as arguments based on the comparative or absolute cost of living are those derived from comparisons with other industries. Comparisons may be either general or particular. Among the general forms the favourite is that which quotes the Ministry of Labour's index of wage movements—in support of a claim for an increase in a particular trade. The principle involved is simple: it is assumed that any occupation in which wages can be demonstrated not to have kept pace with the general advance as shown by this index has a *prima facie* case for an increase of pay. In the manipulation of this argument, as with claims based on cost of living changes, there is some room for manœuvre in the selection of the dates used as the bases of comparison, but otherwise no great subtleties are involved.

Neither the conservative nor the inflationary effects of this argument need any elaboration. The Ministry of Labour has perhaps cause to rue the day when publication of an official wage index made this line of attack so fatally easy; and the parallel risk involved in producing an index of salary changes which will inevitably lend itself to similar use will no doubt be carefully weighed. On the employers' side the obvious answer is simply to emphasize these inflationary consequences, and to leave it at that: the principle that all wages ought to move together is not conceded, and, as with the cost of living argument, discussion of whether they have or have not so moved becomes, therefore, irrelevant. Here and there, however, the challenge is accepted: in one case affecting an important national industry, an ingenious line of reply was developed, designed to show how the claimant industry's proportion of the total advances granted to industrial wage-earners generally compared with its share of the total labour force: one-eighteenth of the country's workers, it was contended, had managed to absorb one-sixth of the total increase in the national wage bill. But such attempts to pursue the argument beyond the general wage index are unusual.

In present circumstances, the practical result of the policy of keeping all wages in step with one another is, of course, likely to be much the same as that of keeping all in step with changes in the cost of living; though the two could diverge if, for example, successful attempts were made to increase wages at the expense of profits, or from the proceeds of improved productivity. The cost of living criterion seems, however, to be the more socially acceptable form of what thus often amounts to exactly the same ground of claim: it is less often openly rejected. No doubt it is easier to concede the principle that no one's standards ought to be reduced than explicitly to admit the permanent rightness of all relativities.

Appeals by claimants to the level of wages obtaining in particular industries supposedly comparable to their own raise more complicated issues. Unhappily, the obligation to treat so many of the relevant documents as confidential presses particularly hardly here; since comparisons between individual employments cannot, in the nature of the case, be scrambled. The illustrations that are given below are therefore inevitably drawn chiefly from industries in which wages and salaries have been the subject of public inquiries; and this overloads the story with the experience of public service industries. I can only say that the confidential material abounds in similar instances.

The outstanding feature of these comparisons is the measure in which they amount to purely circular arguments. The occupations chosen for the purpose of comparison are not so much those which would be judged comparable by objective analysis of the work involved as those which happen to have done a little better than the claimants in the struggle for higher wages: in one case the only common feature of all the trades quoted appeared to be that they had all enjoyed a recent increase of 20s. a week. Occasionally, claimants vary the usual practice of relying upon occupational or industrial parallels by appealing to geographical comparisons. 'Workers in the —— industry,' reads one submission, 'have the same domestic expenditure as other workers employed in surrounding industries, and they do make a comparison between their own earnings and the earnings of their next door neighbour, no matter in which industry he is engaged.' In the selection of 'comparables', there is indeed endless scope for ingenuity; and it is significant that the selection made by a given group of workers often varies from time to time when repeated claims are made over a period.

This, however, is a game at which two can—and do—play. As one group of employers put it, 'the variations both in wages and war increases are so wide that if only favourable instances are selected, evidence can be presented to support the contention of either side'. Nor does the chopping and changing about escape employers' notice. 'The union's representative,' we read in the statement of one group of employers before the National Arbitration Tribunal, 'repudiated a comparison with the agricultural worker's wages when it was 33s. or 35s. a week. Now he quotes it at 63s. in support of his claim, but in fact the agricultural worker is much more highly skilled than the . . . labourers.' In another case, a port authority, faced with a wage claim in 1941, went back to pre-war history in order to illustrate the tendency for workers 'to relate their wages fluctuations to the particular trade group enjoying the temporary advantage'. In 1935 the engineers employed by this authority claimed that they should keep in step with the general workers; next a number of building unions put forward a claim that they should move with the engineers; then the shipbuilders sought to keep pace with the dock-workers; and then, four years after the first move, the engineers started again. Such tactics certainly induce sympathy with the attitude of the 1951 Court of Inquiry into Railway Wages which, after an exceptionally careful study of what was described as the problem of relativity, concluded that, 'The principle of relativity does not provide any secure criterion by means of which a decision can be reached as to the correct basis of comparison between different industries.'[1]

The selection of 'comparable' occupations quoted in support of wage claims is indeed a revealing process in more ways than one. It certainly shows the powerful influence of social and conventional factors. One indication of the force of these is to be found in the practice, to which reference has already been made of carrying comparisons far back into history. A classic example is to be found in the firemen's struggle to get their rate firmly tied to that of the police, which culminated in the issue of parity being specifically referred to a Board of Arbitration under the Industrial Courts Act in January

[1] Court of Inquiry into applications for an improvement in wages and salaries made to the Railway Executive by The National Union of Railwaymen, The Associated Society of Locomotive Engineers and Firemen and The Railway Clerks' Association. *Report*, Cmd. 8154 (1951), p. 37.

1952.[1] The case submitted by the firemen to this Board rested primarily on historical arguments, which were carried as far back even as 1888, though the main weight of evidence rested on experience since 1920; and, in the course of this historical research, it was argued that the Industrial Court had itself on an earlier occasion conceded the principle of parity. So strong indeed was the faith of the claimants in the virture of an established equivalence that they proceeded on the assumption that the onus of proof lay on those who would reject the parity principle. They were not, however, successful.

Similarly the Typographical Association, in 1947, defended a claim for an increase of 9s. per week as necessary to redress an alleged 'injustice' of no less than twenty-five years before, when the differential between London and provincial craftsmen had been increased from 2s. 6d. to 11s. 6d. a week. This claim appeared to be on the verge of acceptance, when the National Arbitration Tribunal issued an award on a dispute between the British Master Printers' Federation and the London Society of Compositors. In the course of this, the Tribunal stated that they 'had had regard to the fact that in recent years the traditional differential between the rates paid to compositors in London and the provinces respectively, as expressed in terms of a percentage, has progressively declined'; and awarded accordingly an increase of 15s. a week to the London compositors, thus increasing the differential to 17s. 6d. over the provincial rate.[2] In this case, it will be noted, the members of the National Arbitration Tribunal, no less than the workers, appear to have accepted the argument from tradition; but by using a percentage instead of a flat-rate calculation they reached an unexpected answer.

A third example of this respect for the remoter past comes from the railway engine drivers. Arguing before a Court of Inquiry in 1951 Mr. Baty of the Associated Society of Locomotive Engineers and Firemen contended that the 'agreements of 1919 and 1920' 'set up a wages structure in which the *proper* value of the Locomotive man in relation to the other grades was recognized. The relativity then established remained more or less intact down to 1939, but it had since been progressively undermined by the granting of successive flat-rate increases, the effect of which was largely to destroy the principle of differentials and to weaken initiative.'[3] Similarly, Mr.

[1] Board of Arbitration in the matter of a difference between the employers' and the employees' sides of the National Joint Council for Local Authorities' Fire Brigades in England and Wales on the Remuneration of Firemen (1952), *Report*.

[2] Court of Inquiry into the causes and circumstances of a dispute between the London Master Printers' Association and the London Society of Compositors, *Report*, Cmd. 8074 (1950), p. 7.

[3] Cmd. 8154 (1951), p. 18. Italics mine.—B.W.

Thorneycroft on behalf of the Railway Clerks' Association (now the Transport Salaried Staffs' Association) deplored the settlement of 1948 on the grounds that it 'fell far short of restoring the *pre-war* differentials between salaried classes which had been impaired by successive flat-rate increases'.[1] The police also used as one of their arguments for higher pay, before the Oaksey Committee of 1949, the contention that their position relative to industry was less favourable than at the time of the previous inquiry in 1920. Thus printers, police and railwaymen, though they have not yet matched the firemen in digging up evidence from the nineteenth century, are all prepared to treat the relationships of anything up to thirty years ago as relevant to the pattern that in their judgement ought to obtain today.

This reliance on precedent smacks more of the law courts than of the human calculating machines postulated by the economic text-books. The implication is that justice must be dispensed, not bargains snatched. 'Proper' relationships are assumed; and should these become disturbed, they must be restored. At the same time the implied standards of propriety are themselves clearly conditioned by conventional factors. 'Equitable comparison,' as Professor Ross has put it, ' . . . runs in limited circuits.'[2] Professional must be matched against professional salaries, clerical against clerical wages, and manual against manual. Mr. Justice Danckwerts, for example, in his 1952 adjudication on the size of the central pool from which general medical practitioners in the National Health Service should be paid, was instructed to have regard to 'the increases which have taken place in incomes in other *professions*'[3]—not, be it noted, to the movement of other incomes generally; and in the teaching profession the need for 'enjoyment of a life of reasonably high cultural standards' was reckoned among the proper determinants of teachers' salaries by the McNair Committee on Teachers and Youth Leaders.[4]

This concept of a proper hierarchy of rates is deeply engrained in current thought on wage questions. It appears again in the principle already mentioned, which demands that supervisors should be paid more highly than those who work under their direction. This principle itself crops up from time to time in explicit form in wage claims; and an attempt to reduce it to numerical form has been made by the Association of Supervisory Staffs, Executives and Technicians

[1] Cmd. 8154 (1951), p. 18. Italics mine.—B.W.
[2] Ross, *Trade Union Wage Policy*, p. 6.
[3] As reported in *British Medical Journal* (supplement) (29 March 1952), p. 2462. Italics mine.—B.W.
[4] Committee appointed by the President of the Board of Education to consider the Supply, Recruitment and Training of Teachers and Youth Leaders, *Report* (1944), para. 118.

(commonly known as Asset), a union which caters largely for fore-men and chargehands, whose rates are in present conditions particularly likely to be overtaken by those working below them: Asset's National Charter demands a basic rate for supervisors $66\frac{2}{3}\%$ above that of those supervised, with further additions for the number of persons supervised, for responsibility for plant, equipment or materials, and for length of service in a supervisory capacity.[1] Though precise figures such as these may be challenged, the basic principle that the supervisor should be paid more than the supervised, appears to enjoy the unique distinction that—alone among all the grounds on which wage advances are advocated—it is fundamentally quite uncontroversial. Employers may question whether in a particular case subordinates do in fact earn more than their superiors; or there may be controversy as to whether the rule should be applied so strictly as to preclude any overlapping incremental scales—as claimed, for instance, by the Society of Telecommunication Engineers in their submission to the Civil Service Arbitration Tribunal in 1951. But no one questions that higher responsibility and higher authority ought normally to carry higher pay. Indeed by the same logic the contention is sometimes made that supervisors ought not to work longer hours than those supervised: the fact that a booking clerk working forty-two hours might be under the supervision of a stationmaster who had to work forty-four hours was quoted as a case of 'serious grievance' in a 1949 railway claim.[2] Although the Railway Executive found difficulty in reducing the hours of supervisors generally on the ground that these were linked to those of other staff working on a forty-four-hour basis, they did in fact agree to a reduction to forty-two hours in the case of stationmasters and agents, in order to meet what they were apparently prepared to accept as the anomaly of these grades being required in some circumstances to work a longer week than their inferiors.

In other cases 'differentials' are defended in more general terms. Thus one group of claimants optimistically declares that differences in wage-rates are 'no accidental circumstance, but the result of a long period of experience, knowledge and assessment of the relative value of work performed'. The importance of differentials is, naturally, constantly stressed by the representatives of skilled crafts. On the railways, particularly, there has been a continual see-saw between claims for flat-rate and for percentage advances—an alternation which

[1] ASSET, *National Charter* (London, n.d.), pp. 15–16.
[2] Board of Conciliation appointed by the Minister of Labour and National Service to assist in the consideration and settlement of certain problems relating to salaries, wages and conditions of service of the Conciliation and Salaried grades on the Railways, *Report* (1949), pp. 22–3.

in fact registers the conflicting interests of the National Union of Railwaymen which speaks for all grades and of the unions representing the Locomotive Engineers and the Salaried Staffs. In 1947 the Associated Society of Locomotive Engineers and Firemen disassociated itself from the claim of the other unions for a flat-rate advance, and proposed larger increases for drivers than for firemen, and more, again, for firemen than for cleaners. The Court of Inquiry which heard this claim found itself baffled by the technicalities and recommended a flat-rate advance all round, while at the same time urging both sides in the industry to get together and to work out a system of differentials which would 'recompense more fairly' the greater skill and responsibility of the higher grades.[1] A few months later, in February 1948, a new settlement did in fact increase these differentials, only to be followed six months afterwards by a fresh though unsuccessful flat-rate claim from the National Union of Railwaymen. At the end of December 1949 the NUR again pressed the case of the lower-paid workers (this time successfully) while the ASLEF and the Transport Salaried Staffs' Association followed up with claims for percentage increases for their own members, designed to improve differentials again. The Confederation of Engineering and Shipbuilding Unions had already declared, on behalf of the railway shopmen, that 'they could not accept any responsibility for an alteration in the rates of lower trades only, and a lessening of the differential between the floor and the ceiling would be regarded as a serious matter'.[2] The ASLEF who, as already mentioned, take their stand on relatively venerable precedents, were still contending in 1951 that the restoration of a 'proper' relativity was the fundamental basis of the Society's claim. The locomotive men—'inheritors of a long tradition of pride in and devotion to their job—were stirred by a profound sense of injustice'—at the repeated narrowing of differentials. As the 1951 Court of Inquiry, which had the task of unravelling this tangled skein, observed, 'one moral, though it is not the only one' to be drawn 'is the impossibility of reconciling, in a period of rising prices and costs of living, the natural desire to cushion the lower-paid workers as much as possible against reductions in their standards of living, with the need for improving the relativity between the lower and the higher grades'.[3] A few months later the Transport Salaried Staffs felt that while they 'did not in any way grudge the Conciliation

---

[1] Cmd. 8154, p. 39.
[2] Board of Conciliation appointed by the Minister of Labour and National Service to assist in the consideration of certain problems relating to wages and conditions of service of Railway Shopmen with a view to promoting a settlement, *Report* (1949), p. 6.
[3] Cmd. 8154, pp. 20 and 40.

Staff the increases they had received' . . . 'the differentials had been reduced far too much'.[1] Once again, the problem of raising the floor without bringing it nearer to the ceiling which, as we have seen, had already troubled Sir Stafford Cripps as Chancellor of the Exchequer, was found to be insoluble.

The need to maintain recognized differentials is, of course, a weapon which can be used against, as well as on the side of, wage claims. In one case heard by the National Arbitration Tribunal in 1948 this argument was translated by employers into terms of the highest public responsibility. 'We believe,' they said, 'we should be doing a disservice to the country if the agreed minimum rates for craftsmen in a big industry like —— were to get seriously out of step or in advance of the rates for craftsmen in other industries.' 'We have, therefore, taken the trouble to get together an up-to-date list of the minimum time rates for men in other industries. . . . We have not just picked out half a dozen industries and we do not suggest that the skill in each and every industry is comparable, but the Tribunal will note that the minimum rate for the —— is one of the highest in the list.'

Differentials can be defended on historical, ethical or prestige grounds, and the degree of emphasis laid upon each of these considerations varies from one industry or service to another. It is, as one would expect, in such formally hierarchical services as the police that the association of rank with pay stands most solidly in its own right. Even here, however, the complications that result from the impossibility of raising minima without reducing differentials have not been entirely avoided. Two months after the publication of the 1948 White Paper on Personal Incomes, a committee appointed to consider the pay of police superintendents made certain recommendations which were accepted in principle by the Government, but subsequently suspended in deference to the White Paper policy of restraint. Representatives of the police superintendents argued before the Oaksey Committee of 1949 that these proposals had been intended to establish the 'proper' relationship between the pay of superintendents and that of lower ranks, and that it was only on account of the general standstill that a, so to speak, improper relationship had been allowed to continue. This line of argument, as the Oaksey Committee acknowledged, led to the conclusion that any increases which they might recommend in the pay of the lower ranks would necessarily require commensurate advances in the superintendents' scales. The Committee refused, however, to admit the premise from which this conclusion was

[1] British Railways, *Railway Staff National Tribunal*, Decision No. 13 (7 November 1951), p. 13.

derived, regarding themselves as free to 'consider the subject afresh'; and the upshot of their consideration was that, while increases were recommended in the pay of the lower ranks and in the superintendents' minima, the maxima in the scales that were held up by the White Paper were retained. Though rejecting one premise, the Committee did not, however, disclose from what alternative they had reached their own conclusion: no reasons were given for the change in differentials.

In this context it is of interest to reflect upon the significance of the common practice of reckoning differentials on a percentage rather than an absolute basis. Flat-rate advances to all grades, although they leave the absolute differences between one grade and another unchanged, are generally said to reduce differentials. Yet the concrete advantage of a higher wage to any individual is measured by the additions that the extra money makes to the actual goods that he is able to buy. A worker with £500 a year can make certain expenditure which his colleague at £400 cannot afford. If both receive an increase of £50 a year, the one is still ahead of the other to the tune of £100 worth of commodities: only in the case in which the increment just matches a deterioration in the value of money will the visible difference between their respective styles of living be unavoidably changed to the detriment of the better paid. In ordinary life there are, no doubt, occasions when it is appropriate to reckon differentials in absolute terms, and occasions when percentage comparisons are more appropriate. One may, perhaps, hazard the speculation that most of us think in absolute figures when considering possible changes in our own position ('what could I buy with another fifty pounds a year?') but in percentage terms in comparing ourselves with others.

This point may have considerable significance in connection with the supposed incentive value of differentials, which is an important, though usually subsidiary, line of defence for the privileges of the more highly-paid grades, and has been particularly prominent in the various ASLEF claims on behalf of the footplate men. Claims for the maintenance or increase of differentials on incentive grounds are, however, only a special case of the general argument from undermanning and are discussed more fully in connection with that topic below. But it may be worth noting here that the practice of reckoning differentials on an absolute, rather than on a percentage, basis appears to be yet another indication of the great weight given to social prestige in our wage and salary structure. It seems to imply that we are more interested in keeping our distances above other people than in the actual level at which our earnings make it possible for us to live. Standards of living can be reckoned in terms of absolute quantities of meat and bread and motor-cars and holidays abroad; whereas prestige is inherently relative.

IV

From time to time attempts are made to break away from traditional comparisons and to determine standards either by some supposedly absolute standard of 'merits', or by reference to more scientific methods of comparison. The 'merits' argument, as will be seen from the quotations that follow, merges easily into the concept already discussed, of standards of living that are appropriate in an absolute sense; though there remains in principle a definite, if subtle, distinction between a standard that represents a proper way to live, and one which correctly measures the value that, it is supposed, ought to be set on a particular job—in some sense other than that of its crude economic value as determined by market forces of demand and supply. The 'merits' argument need not, however, be taken very seriously in any of its versions. It is obvious enough that absolute standards of remuneration can have no meaning; and the appeal to merits, accordingly, always itself involves implied comparisons: it is used, as a rule, either as a tactical device for escaping from some particular comparison, or as a last resort to which recourse is indicated when there is no hope that conventional comparisons will yield the result desired. Thus the Board of Arbitration which rejected the firemen's claim to equality with the police expressed the view that this comparison was 'not . . . very rewarding'. 'The two services are doing different things and it is in our view not profitable to attempt to weigh up their respective responsibilities or advantages. It appears to us that the proper way of deciding the remuneration of the Fire Service is not to relate it to police remuneration but to determine it on its own merits.'[1] Similarly a writer in the *Local Government Chronicle* for 26 January 1952, deprecated the practice of 'negotiation by comparison' in relation to local government salaries on the ground that 'it weakens the case for dealing with each category of workers on the merits of their claims'. 'We are not arguing,' writes another group of claimants, 'and never have been arguing, about the relations of our basic rate to any other industry's basic rate, but rather on the relationship of the rates that we *had* to the rates that we have, which is a totally different

[1] Board of Arbitration on the Remuneration of Firemen, *Report* (1952), para. 35.

question.' Again, in the course of what was in effect an inter-union dispute, we find a complaint of 'the tendency for independent wage-fixing bodies to judge a local claim against a national background, to compare conditions in one industry with conditions in another, and against that background the union did not get a fair answer'. In the professional field, the Spens Committee, which thought that 'comparisons are proverbially odious but they are sometimes inevitable', felt that it would be 'affectation to ignore the fact' that comparisons would be made between their recommendations for dental and for general medical practitioners.[1] When dealing with the latter, however, the same Committee started from the proposition that before the Second World War, 'Having regard to length of training, to the arduousness of the general practitioner's life compared with that in other professions, to the greater danger to health, to the skill and other qualities required and to the degree of individual responsibility', 'the percentages of low incomes are too high'.[2] They therefore recommended additions which would have the effect (in 1939 prices) of augmenting pre-war net incomes by £200 in the case of incomes between £400 and £1,200, and by smaller sums above that figure. 'Too low on merits' was also the verdict, though at a much humbler level, of a group of industrial workers whose submission took the simple line that 'there is no reason, other than that of social responsibility, why we should give any consideration to the standards of 1939—they were much too low'; whilst, in yet another case, pre-war comparisons were dismissed as inappropriate on the ground that no increase had been given for twenty years before the war owing to the high rate of unemployment and depressed state of the trade in question.

Similarly, the Desborough Committee which reviewed the conditions of service of the police in 1920 emphasized that 'a policeman has responsibilities and obligations which are peculiar to his calling and distinguish him from other public servants and municipal employees'; and a sketch which they gave of the qualities expected of the police constable (which was repeated by their successors, the Oaksey Committee of 1949) indicated that this occupation demands a very high standard indeed. According to these authorities the policeman must not only have 'general intelligence, memory and powers of observation' 'distinctly above the average': his character must also be 'unblemished'; he must be 'humane and courteous'; and he should possess 'a combination of moral, mental and physical

[1] Inter-Departmental Committee on the Remuneration of General Dental Practitioners, *Report*, Cmd. 7402 (1948), p. 10.
[2] Inter-Departmental Committee on the Remuneration of General Practitioners, *Report*, Cmd. 6810 (1946), p. 5.

qualities not ordinarily required in other employments', besides being able to act with 'tact and discretion, and on his own initiative and responsibility, in all sorts of contingencies'. Police witnesses before the Oaksey Committee urged in addition that a constable is 'subject to social disabilities by reason of his employment', and that he must 'at all times, both on and off duty, maintain a standard of personal conduct befitting to his position'.[1] The Committee to whom these observations were addressed expressed entire agreement with them, and appeared to accept the implication that they constituted, without further argument, grounds for relatively high standards of remuneration.

For an unusually frank and sceptical discussion of the whole subject of relativities we may refer again to the report of the 1951 Court of Inquiry into railway wages. 'Relativity,' as this report observed, 'can refer to the relation between the wages and earnings in railway employment as compared with those prevailing in outside industries, or it can refer to differentials between different grades within the railway industry itself.' In the discussion which followed of the former type of relativity, the Court made the point (the significance of which is discussed below)[2] that the more rapid advance of some of the industries which had outstripped the railways was justified by the fact that these industries must be counted undermanned by the standards of national economic policy; and stressed, in addition, the need to make comparisons, not in terms of money alone, but on a basis which takes account of all that the economist would include in net advantages or disadvantages—such as, in the case of railways, the privilege of free or cheap travel on the one hand, and inconvenient hours of duty, liability to accident and so forth on the other. However, while admitting the 'immense practical driving force' of relativity between different industries as a factor in wage negotiations, the members of this Court reached the conclusions that 'there is no objective method by which these advantages and disadvantages can be evaluated or brought into a balance', and that the 'principle of relativity does not provide any secure criterion by means of which a decision can be reached as to the correct basis of comparison between different industries'.[3] They did not, however, rival the practical optimism of their predecessors on the 1947 railway Court of Inquiry who, after a somewhat similar discussion of the 'net advantage' of railway employment, put forward the remarkable claim that 'although we are unable to evaluate the respective merits and demerits, we

[1] Committee on Police Conditions of Service, Part I, *Report*, Cmd. 7674 (1949), pp. 7–8.
[2] See pp. 157 ff.   [3] Cmd. 8154, pp. 36–8.

have endeavoured to have due regard to them in reaching our conclusions'.[1]

Much less sceptical is the attitude taken by the authors of the considerable body of literature—on which many firms now seek to base their practice—dealing with 'scientific' methods of job evaluation designed to establish relativities that might prove less vulnerable to charges of opportunism. Thus Mr. C. W. Lytle, in a standard American work on the subject, writes, 'We do not find it necessary any longer to haggle for hours over the price of an automobile. Why should we find it necessary to haggle over the most vitally important commodity of all—human service? The answer is that it is not necessary to bargain on each individual job. Job evaluation is merely a convenient name for systematic and impartial pricing in the labour market, quite closely comparable to modern pricing of merchandise. The latter is made possible by adequate cost analysis, the former by adequate job analysis.' In general this 'systematic and impartial pricing', since it is designed for use within a particular firm, relates, at least by implication, to intra-industry rather than to inter-industry comparisons; but this does not preclude attempts to extend the standards thus arrived at to jobs of widely differing character. The procedure generally adopted is, in outline, as follows. Jobs are first analysed in terms of four major characteristics, namely, skill, effort, responsibility and working conditions. These characteristics are then sub-divided to suit the circumstances of individual occupations: Mr. Lytle, for example, suggests that skill should be sub-divided into mental ('intelligence, education, experience, training, reaction time, etc.'), and physical ('manual dexterity, accuracy, etc.'); that effort should be similarly divided into mental and physical: that responsibility should be classified according to whether it relates to people or to material things; and that working conditions should be divided into 'hazardous' and 'disagreeable'.[2]

The next step is to assign weights to these various factors or sub-factors. In the words of another American manual, 'The analyst will assign point values to the factors as defined in order to provide a fair weighting of the varying degrees of importance attached to each factor': skill, for instance, in a hypothetical example subsequently quoted, is rated at 35%, effort at 15%, responsibility at 30% and working conditions at 20%. Every job is then assessed for its rating in terms of these factors and sub-factors—a process which the author

[1] Court of Inquiry into applications by the trade unions representing the employees of the railway companies for improvements in wages and reductions in weekly hours of work, *Report*, Cmd. 7161 (1947), p. 29.
[2] Lytle, C. W., *Job Evaluation Methods* (New York, Ronald Press, 1946), pp. 3 and 61.

just quoted reckoned to be 'a very formidable and significant one'. 'The analyst must exercise impartial and honest judgement in weighting the value of the various factors and minor factors for each job on the basis of the job data assembled and the job classification set up.'[1] The final step is to convert the point values thus calculated into monetary terms. For this purpose a conversion formula must be supplied from outside the evaluation process in the form of a given rate or rates for a particular job or jobs, the characteristics of which have been analysed in the manner already described.

Theoretically, if the system were perfect (which nobody would claim that it is) the appropriate pay for all other jobs could then be calculated from a single known rate. In practice much more modest objectives are set as when job evaluation is applied only to determine the pay of a limited range of employments falling between a top and a bottom rate which are taken as given.

This sketchy description hardly does justice to what has now become a formidable professional skill. The claims of brevity compel the omission of many refinements and variants in the methods employed by experts in this field. But the principles are, I hope, clear. Useful examples of the kind of equations that result at the salaried level will be found in the evidence submitted by the BBC to the Broadcasting Committee of 1949:[2] these are of particular interest inasmuch as the Corporation is faced with the task of comparing posts in the widely differing spheres of administrative, programme-editorial and engineering employments; so that we find the picture editor of a weekly publication for overseas listeners equated with, on the one side, the senior maintenance engineer for outside broadcasts and, on the other side, an administrative assistant responsible for the secretarial and clerical staff of a department.

Most of these attempts at scientific grading of occupations originate on the employers' side. In some industries, however, joint efforts have been made to 'rationalize' the wage structure. Both the spinning and the manufacturing sections of the cotton industry have, for instance, undertaken comprehensive investigations for this purpose. In the manufacturing section a commission, consisting of representatives of both sides of the industry, together with a chairman and two independent members appointed by the Minister of Labour, were faced with a situation of extreme complexity, in which wages were governed by uniform lists of piecework prices dating back to 1892 and encrusted with a mass of subsequent interpretations and additions. In their

[1] Stanway, H. Geddes, *Applied Job Evaluation* (New York, Ronald Press, 1947), pp. 21 and 28.

[2] Broadcasting Committee, *Report*, Cmd. 8117 (1951) Appendix H, pp. 119–24.

attempt to design a completely new system this Commission laid down a number of principles to which in their view any new wage structure must conform. These included the principle that 'the wage earned by a weaver should be related to the skill and the effort which the task requires and the efficiency with which it is discharged'; that the system should 'encourage the fullest use of skilled labour, and a proper reward for the efficiency of operatives and management'; that 'the benefit of increased productivity from the same manpower' should be 'fairly divided'; and that the system should be comprehensible and easily checked. Significantly the Commission felt themselves bound by the limitation that any new system ought to 'reproduce broadly the existing level of wages'; but within this limitation they claimed to have succeeded in presenting the industry with a 'sound, workable, and intelligible system of payment, which will give enterprise, efficiency and hard work its due reward'.[1]

On the railways also one of the conditions on which a threatened national strike at the end of 1953 was called off was a promise by the Transport Commission to undertake, in association with the three railway unions, a comprehensive review of the wages structure. Meanwhile, the union known as Asset, in presenting its 'National Charter' for supervisors and technicians, deprecates the view that to ask, 'What is a foreman worth?' is like asking, 'How long is a piece of string?' and upholds the proposition that 'minimum values can be set' for the qualities which a foreman has to possess to do his job, over and above the qualities needed by those whom he supervises. As already mentioned, this charter includes a mathematical formula for calculating the responsibilities of supervisors. Such an active interest in job evaluation is on the whole unusual in the trade union world; but obviously a union which caters primarily for supervisory grades is in an exceptional position.

'In every wage problem there is a scientifically right level of wages for the particular conditions,' writes Mr. Hubert Somervell with magnificent optimism in the *Observer* of 26 October 1947. Certainly the hope that a scientific basis might be found on which to settle wage relativities has much to commend it to the temper of the age: equal pay for equal work is an attractive slogan in more than the restricted sense of equality as between the sexes. And job evaluation even promises in addition the happy marriage—so rarely found—of science and equity; for, in the words of Mr. Lytle, it seeks to establish 'not what the management thinks it ought to pay, nor what the

[1] Ministry of Labour and National Service, Cotton Manufacturing Commission, Inquiry into Wages Arrangements and Methods of Organization of Work in the Cotton Manufacturing Industry, *Interim Report*, 1948, pp. 21–3, 36–7.

worker, or his union, thinks he ought to get, but *the fair share*, to which a satisfactory performance of that job should entitle the man who performs it, of the profitable result to which his performance contributes.'[1]

These attractions are, moreover, enhanced by the apparent irrationality, as judged by *any* standard, of our present wage and salary structure. One may search in vain for the rational compound of skill, responsibility, effort and working conditions of a system which would explain why the ward sister in a general hospital should be paid (at the top of her scale) about one-sixth of the salary of the Dean of Westminster; why the male probation officer should start at about one quarter of the top transatlantic airpilot's rate, and at his maximum just pass the starting-rate of the university lecturer in Greek; or why the sub-officer in the fire brigade should end a little above where the graduate school teacher began, and the police constable after six years experience get for his full-time employment about five-sixths of the salary of a part-time governor of the BBC.[2] There may indeed be those who find this structure entirely intelligible and commendable; but such judgements (as much as their opposites) are essentially subjective, and based on personal preferences: one is at a loss to see by what process of reasoning they could be made convincing to those whose prejudices were differently orientated.

It would indeed be of interest to see how half a dozen job analysts working independently on, say, the formula of 35% skill, 15% effort, 30% responsibility and 20% conditions, would grade such cases as those quoted in the preceding paragraph. Whether or no their various findings agreed with one another, the results could hardly fail to prove revolutionary by the standards of existing practice: in the light of such an analysis the last might well find themselves first, and the first last. For in one respect, the job evaluator's approach to wage problems is, theoretically at least, distinguished from virtually all others. It is not—in theory—conservative—but, by contrast, a lonely exception to the rule that wage discussions are only an elaborate rationalization in defence of the existing order.

The gulf between theory and practice remains, however, wide; and for good reasons. For even in the simplest cases the objectivity of job analyses is far from absolute. At two points the contingent quality of the measures employed betrays itself. The first is in the assignment of weights to the various factors involved. This is obviously bound to be arbitrary: effort, skill, responsibility and environment are mutually inconvertible. The second is inherent in the translation of job-points.

---

[1] Lytle, *Job Evaluation Methods*, p. 3. Italics mine—B.W.
[2] All comparisons refer to rates paid in London in 1951.

into money-wages—quantities which are even more patently inconvertible, for to attempt directly to translate job-points into money-
values would be like comparing Hyde Park Corner with the members
of the House of Lords. Some wage, therefore, which is not itself
derived from any evaluation process, must, as we have seen, be introduced as a datum; and on this all subsequent calculations depend.

In job analysis as ordinarily practised—that is, in the assessment of
posts inside a single enterprise or in a narrow industrial area where
the wider framework can be taken for granted—these limitations can
be forgotten. But any attempt to use the same methods to establish
scientifically defensible relativities over a wider field quickly runs into
formidable difficulties. In particular, the arbitrary element involved
in weighting the major characteristics of widely different employments must become much more obtrusive. 'Responsibility for people',
for instance, must be broken down into responsibility for the work
of subordinates, and responsibility for the bodily health and safety,
or for the mental and spiritual welfare, of members of the public. But
in the assessment of these factors the most profound social judgements
are involved; and to these job analysis gives no clue. The fact, for
instance, that today the medical professor earns anything up to
double (and occasionally more than double) the salary of his non-
medical colleague in the universities, and anything from four to ten
times the pay of a clergyman, undoubtedly reflects the tendency of a
materialistically-minded civilization to esteem more highly those who
care for our bodies than those who look after our minds or souls.
Certainly it is difficult to believe that these relationships would not be
disturbed, were the fear of death less vivid, and the expectation of
immortality livelier. But on the merits of these attitudes, the job
analysts would hardly claim to pronounce: they could but accept the
values of the society in which they live, and construct their measures
accordingly.

If only for these reasons the proponents of job evaluation are wise
in confining their activities as a rule to restricted areas of industry.
When they do look further afield, their view tends—perhaps inevitably—to be conditioned by the standards of remuneration that happen
actually to prevail. In selecting from industry and from the public
service posts that are comparable in terms of their formulae, they
choose examples from among those which already stand at about the
same level of pay; and, since such examples are not as a rule difficult
to find, they feel no need to make excursions into startlingly dissimilar
ranges of income. The scope of their science is in fact confined
within the boundaries of a circular argument.

The heavy silent pressure of the established order thus makes itself felt again. This pressure is apparent also in Mr. Lytle's assumption (which is not peculiar to this author) that 'for salaried positions the major characteristics may be the same but most of them must be sub-divided differently and reweighted'.[1] One is tempted to ask why? It is true that in salaried posts, responsibility is likely to bulk larger, and disagreeable conditions to be less conspicuous, than is usual at the wage-earning level. With a fixed system of weighting this result would, however, appear in the final evaluation: salaried jobs would tend to be upgraded for their heavier responsibilities and down-graded for their pleasanter conditions; whereas, by contrast, any reduction in the weight allowed for working conditions would redound to their advantage on every count. Impartial application of a constant system of measurement from top to bottom of the wage and salary system would, in fact, almost certainly have the effect of materially narrowing the present spread. In this also its potentially revolutionary nature is manifest.

This use of one set of standards for job analysis in salaried, and another in wage-earning, employments, cannot be defended by ana-logy with the common practice of using different weights in com-parisons of changes in the cost of living at different levels of income, and for two reasons. In the first place, a comparison of the impact of changes in the value of money upon a particular income-group at successive dates is an entirely different thing from any comparison affecting different groups at the same time; and, in the second place, the weights used in cost of living indices are not, like the weights given to job-characteristics, subjectively determined: they are ordi-narily derived from the proportions of a person's or a family's total outlay which is absorbed by various items—such as food, rent, fuel, etc. These proportions demonstrably vary from one social class to another—so that in measurements of the amount of money needed by a given class to maintain its particular standard at different price levels, it would be wholly inappropriate to use weights derived from the spending habits of some other class. To argue that in job com-parisons, on the other hand, if one unit of effort is reckoned as equiva-lent to half a unit of responsibility for a miner, it must be worth only one-sixteenth of a unit of responsibility for a mine manager, is like using a ten-inch foot to measure a mannequin's waist, and the usual twelve-inch rule on the rest of us.

Any attempt to formulate a comprehensive wage policy upon even the most skilful grading of the content of different jobs raises, indeed, even more fundamental difficulties. Paradoxically (for there is no cause to suspect professional personnel managers or job-analysts as a

[1] Lytle, *Job Evaluation Methods*, p. 61.

group of any predisposition to Communist opinions), such a proposal is a thoroughly Marxist conception. In effect the labour theory of value knows no more effective exponent than the job-evaluator; for the job-analyst, like the Marxist, considers only what is involved in the actual performance of a job: to him, as to the Marxist, the harder the job the higher its rating—though each might, of course, put his own interpretation on the meaning of 'harder'. Neither, in fact, takes any account of what the economist would call the forces on the side of demand. According to job-evaluation scales, a highly skilled job would remain highly rated, even though the techniques that it involved had become obsolete. From this it follows that no system of wage relativities which is constructed from such an evaluation can fulfil the function of directing workers to the industries and occupations in which they are most urgently needed: and that will be true, whether the criterion of need is taken to be money demand in the market, or a scale of priorities determined in the light of some socially planned policy. 'Scientific' job-evaluation must therefore be reckoned amongst the ethical, rather than among the economic, determinants of wage policy; for in the last resort a system which pays more for a job because it is hard and disagreeable commends itself because it is *fair*, rather than because it is consistent with the harsh realities of the economic situation.

Similar issues are raised even by what on the face of it would appear to be the most convincing of all the arguments from comparison—that is, the contention that the same rate should be paid for the same job wherever and by whomsoever it is performed. This plea occurs in various contexts: as, for instance, when the same occupation plays a part in more than one industry, or, alternatively, when equal pay is demanded for members of both sexes when engaged on similar work. In the former case economics and ethics, at least as seen from one angle, appear to march together: if, for example, typists in some area receive an appreciably lower rate in railway service than in the municipal offices, it can be argued both that this is ethically indefensible, and that it is likely to result in railway officials having to spend time in writing their letters by hand. But from another angle this is only half the economic side of the story. In a dynamic economic system the varying rates in different industries must be presumed to reflect the varying economic condition of these industries. Artificial standardization would, in fact, merely impede the operation of the invisible hand without substituting a visible one.

It is not, therefore, surprising that arguments about wage relativities are apt to founder in unresolved conflicts about occupational as against industrial comparisons. The question whether the wages of electrical engineers in the flour-milling industry should be adjusted to the classification of different mills which governs the wage structure in that industry, or whether the rates for electrical engineers should follow an independent course of their own, has been the subject of more than one reference to the National Arbitration Tribunal;[1] while similar issues have arisen in regard to (amongst many others) the position of box-makers in the tobacco industry[2] and of engineers in printing;[3] to the relation of mental hospital workers (prior to the establishment of the Regional Hospital Boards) to other hospital employees on the one hand, and to their colleagues in local authority employment on the other; and to the position of enginemen and firemen employed by the Port of London Authority in relation to similar workers on the railways.[4] This last case (heard in 1946) has perhaps a special interest inasmuch as it appears that the port employees succeeded in getting their wages disassociated from those of their colleagues on the railways before the war at a time when railway wages were particularly depressed; that during the war they succeeded in restoring the link so as to share in advances made to railway workers generally; and that when the war was over they put forward a claim (though without success) that the previous differential should be restored. It is shifts like these which betray the dominance of expediency over principle in the argument by comparison; and the fictitious element in what purports to be objective selection of 'comparables'.

These cross-industrial issues are determined, often after reference to arbitration, independently in each instance; and there is, of course, no case-law which might lead to the establishment of generally accepted principles: each industry must settle the problem in its own way. But it is significant that in the discussion of this type of case historical argument takes a large place. 'Proper' relativities, it is assumed, are matters to be governed by policy and precedent, rather than uncontrollable incidents of the bargaining process envisaged in the economic textbooks.

Even more marked are the ethical and social factors in that version of the claim for 'the rate for the job' which demands equality as between the sexes. It will hardly be denied that on the women's side the driving force in this controversy is the sense of injustice which is felt when pay is differentiated according to sex. The terms of reference of the Royal Commission on Equal Pay were so drafted as to preclude its members from giving an opinion on the merits of the

[1] See, e.g., *National Arbitration Tribunal*, Awards Nos. 886 (1946) and 996 (1947).
[2] See, e.g., *ibid.*, Award No. 928 (1947).
[3] See, e.g., *ibid.*, Award No. 302 (1943).
[4] See, e.g., *ibid.*, Award No. 887 (1946).

question of principle involved here. They were permitted only 'to examine the existing relationship between the remuneration of men and women in the public services, in industry and in other fields of employment', and to 'consider the social, economic and financial implications of the claim of equal pay for equal work'; and the instruction to 'report' did not (contrary to the usual practice) include an obligation also to make recommendations. Even so, however, the Commissioners were not able wholly to escape reference to the question of equity, and of the 563 paragraphs of their report two are specifically devoted to this subject. 'It will be evident,' they say, 'that, apart from the purely material aspect of these consequences, a question of equity is also involved. The claim for equal pay relies for its appeal largely on "plain justice".' The report then develops the thesis that 'plain justice' is not as plain as she looks. Equal pay, in the view of the majority of the members of the Commission, would 'not only affect the comparative remuneration of a minority only of women (viz. employed women) as against that of men': it would at the same time disturb the balance as between those women who work in purely feminine and those who work in mixed occupations. In their concluding remarks the majority return to the same theme, with the observation that they are 'not called upon . . . to attempt any final summing-up of the relative importance of ensuring exact justice between individuals on the one hand and oiling the wheels of economic progress on the other'. The 'cases of departure', they continue, 'from perfect individual justice which are apt to arise under a system of unequal pay are, as it seems to us, illustrations of a broader principle in human affairs, which applies also to matters quite unrelated to our present problem. The achievement of perfect justice in respect of reward between individuals at every moment and at every point appears to be scarcely compatible with the working of an economic system in which it is desired on the one hand to preserve free choice of occupation and on the other to make provision for continuous adaptation to changes in technique and in demand. For in such a system it is only through the emergence of inequalities in the reward obtainable for similar effort that the desired flexibility is maintained. If every such inequality is forcibly ironed out so soon as it appears, its economic function remains unfulfilled. It may not be just that work by hand or brain in a rising trade should command a higher reward than work by hand or brain in a decaying trade; yet if it is prevented from doing so it is hard to see how, except under a completely regimented system, response to the changing needs of the community could be secured.'[1]

[1] Royal Commission on Equal Pay, *Report.* Cmd. 6937 (1946), pp. 1, 133, 170.

These paragraphs afford one more illustration of the conflict, or the supposed conflict, of the ethical and the economic aspects of wage and salary determination—or at least of the attempt to meet ethical arguments with economic ones. In view of their restricted terms of reference, the Commissioners could hardly carry the argument further. Perhaps, however, that limitation had its advantages; for the illustration chosen was far from fortunate; the principle that every wage has an economic function in directing workers into 'rising' and away from 'decaying' trades is scarcely relevant to discriminations between the sexes. From the economic point of view it is clearly important that trades should rise and decay in accordance with the changing needs of the public; and that the work that is done should be the work that needs to be done; but the degree in which that objective is achieved is not affected by the question whether that work is done (so long as all do it equally well, which the principle of equal pay for *equal* work by definition demands) by males or females, by the old or the young, the fat or the thin.

The three women members of the Commission, who were responsible for a minority report, found their colleagues' line of argument unconvincing. Though clearly themselves also inhibited by the restrictive terms of reference, and unable accordingly to argue the whole case on its ethical merits, they began with a reference to the 'tendency in the human mind', when 'confronted with any existing state of affairs', to accept 'any explanation which seems at all plausible', even when 'in origin it may be merely what psychologists describe as "rationalization", without any basis in reality'. For their part they were unable to find any necessity for choice between 'exact justice' and 'oiling the wheels of economic progress'; and they did what they could to establish that, on the contrary, 'the claims of justice between individuals and of the development of national productivity point in the same direction'.[1]

The lameness of the *economic* arguments on the subject of equal pay has already been commented upon.[2] As we have seen, the existing situation is not explicable in terms of economic theory; though once that situation is there, any change would involve economic consequences about the merits of which it is possible to argue, as the thrusts and counter-thrusts of the various Commissioners show. The existing situation is, in fact, before anything else, an expression of social attitudes; and the urge to change it springs, not from the conviction that it is economically inexpedient, but from an—often passionate—sense of injustice.

[1] Royal Commission on Equal Pay, *Memorandum of Dissent*, pp. 187 and 196.
[2] See pp. 62 ff.

It is perhaps indicative of the contemporary inclination to give pride of place in wage issues to social and moral considerations, that the case for equal pay as between the sexes is now, 'in principle' generally conceded. 'In principle' it is the official policy of the Government as well as of the opposition parties—so much so that the Treasury offered no evidence on this subject (other than purely factual statements as to current practice showing differentiation in favour of men) to the 1954 Royal Commission on the Civil Service, on the ground that policy was already determined in favour of equality. Nor is much now heard of the arguments which occupied the time of the Equal Pay Commission: the only reasons today adduced for deferring the translation of principle into practice and for failure to remedy what is now officially admitted to be an injustice is that it would be expensive to do so.[1]

V

A third argument for wage advances that ranks in popularity close behind those two main stand-bys—movements in the cost of living and the need to maintain relativities—is that derived from undermanning. In the period under review references to under-manning are frequent, though one has the impression that they do not carry quite the weight that attaches to the arguments already discussed: their role is more often that of extras to be tossed in towards the end of a case.

Here at last we abandon ethical for economic territory. The argument from undermanning is conceived in the terms of the most orthodox economic theory, and implies that the test of adequacy of any wage is its effectiveness as the supply price of the kind of labour for which it is paid. In strictly economic terms, value is linked to scarcity: you pay for what you cannot otherwise get: skill, social standing, responsibility and so forth have no virtue in their own right, but only in so far as they are the prerogatives of the few. Such a conception is obviously liable, in a changing world, to run headlong into conflict with traditional notions of proper relativities; for it is indeed unlikely that the ratios which twenty or thirty years ago happened to regulate the flow of labour correctly (in whatever sense that word is used) as between alternative occupations or grades will still produce the same result today: on that point the 1951 Railway Court of Inquiry showed a

---

[1] Since the above was written, the Government has announced its intention (May 1954) of introducing equal pay into the Civil Service by—apparently unhurried—instalments.

troubled, though exceptional, awareness. But if particular relativities are defended on the ground that they are necesssary in order to keep the flow of recruitment as between two closely related occupations stable, complications will arise when the differentials indicated by accepted conventions as to responsibility and so forth are not easily reconciled with the rates that are thus thought to be necessary to adjust recruitment. The 1949 Committee of Youth Leaders and Community Centre Wardens was clearly disturbed by this problem. In principle they wished to link these professions with teaching 'as part of a common educational service', and to fix salaries and pensions 'such that they present no obstacle to freedom of movement between one part of the educational service and another'. At the same time, they were faced with the argument that, whereas in teaching only a proportion of posts carry special responsibility justifying an additional allowance, the club leader, even in his first post, commonly has full responsibility for his club. 'Unlike a teacher, all too rarely has he had a period of experience as an assistant'[1]— from which it would seem to follow, in terms of the convention which links pay with responsibility, that all club leaders should receive salaries above the normal teacher's rate. The Committee, however, resisted this demand on the ground that, unless the practice in both services followed a common pattern, the interchange between youth leadership and the teaching profession which they considered so desirable would be hampered.

In contrast with claims that rest on cost of living changes, arguments based on undermanning are seldom supported by any serious statistical evidence. A remarkable case in point is that of the Spens Committee, who were instructed by their terms of reference to have regard not only to the proper social and economic status of general medical practice but also to its 'power to attract a suitable type of recruit to the profession'. In their report, however, the Committee made no attempt whatever to examine the state of recruitment to the profession, but merely expressed the opinion, unsupported by any factual evidence, that, on the basis of pre-war pay, 'the recruitment of general medical practice could not, in the long run, be maintained . . . even apart from proposals for a publicly organized general medical service'.[2] The only specific aspect of recruitment upon which they felt it necessary to comment was the possibility that, with the establishment of a national health service, the financial risks incurred

[1] Ministry of Education, Report of the *Committee on Recruitment, Training and Conditions of Service of Youth Leaders and Community Centre Wardens*, 1949, *Report*, p. 10.
[2] Inter-departmental Committee on the Renumeration of General Practitioners, *Report*. Cmd. 6810 (1946), pp. 1, 5.

by specialists would diminish, and that in consequence an undue proportion of practitioners would be tempted away from general practice. In view of the immense pressure on entry to medical schools which has prevailed since the end of the war, recruitment would, in point of fact, have been the worst possible ground on which to base any claim for increased remuneration for the medical profession.

In the few cases in which figures are produced in an attempt to prove undermanning the effect is apt to be somewhat inconclusive. The Locomotive Engineers' Society quoted records of wastage amongst drivers, firemen and engine cleaners, before the 1951 Railway Court of Inquiry, showing rates of voluntary resignations (other than retirements) as a percentage of the numbers in each trade: the figures ranged from 0·28% for drivers to 33·91% for junior engine cleaners. 'In grades where so much depended upon having a stable and experienced staff,' those figures were, in the Society's view, 'extremely disturbing'.[1] Nevertheless, the union's claim, which was calculated to give approximately 15% to each grade, was not in any way adjusted to meet the very great difference which these figures show in the wastage at different levels. Nor was any comparison made between the wastage of footplate men and that experienced in other branches of the railway service—although the locomotive engineers throughout stressed the need to restore differentials said to have been reduced by the practice of granting flat-rate advances throughout the service. It would seem that the logic of the argument called for larger increases at the points at which wastage was most pronounced, and for evidence that losses amongst footplate men were above the average for the industry as a whole.

In the example just quoted, the state of recruitment is discussed with reference only to conditions in the industry in which a claim is under consideration. This is common practice; though, as will be argued later, the habit of treating each industry's recruitment problems in isolation from those of every other deprives these arguments of any real foundation—at least from the angle of any coherent wage policy. Exceptions are rare, but in one case, that of the firemen, which was the subject of arbitration in 1952, the claimants took their stand upon ground which made it impossible for them to treat the subject with the customary isolationism. The firemen, it will be recalled, based their case primarily on a claim to parity with the police. It followed that they had to show, not merely that the fire service was understaffed, but that it was in at least as serious a position, in this respect, as the police. Actually, the Oaksey Committee had estimated the police deficiency at 17·4%, at the end of 1948, as

[1] Cmd. 8154, p. 18.

against a shortage of 8·3% in the fire service. The firemen claimed, however, that this figure was based upon an unusually large increase in police establishment, and that if allowance were made for this, the true deficiency would be only 9%. On their side the employers countered this argument with the contention that the fire service figures were in need of adjustment on account of increased establishment, and that such an adjustment would approximately halve the apparent deficiency in the fire service. Whichever of these estimates may have been the more accurate (and of their views on that subject the arbitrators gave no hint), the introduction of comparative material of any kind is most unusual; though its significant relevance to the issue under discussion is obvious enough.

Actually, the Oaksey Committee was responsible for one of the most systematic attempts at an objective estimate of the relation between pay and recruitment which has yet appeared; and this is not less instructive by reason of the fact that its conclusions were largely negative. This committee approached the problem by forming an estimate of the total deficiency in the police forces in England and Wales at the end of the war, and by a comparison of the post-war with the pre-war rate of recruitment, in the light of which the latter was judged to be 'reasonably good': recruitment had, in fact, been running since 1946 at about 2½ times the normal pre-war rate. Shortage was found to be due not to insufficient entry, but to resignations and retirement. The Committee accordingly analysed in some detail the exact points in period of service at which losses from these causes were particularly pronounced; and they also reviewed the experience of different parts of the country, which proved to be very variable. From this they reached the conclusion that, although 'the pay of the police must be an important factor in attracting recruits and retaining serving men . . . it would be unwise to overlook certain other considerations which affect the problem. The pay is the same in all forces and many have succeeded in reaching and maintaining a full complement. Increased rates of pay introduced in November 1946, and the higher levels of rent allowances introduced in 1948 seem to have had no significant effect upon rates of recruiting and resignation.' Wastage, moreover, as the Oaksey Report Committee recognized, cannot be intelligently estimated in any one occupation by itself; but, apart from a reference to the increased post-war wastage amongst the employees of London Transport, this aspect of the matter was not pursued.[1]

It would seem that an analysis on at least as elaborate a scale as

[1] Committee on Police Conditions of Service, *Report*, Part I.Cmd. 7674 (1949), p. 6.

this is necessary before even the most tentative conclusions can be reached as to the relation between remuneration and recruitment in any occupation. The weakness of the typical contemporary reference to undermanning as a criterion in wage determinations is the absence of any standard of what constitutes 'adequate' recruitment— itself aggravated by the habit, already noticed, of treating every case independently. Here two alternative standards are possible. The first is that postulated by classical economic theory. In terms of this criterion an occupation ranks as undermanned if the supply of labour forthcoming at the wage offered is not as large as employers would be willing to employ at that wage: in such a case the current wage would be said to fall short of the 'marginal net product' of the workers employed. In these circumstances, according to the text-books, an increase of wages is clearly indicated; in fact, thanks to competition between employers to get hold of scarce supplies of labour, such an increase is likely to come about of itself even in the absence of any trade union demand for it; and in the long run either additional workers will be attracted into this 'undermanned' industry, or, if for some reason none such can be found, the remuneration of those already employed there will be permanently increased.

By the canons of classical economic theory, this is the proper mechanism for encouraging the growth of desirable (or at least of desired), and for discouraging the survival of unwanted, industries. It is public demand for the goods which he has to sell which makes an employer willing and able to pay higher wages or to increase the number of workers that he employs at existing rates. It follows that, in terms of this theory, it makes no sense at all to speak of shortage of labour as an *independent* reason for a wage increase; since shortage is itself defined in terms of the wage which employers are prepared to pay for any given supply of labour; and the argument from undermanning is, in consequence, tautological.

In the light of post-Keynesian economics (as also of common observation), on the other hand, this is not the whole story. An industry that is 'undermanned' in whatever sense must make good its shortages from somewhere. But in conditions of near-full employment, in which jobs compete for workers rather than workers for jobs, filling up one place may just mean emptying another; and there is nothing to prevent all industries from being simultaneously undermanned. In these conditions, to prescribe wage advances as a remedy for specific cases of such 'undermanning' is, of course, merely to aggravate the disease; since, in post-Keynesian economics, such an indulgence of the propensity to consume only stimulates additional public demand for the products of industries that are already extended to the limit, and for the services of still more non-existent workers to satisfy this demand. Chronic pandemic shortage of labour is in fact an elementary, and an all-too-familiar, symptom of an inflationary situation.

For these reasons arguments from undermanning which take note only of the state of one industry or calling at a time must be viewed with suspicion even by those who accept the principle that economic development ought in general to be ruled by the ballot box of the market-place and to follow the lead of effective public demand. Indeed, perhaps the point should be put more strongly; for these arguments tend in fact to be compounded of a nice mixture of the meaningless and the dangerous.

The alternative criterion of adequacy in staffing is based, not on market demand, but on planned public policy. This has the merit that it is, or at least could be, stated in reasonably precise figures— as in the forecasts of occupational distribution, which, as already mentioned, used to be included in the annual Economic Surveys. Occupations which fail to achieve their planned scale of recruitment can be said to be undermanned in a sense of their own, and to have a special title to favourable consideration of their wage claims. No doubt the high priority enjoyed by coal and agriculture in the economic plans of post-war Britain has helped the miners and the farm workers to improve their position in the wage hierarchy. But as long as other industries find themselves undermanned in the economic sense, and have unfilled vacancies to offer, it is extremely difficult for them to appreciate these special cases; and that as a rule goes for both employers and employed. The attitude of the road haulage employers who declared before a Court of Inquiry in 1947 that there was 'no great difficulty in increasing the industry's man-power as men were very willing to enter it'; but that 'this would mean taking men away from other industries, which might have serious repercussions on the general man power position'—this attitude is quite exceptional.[1] In this case the circumstances were unusual, as the claim related primarily to a reduction in hours of working which would of itself have necessitated the employment of larger staffs in order to keep the industry running on its existing scale. No doubt it goes against the grain for either side in any industry to admit that it would be in the national interest for that industry to suffer contraction; and doubly so, if employers see the prospect of profit in

---

[1] Court of Inquiry into the differences which have arisen between the two sides of the National Joint Industrial Council for the Road Haulage Industry on the Trade Union Claim, *Report*. Cmd. 7025 (1947), p. 8.

expansion, and unions can use unfilled vacancies as a weapon in the battle for increased wages.

Serious appreciation of national priorities certainly has no habitual place in the background of wage discussions which bandy arguments about undermanning. In overwhelming degree each industry tends to look only at its own corner of the picture, and to reckon undermanning primarily as a matter of keeping its own strength up to the level that happens to have been already achieved. The practical issue at the wage conference table is the question whether workers will or will not in fact be attracted by the wages prevailing to enter a particular industry—not whether the industry ought to have them; and, in consequence, the one line of argument in wage negotiations which is virtually free of ethical content, and which must be reckoned a potentially powerful instrument of economic change, becomes almost as vigorously conservative in operation as the most frankly ethical concepts of justice and fairness.

VI

The pages of contemporary wage claims are spattered also with a number of other arguments, though none in recent years is so conspicuous as the trio composed of the cost of living, of relativities and of undermanning. References to increased productivity are, for instance, not uncommon. From one angle these might be expected, perhaps, to play a larger part than in fact they do; for wage advances which are met from increased output can at least claim to be innocent of all inflationary consequences. Perhaps the extensive use of methods of payment by results, under which the individual workers' productivity is automatically reflected in earnings, accounts in some degree for the relatively modest role of these arguments; for, where such systems prevail, to use increased output as an argument for higher rates might look a little like counting the same factor twice over. Fairly frequent references are made also to the ability of employers to pay the rates that are asked of them: though, as might be expected, in claims affecting the nationalized industries, it is the employers rather than the unions who are apt to bring balance sheets into the discussion. In the engineers' claim of 1953 considerable play was made with the allegedly substantial profits made by firms in the industry; and it will be recalled that one of the main arguments used by the speakers who persuaded the Trades Union Congress to abandon support of wage restraint in 1948 was the expectation that substantial advances (estimated by

Mr. Stevens of the Electrical Trades Union at 2s. 5d. in the £) could be extracted from profits. But in the prevailing tone of post-war wage claims, balance-sheet arguments play a definitely subsidiary role. The unions quote profit figures, less as evidence of what they ought to have, than as proof that what they regard as due on other grounds can in fact be paid; and employers, in the typical post-war situation, have found the national interest a better defence than their own pecuniary difficulties.

In general, the shift of emphasis away from economic and towards social and ethical considerations cannot fail to strike anyone who has followed the trend of wage discussions over the past thirty or forty years. The contrasts are striking. Once a battle-ground in which rivals fought each other over the division of the proceeds of their joint plundering activities, today wage negotiation has developed into a conference of industrial statesmen debating questions of justice, precedent and public interest. Yet at the same time this revolution is incomplete; and on that account any prolonged study of wage negotiations induces a certain cynicism. For choice within the range of socially acceptable arguments is manifestly dictated by expediency alone. In default of clear policy or overriding principle, the question whether appeal is made to movements in the cost of living, and if so between what dates; or to changes in the general level of wages; or to the position in comparable employments, and, if so, which are reckoned as such—these questions are settled in the light only of the strength of the support which the various possible answers lend to claims already drafted upon quite other grounds. And—again in default of policy or principle—neither members of the public, nor those who speak for them on wages boards and tribunals, are equipped to make any more rational assessment of the merits of those claims.

CHAPTER VI

Towards a Rational Wage Policy

I

THE purpose of the preceding chapters has been to show the contemporary wage and salary structure of this country as the accumulated deposit laid down by a rich mixture of economic and social forces, operating through considerable periods of history. The attempt to explain the curious contrasts of the picture as it now stands, in purely economic terms, is found to be inadequate: such explanation can indeed be made intellectually coherent; but only at a heavy price in the sacrifice of contact with reality. On the other hand, we have to live: political and social factors do not operate in complete disregard of economic realities. At every point the economic and the sociological forces act and react upon one another to produce a result which is quite inexplicable if either is left out of the reckoning. The operation of all these forces is, however, strikingly different from what it was even fifty years ago. In the past half century, the role of trade unionism in British society has been changed out of all recognition. Trade unions and their leaders have not only moved from the position of social outcasts to one of the highest respectability: what is no less important, their techniques have been copied at the most exalted professional levels; and—perhaps most significant of all—this development seems to be welcomed by the organized trade union movement itself. In the same period, statutory wage regulation has been invented and applied to a number of industries, mostly small, but some, such as agriculture, of major importance by any standard; permanent arbitration machinery has been established; and wage disputes have constantly been the subject of public investigation by Courts of Inquiry. These are big changes; and with them goes a not less notable change in the implied major premise of all wage discussions. No longer the private concern of the worker and his employer alone, every wage bargain is now a matter of threefold concern; at least a watching brief, if not a place at the conference table itself, must be assigned to the representatives of the general public; and wage policy is, if not born, at least conceived. Policy, moreover, in this as in other spheres, has to be defensible in terms of justice no less than of expediency. Indeed, in this case expediency has been swamped by justice—swamped by a confluence of the political manœuvres of the professional negotiator, the social conscience of the legislator and the judicial impartiality of the arbitrator.

On the other side of the picture, the economic changes are hardly less remarkable. For some thirteen or fourteen years most wage negotiations have been conducted with no significant threat of unemployment in the background; while even the most stalwart adherents of private enterprise are no longer prepared to leave great national industries to wax and wane in accordance only with their profit and loss accounts.

These changes do not, however, all pull in the same direction. Indeed, the present seems to be a moment of particularly sharp conflict. As we have seen, the weight of the social influences involved falls overwhelmingly on the side of conservatism. That every wage bargain must be 'fair' or 'reasonable' now goes without saying. Also unspoken—though for a different reason—is the rubric by which the fair and the reasonable are defined; nobody knows in this context what justice is, and no Socrates walks the streets pestering us to find out. That is where conservatism comes to the rescue. Change—always, everywhere, in everything—requires justification: the strength of conservatism is that it is held to justify itself. It is not therefore, surprising that the maintenance of standards, absolute or comparative, should be woven as warp and woof into the texture of wage discussions; or, to change the metaphor, that history should be summoned to fill the void when moral actions must be performed without moral principles to guide them.

This lack of guiding principle affects, moreover, equally those who pay and those who receive wages. Conservatism does duty on both sides. On the one side, the unions, as we have seen, appeal to precedent, and defend their proposals as necessary to restore the *status quo*—if not literally *ante bellum*, at least before some selected date-line; whilst employers, on the other hand, take their stand on the simple rule of 'no change'. The dispute between them turns, not so much on the choice of the direction in which to move, as on rival interpretations of what is meant by standing still. Indeed, of all the arguments now commonly used in support of the justice of wage claims, two only can be said to imply recognition of some principle other than the virture of established practice. The first is the plea for equality of payment as between the sexes; the second derives from the concept of the scientific grading of posts according to the nature of the work involved. Of these the first has, to date, been fairly effectively nullified by the cynical device of acceptance in principle and deferment in practice; and the second, as we have seen, respects in practice the boundaries set by conventions to which in theory it might offer serious challenge.

In the preceding pages it has been argued that not only are the forces making for conservatism in wage discussions themselves strong: the whole tendency of modern methods of wage determination is also to make them progressively stronger. This means that the simultaneous demands of the changing economic picture have to pull against increasingly powerful resistance. Of these demands, those which spring from considerations of national policy are relatively feeble; while the old-fashioned market mechanism has become an altogether ineffectual instrument for making their presence felt. National policy would give very high priority to the coal industry; but this industry, for all its acknowledged national importance, enjoys no magic power of buying labour at the top of the market. Only with the utmost difficulty have the miners succeeded in improving their relative positions in face of the sanctity attaching to traditional relationships; and the chronic shortage of labour in the mines (as measured by the standards set by declared national policy) is evidence that even this success is only partial. At the same time, some at least of the purely economic factors in wage determination are in a good position to increase their strength. With near-full employment, there is little inducement for anyone to enter the dirty, disagreeable, socially despised—and traditionally ill-paid—occupations. For the first time, under pressure of true economic scarcity, the balance of 'net advantages' begins to be translated from fiction to fact, and the economists, at long last, can point beyond their own hypothetical deductions to the actual closing of the gaps between manual and non-manual, or between skilled and unskilled, rates as evidence of the truth of their theories.

This situation is not without its ironies. Orthodox economic theory has not—at least in the present century—generally found itself on the side of drastic social change. The main effect of classical wage theories has been to justify an existing situation by explaining an imaginary one. The belief that rough work and long hours tend to be compensated by handsome pay is comfortable doctrine for those whose bread is buttered on both sides—so long as it remains a fantasy. But now the fantasy threatens, at least at some points, to become real. The prestige values inherent in the traditional wage and salary structure find themselves not supported, but menaced, by the realization of an academic dream; and the economists are driven by the force of their own logic to desert the established order to which they have so long been loyal friends. The 'professional men who have to present a smooth façade to the world', 'paying rents of £400 and £500 a year for their homes' as well as membership fees of a 'London club (at least twenty guineas a year), and of a golf club (five or ten guineas)', and 'the "successful" practitioner' spending '£150 a year, at present prices, on sherry and spirits for consumption at home',[1] are thus deprived of their best defence, as they watch the slaughterman, the road sweeper, and even the female typist creeping slowly up on their position.

In the absence of any effective wage policy, the outcome of this struggle between the static social, and the dynamic economic, forces is unpredictable. My own guess would be that, in spite of the loss of some ground during and immediately after the war, the present balance of power is at least unfavourable to radical change. The view that wage questions ought to be settled in reasonable fashion is very much in the air and, pending the clear acceptance of any other standard, 'reasonableness', it must be repeated, means 'conservatism'.

Nevertheless the side-effects of this effort simultaneously to move and to stand still are inescapable; and they threaten to be economically disastrous in both their general and their particular consequences. In the economy as a whole they produce the familiar picture of continuous and cumulative inflation as one claim follows another in regular succession. Even in the five years from 1946 to 1950, (which, it will be recalled, included the period of the 1948 White Paper and the devaluation standstill), there were not less than three general increases in the engineering, shipbuilding and ship-repairing industries; three[2] for underground and surface workers in coal-mining; three in agriculture; four in furniture manufacturing; eleven (owing to sliding-scale arrangements) in building; four in hosiery manufacture; four in baking; three in the principal branches of retail food distribution; three in gas[2] and electricity production; three in the wool textile industry; four in cotton[2] spinning and manufacturing; three on the railways; three for the main civil service classes; two or three in the principal local government classes; two in teaching; one in the universities; and so on. And the pace has become much hotter since.

Cumulative inflation, it is sometimes argued, is not a necessary consequence of the present scramble. The argument of those who persuaded the Trades Union Congress that policies of restraint could be abandoned without disturbance to the cost of living may have considerable force today in particular industries. The tide

[1] Lewis, R. & Maude, A., *Professional People* (London, Phoenix, 1952), p. 253.
[2] Including one designed to compensate for shorter hours.

may already have turned, and the division of the proceeds of industry as between capital and labour may well now be moving to the disadvantage of the latter; and, even if it is not, there is nothing sacrosanct about the proportions that exist at any given moment. But though it may be a fact that, in certain industries, higher wages could be paid without inflation, it is also a fact that in others— notably in the nationalized industries and the public service—this is not possible. This means that, with the present pressure to maintain relativities, even a non-inflationary advance in one place constantly produces inflationary reactions in others.

The absence of any coherent wage policy is liable therefore to produce on the one hand cumulative inflation in the economy as a whole, and on the other hand a breakdown of the machinery for controlling the distribution of labour between different industries and occupations—or, if not a breakdown, at least a failure to adapt this to the conditions of a planned, or semi-planned, economy. From an economic angle, the situation could hardly be worse.

Nor is there anything particularly admirable in the social aspects of the present wage and salary structure. Its best defence, as we have seen, is the fact that it exists. In spite of some tendency for manual-working occupations to gain upon the lower professions, and unskilled workers to gain upon the skilled, that structure still, as a whole, honours more than anything else the rule that to him that hath shall be given. The well-paid jobs are those in which satisfaction is to be found in the work itself; and by and large these are also the jobs with long periods of notice, good holidays and prospects of comfortable superannuation. From top to bottom inequalities are still great; and these inequalities must carry the lion's share of responsibility for the division of our society into a hierarchy of social classes, a division which (as those who see its consequences at close quarters cannot fail to observe) still has to its discredit a heavy toll of unhappiness and discomfiture, as well as of wasted ability— fashionable though it may be to pretend that class distinctions have either disappeared or ceased to matter.

Opinion will, naturally, differ as to the shape of the income distribution which is felt to be socially desirable. Equalitarian trends which hearten Professor Tawney[1] disgust Messrs. Lewis and Maude.[2] But that the character of our society is profoundly influenced by its distributive habits will hardly be denied. The opportunities for self-realization, available at different social levels, the

[1] Tawney, R. H., *Equality* (London, Allen & Unwin, revised ed. 1952).
[2] See Lewis & Maude, *Professional People*.

prestige attaching to particular callings and to those who pursue them, even the blend of worldly and unworldly elements in our civilization, are all sensitive to changes in the wage and salary structure. The secrecy about income, to which reference has already been made, is a sign not only of uneasy conscience: it testifies no less to the significance of the issues involved. Wage policy is in fact the instrument as much of social as of economic purposes; and on economic and social grounds alike, *some* policy is imperative. Even those who find least to cavil at in the present picture will hardly contend that this ought to be stereotyped for ever: the only question at issue is whether change will be voluntary or involuntary, in a desired or an undesired direction. That issues so vital to the whole way of life of the community as those involved in its concept of just rewards should find no place in the topics of political discussion is fantastic: that for lack of such discussion we should live in a chronic state of economic hypertension, in which the aged, the infirm and the unfortunates are the worst sufferers, is almost unbelievable. And these developments are, moreover, the more paradoxical, in that no one any longer pretends that wage bargains are merely the private concern of the two parties immediately involved in them. Yet in this field, and in this field alone, it seems, we are expected to believe that public issues are best left to organized private interests to decide; and that justice is best dispensed independently of statute, case law or principle.

The first step, therefore, is to induce the ostriches to take their heads out of the sand, and to bring the whole subject into the arena of intelligent controversy; and that means the arena of *political* controversy: the ostriches in the picture are the politicians. For the pattern of income distribution is essentially a political question. It embodies social valuations which affect the whole community, and in which conflicting interests are involved; and the issues raised by these conflicts are germane to the differences which divide political parties—so long at least as those differences can claim to be in any sense the expression of alternative social philosophies, or of designs for achieving alternative social ends. The place for the discussion of wage policy is on the agenda of the political conferences; and the responsibility for consequent action must lie on governments.

Today the Royal Commission or other 'impartial' body is so popular a mechanism for the exploration of awkward issues that it is perhaps desirable, at this point, explicitly to recognize the futility of any resort to this superficially tempting device, except for purely fact-finding purposes, as defined below. At the time of writing (1954) one proposal to have recourse to some such body has just emanated from a Court of Inquiry into a dispute over engineering wages; and is now the subject of (very cautious) discussion between the Trades Union Congress, the British Employers' Confederation, the nationalized industries and the Minister of Labour. The Court in question expressed itself as concerned about the 'wider problems affecting the national economy' which were raised by the particular case before it, and proposed that an 'authoritative and impartial body' should be appointed to consider these issues. The exact scope of this proposal is not elaborated in the Court's Report; but it appears that something more than statistical fact-finding was in mind. At least it was suggested that the proposed impartial body should not only 'consider' the wider problems involved in specific wage claims and the 'complex and sometimes conflicting economic arguments which surround them', but that it should also 'form a view upon their implication for the national economy and our ability to maintain our present standards' and should 'give advice and guidance as to broad *policy* and possible action'.[1] The last clause certainly seems to imply trespass beyond the boundaries of the strictly factual.[2]

The hope, however, that any issue can be 'taken out of politics' by the simple device of handing it over to a non-political body is vain. (Twenty years ago the government which tried to 'take relief out of politics' by entrusting its administration to a non-political Assistance Board made that discovery.) Decisions on issues of social policy involve judgements of value; and it is an illusion to suppose that, however 'authoritative' its character, any tribunal could make such decisions 'impartially'. Wage policy comes as close as any topic to the issues which have traditionally divided the main political parties in this country. Unless and until those parties have reached substantial agreement as to the pattern of distribution which they applaud, it must, in consequence, remain intractable to impartial treatment on a non-political basis. No group of investigators can tackle a problem unless they have a common mind as to the purpose

[1] Court of Inquiry into a Dispute between employers who are members of the Engineering and Allied Employers' National Federation and workmen who are members of Trade Unions affiliated to the Confederation of Shipbuilding and Engineering Unions, *Report*. Cmd. 9084 (1954), pp. 47–8. Italics mine—B.W.

[2] Since the above was written, it has become evident that no action is likely to be taken on this proposal. Instead, it is announced that the Government is to issue a purely factual statement on 'the country's economic position, with special reference to prices, wages, and profits'. 'The terms of reference of those responsible for preparing the statement are narrower than those envisaged by the courts of inquiry for the proposed impartial body, which was to give definite advice and guidance on policy and action. The proposal for this body was dropped mainly because of the opposition of the T.U.C.' (*The Times*, 29 July 1953.)

of the whole exercise. The membership of a modern commission, or other impartial tribunal, is—for good reasons—carefully chosen so as to avoid political homogeneity; and these bodies can, therefore, only function effectively in respect of topics which are either not themselves the subject of political difference, or on which they have accepted precise instructions. An impartial commission could explore the steps necessary to carry into effect a wage policy based upon given principles; but itself to discover those principles would be a task wholly beyond its capacity.

II

Any wage policy, irrespective of its particular bias, is bound to meet with formidable difficulties, some real, some imaginary; and the effectiveness of any policy will depend upon the skill and courage with which these are faced, as well as upon appreciation of the factors that make for success. Chief among the real difficulties must be reckoned the fact that no wage policy other than one hundred per cent conservatism can be equally advantageous to everybody. If the shape of the present picture is to be altered, the change will benefit some people more than others: which means (and this is what creates the uproar) that it will benefit other people less than some. No doubt it is for this reason that all political parties are afraid of it: this is why all alike shelter behind a façade of respect for the 'independence' of collective bargaining, or the impropriety of 'tampering' with arbitrators. But unless we are to accept the doctrine that the particular relationships now prevailing are sacred for all time, there is no escape from this difficulty. It has to be faced. No policy of change can please all the people, at all levels from top civil servants to bus conductors, all of the time: one can only take heart from the fact that, in the absence of any policy at all, hardly anybody seems to be pleased any of the time.

Any policy has, moreover, to be woven into the texture of British institutions, with their tradition of voluntaryism and of independence. Since no plan makes sense unless it includes restrictions on movement upwards as well as downwards, any legally binding policy would imply statutory maximum wages: penalties for paying too much as well as too little. That is not a proposition which can be seriously advanced—at least not in relation to wages generally—in this country. Even in the most critical period of the war and through all the successive economic crises that followed, wage increases in Britain have never been subject to government approval; though bolder measures have been applied elsewhere—including, paradoxically, the United States, where, although the fear of government interference is generally supposed to be stronger than it is in this country, such a requirement was in force during the war; while in Holland, even today (1954), a tripartite body representing the State, employers and workers has to approve rates and differentials for skill in a number of important industries, and penalties may be imposed on employers who pay 'black market wages'. Yet even in Britain the thin ends of wedges are here and there discernible. Under the regulations which govern the remuneration and conditions of service of officers employed by Regional Hospital Boards or Hospital Management Committees, salaries are fixed by ministerial regulation, after they have been the subject of negotiation between the parties, and after the Minister has considered the result of such negotiations. These regulations, which have statutory force, expressly require that the salaries paid shall be *'neither more nor less than the remuneration so approved'*, except in cases where the Minister thinks fit to allow individual variations.[1] In the case of certain local government employees also—such as police and firemen—salaries are fixed by ministerial regulation, the function of the negotiating bodies being merely to advise the Minister; and, although in this case the no less and no more rule is not explicitly laid down, any local authority which exceeded the prescribed figure would certainly run a grave risk of surcharge.

Milder, alternative measures are, however, available, and not necessarily less effectual. A mere declaration, at the highest governmental levels, of some clear and consistent policy would be itself a significant step: the possible content of such a policy and the degree of precision with which it might be formulated are discussed below. Consistency is certainly important, for a situation in which Ministers have to declare themselves baffled by the mathematics of raising the lowest levels without disturbing relativities is neither dignified nor defensible. And the more such a policy can be agreed between the unions and employers' organizations, the more hopeful, naturally, will the outlook be. True, the gradual translation of the trade unions from the role of representatives of the under-dogs into that of champions of sectional interests makes it unlikely that this co-operation will be easily won. But one should not despair. The enormous revolution in the attitudes of union leaders recorded during the past twenty years suggests that they are by no means rigidly set in their ways; and the position of these leaders, trapped

[1] National Health Service (Remuneration and Conditions of Service) Regulations, 1951. (SR & O, 1951, no. 1373.) Italics mine—B.W.

12

in the chaos erected by their own activities, is by no means altogether happy. Certainly we must not assume in advance that they would reject out of hand every policy which embodied an honest attempt to combine social goals with due regard for economic necessity.

If such a declaration of policy were authoritatively made, it might perhaps be taken for granted that arbitrators and courts of inquiry would take notice of it. But whether this comes about directly or indirectly, a change in our attitude towards wage arbitrations is long overdue. The practice, as described by Sir Walter Monckton, of not issuing 'instructions or guidance of any sort' to arbitration tribunals is not a satisfactory way of expressing 'scrupulous respect for their independence'.[1] So long as this practice prevails, the task of these tribunals is as plainly impossible as would be that of Her Majesty's judges, if the condition that they should observe statute and case law were regarded as 'tampering' with justice. Far from ranking as improper interference, guidance as to policy ought to be accepted as a necessary condition for the effective functioning of arbitral bodies: without it they cannot be expected to do their job properly. That some courts at least are oppressed by the impossible nature of their task under present conditions is evident from the 1954 engineering Court of Inquiry's plea for review of the wider issues of wage policy. The solution which this Court proposed may not have been appropriate; but the true nature of the problem here was explicitly stated at last. Members of this Court reported that they had 'inquired of those who appeared before us whether there was any common ground as to the principles which guide them when wage adjustments in the industry are under consideration. From the answers that we received it seemed to us that there was no mutually accepted formula and no expressed common assent in regard to guiding principles.' This nihilistic conclusion was, it is true, qualified by the addition that there was a 'considerable measure of underlying and implicit agreement'— notably on such propositions as that changes in the cost of living and the general prosperity of the industry were relevant considerations. Faced with the task of translating these generalities into concrete monetary terms, the members of this Court, however, like all their colleagues, found themselves left without any helpful directions. Arguments based on cost of living changes, in particular, as they were at pains to demonstrate, could be dressed up to lead to very different conclusions according to the dates chosen as the basis of comparisons; nor did they feel able to 'assess or quantify the dangers to the national economy which might arise from action which provoked a general and substantial increase in production costs'.[2] Their

[1] See pp. 90, 91.   [2] Cmd. 9084, paras. 110, 145.

whole report reads, in fact, like a distress signal. Commenting favourably on their proposals, a leading article in *The Times* of 27 February 1954 remarked: 'The arbitrators absorb a vast quantity of information and statistics, all of it provided by interested parties and little of it adequate, and then, without any accepted principles to guide them, ponder it until there emerges, by some means that must go far beyond logic, a conclusion. The mystery is that the conclusion is so often generally felt to be about right. . . . But it is clear that tribunals could depend rather less on inspiration and more on reason if they were provided with fuller facts from impartial sources.'

Nor would the effect of clear guidance as to policy be confined to those to whom it was specifically addressed. The mere fact that arbitrators were known to be following explicit principles could not fail to have repercussions in wage negotiations. Even if (which is hardly likely) it did not materially influence the actual figures put forward, it would be bound to shift the plane of the discussion: the onus would lie on each side to show that its proposals were consistent with declared national policy; and it would for the first time be possible to judge the merits of this defence in terms of an accepted standard.

A rational wage policy cannot, however, be either constructed or executed in the dark. Somehow or other the secrecy which invests the subject of personal earnings, and particularly the upper reaches of the income-pyramid, must be dispelled. If labourers, including even those that are relatively exalted, are worthy of their hire, it is to everybody's advantage that this should be known and recognized. If they are not, it is only in the light of the facts that the matter can be put right. Present sensibilities are quite absurd, the more so, since they cannot, in the nature of the case, be universally respected. If the Chairman of the Electricity Authority's £8,500 or the Civil Service Permanent Secretary's £4,500 can be matters of common knowledge, why should the chief executive of large industrial concerns be so shy about their own figures? Those who control the policy of the large joint-stock companies of today constantly stress their consciousness of a duty to the public; and indeed there is some evidence to support the late Lord Keynes' thesis that the great industrial undertaking tends, at least in some cases, in a sense to socialize itself. Candour on the subject of remuneration, as on other matters, would be the best proof that there is nothing in present practice to be ashamed of. Times, in fact, change. Indeed it is not so long since the notion that the accounts of privately owned undertakings should be subject to independent audit evoked expressions of horror and dismay; yet it is a far cry from that state of mind to the requirements, mostly now accepted as a matter of course, of the contemporary Companies' Acts. Little by little industrialism is growing up to maturity; and an adult attitude on the subject of rewards for services rendered would mark another stage of its progress towards years of discretion.

III

We must now approach more closely the question of the *content* of wage policy. Here we have to face the certainty of at least some measure of conflict between social and economic ends: it would indeed be an extraordinary stroke of luck if our chosen social ideals proved to be one hundred per cent economically viable. The severity of that conflict will depend upon factors on both sides. A policy of social equality, for instance, is much better adapted to some economic environments than to others; and it is generally least difficult to change relativities in any socially desired direction when economic conditions allow of fairly lavish increases all round.

In principle the problems of policy fall into two distinct groups—those concerned with the size of the whole cake, and those concerned with its division into appropriate slices. The former involve mainly, but not exclusively, economic considerations. Obviously at some point the scale of output sets a limit to the levels of wages and salaries which can be sustained without inflationary consequences. In order to determine this point, economic data are primarily required; and the provision of such data is the one part of the whole exercise in which impartial investigation has an important function. The need for such investigation has indeed been repeatedly voiced in recent years in more quarters than one. Anticipating the 1954 engineering Court of Inquiry's proposal, we find that experienced arbitrator, Mr. C. W. Guillebaud, advocating in 1951 that the 'Government should publish annually an estimate of the amount by which, in the opinion of their statistical experts, the total sum of wages and salaries could rise during the ensuing twelve months without adding to inflationary pressure';[1] though his view of the prospect of any centrally controlled policy being adopted in this country in the near future was pessimistic, since he saw little 'likelihood of the people of this country, whether employers, trade union officials or individual workers, being willing to allow such a system to be operated. Past traditions, the institutional framework, and the whole climate of opinion here, are against it.' Similarly, the Labour correspondent of *The Times*, in an article published on 20 November 1951, urged that the 'Government might

[1] Ministry of Labour, *The Worker in Industry*, Centenary Lectures, 1951 (1952), p. 53.

estimate total wages and salaries as part of consumer expenditure related to Government expenditure and expenditure on capital investment, and calculate the overall percentage increase or decrease desirable'. This correspondent also, while emphasizing that the initiative must lie with the Government, took the view that it 'would also be folly at the present time for the Government to attempt any detailed or compulsory wage control': pronouncements should not be regarded as 'anything more than guidance, and their effectiveness would depend on the extent to which they were taken into consideration by employers, trade unions, and negotiating and arbitrating bodies'. And a year earlier, an article in *The New Statesman and Nation* (6 May 1950) had advocated as the first stage in a comprehensive wage policy an 'attempt by the Government in consultation with the trade unions and employers (including the nationalized section) to reach agreement about the total sum that can be afforded each year for the "wages fund", with the necessary elasticity in relation to changes in actual production'.

Necessary though the facts are, however, even this stage cannot be regarded as purely an expert matter. An expert calculation as to the 'total sum by which wages and salaries could rise without adding to inflationary pressure' is necessarily itself subject to a number of assumptions. Obviously, as Mr. Guillebaud himself went on to point out, wage policy cannot be considered without reference to what is happening to prices and profits. For many years past the concept of a fixed wages fund has been treated as a classic illustration of fallacious economic reasoning; and the reappearance of the phrase (even safeguarded by marks of quotation) in contemporary discussion should be viewed with suspicion. 'So long as prices and profits continue to increase, it is of course senseless even to talk of a wages policy, if by that is meant a policy of wage stabilization.' A government which applied dividend control would certainly find itself able to aim at a more substantial increase in wage incomes than one which would not admit any interference with the distribution of profits. Accordingly, in what follows it is assumed that general economic policy is directed towards maximizing the sum available for distribution without risk of inflation amongst the working community. Such an assumption is in keeping with the mental climate of an age which, ostensibly at any rate, seems disposed to accept as axiomatic the principle that the standard of living of those who do the world's work should rise as far and as fast as possible; and to quarrel only over the question of how far and how fast that can be. But axiomatic though this assumption may have become, it is essential that it should be clearly understood to underlie *any* considered wage policy—and not only a proposal for general stabilization. For since any wage policy must involve some claimants getting less than they might have hoped for under a régime of uncontrolled smash and grab, groups which are asked to exercise restraint in favour of some of their fellow-workers have a right to demand assurance that this conflict of interest cannot be resolved by enlarging the total to be shared by all.

In practice, however, the whole concept of an undifferentiated national income, subsequently divisible into the respective 'shares' of labour, capital and other 'factors of production', which is the traditional mode of economic analysis, is highly artificial. In practice the question of how much we can afford without running into inflation cannot be disassociated from the question of how any increases are to be distributed; or of what, if any, rules should govern relativities. If, for example, the principle that all differentials must at all costs be maintained is to be followed, then it would almost be accurate to say that no increase at all is possible without inflation. It is, therefore, by deliberate choice that in this book little attention has been paid to questions of wages as a whole, or to the share of wage payments in the distribution of the total national income, as distinct from matters affecting the determination of particular rates paid for particular jobs. For wage questions are, in practice, not handled *in general*; the complete picture is the result, and mostly the undesigned and unintended result, of innumerable decisions scattered throughout the parts. That indeed is the crux of the whole problem. Cumulative inflation, like cumulative armament, is the consequence of a chain-reaction, any individual stage of which may be negligible; and as we have seen, pious exhortations to wage retraint *in general* (like pious exhortations to disarmament) are futile unless everybody can be confident that everybody else will pay equal respect to them.

This situation will not be changed merely because efforts are made to reckon the total room for manœuvre. A bare announcement that, say, a 15% rise is practicable without inflation is little help to anybody. If it is interpreted to mean that everybody everywhere is to be raised by 15%, it will serve only to standardize all relativities at the level at which they happen to be. In the end such a stereotyping of what are after all the fortuitous accidents of a particular historical situation must become an absurdity. But if a given total increase is not to be applied equally everywhere, then guidance must also be forthcoming on the consequential problem of distribution. We have to recognize that wage determinations are in fact made, and will continue to be made, at the level of the individual trade or profession. Even if we disregard the fact that it is at this level that wage decisions regulate the flow of workers into various occupations, no general wage policy, designed merely to obviate inflation, has a chance of success unless it is reduced to particular terms. In this matter it is not the whole which determines the parts; it is the parts which govern the whole.

The first stage in the formulation of a wage policy—that of calculating the devisible total—is thus an abstract, theoretical task; and, as such, likely to be much less formidable than the second stage, in which the practical business of translating the resulting figure into concrete proposals for individual occupations has to be faced. And it is at this second stage, also, that social factors come to the fore, which may be found difficult to reconcile with the demands of economic realism. This, therefore, is at once the most difficult and the most controversial part of the whole business. For not only, as we have seen, is the habit of discussing concrete wage bargains in social and ethical terms now firmly established: distributive policy is itself also necessarily an expression of social relations; and about these reasonable—and for that matter unreasonable—men may differ. Some would *like* to see the dustman paid as much as the surgeon, and will, therefore, wish to explore how far this is economically practicable. Some would not. Each group's views on the objective to be aimed at will be a contradiction of those held by the other. Calculations of the total 'wage fund' available at any time can at least be guided by the rule that advances must not be carried to the point at which inflation begins; but for the determination of *particular* rates no equally acceptable formula exists.

The crux of the controversy here lies in the rival claims of equalitarian ideals and of the sanctity of differentials. Equality as a social ideal has been much blown upon in the past thirty years or so; or perhaps it would be more correct to say that it has simply been allowed to fall into neglect. Between the first publication of Professor Tawney's *Equality* in 1931 and the appearance of the revised edition in 1952, silence on this subject was seldom broken. Among the reasons for the decline and fall of equalitarian social philosophies one may guess, perhaps, that the conversion of the trade union movement from its role as the defence of the manual workers against the depredations of their economic betters into a highly organized machine, professionally operated for the protection of sectional interests at all levels, has a significant place. And the Labour Party, also, which in this century has been the traditional champion of equality in the political arena, has itself experienced a similar, and no less profound, change of heart. The establishment, after the First World War, of constituency Labour parties open to individual membership gave, it is true, the Party a chance to develop, at least up to a point, a mind of its own, independent of the unions. But the simultaneous decision to welcome to its ranks workers by brain as well as by hand was a guarantee that sooner or later the political no less than the industrial wing of the Labour Movement would abandon its position as champion of the under-dog: the professional classes have to do too much dressing up in order to present themselves convincingly in this role, on a stage on which old age pensioners and unskilled labourers are also present. If the change has been slow, that shows only that tradition dies hard: the process has certainly been effectively accomplished in the end. Whatever else may be said about it, *Challenge to Britain* does not read like an equalitarian manifesto.

I write as one who deprecates this change; and who believes incidentally (though this aspect of the matter has no relevance in the present context) that it is the chief agent responsible for the failure of the Labour Party to maintain its dramatic rise in electoral popularity. It is not only that gross economic inequalities are incompatible (or at least in practice extraordinarily difficult to combine) with respect for individual human dignity: political democracy itself—and to respect for political democracy all parties are alike committed—degenerates into a sham in a privilege-ridden environment. This has often been said, and never better than by Professor Tawney. 'Whatever conclusions,' he wrote in 1952, 'may be drawn from the history of the last decade, one, at least, is indisputable. It is that democracy is unstable as a political system, as long as it remains a political system and nothing more, instead of being, as it should be, not only a form of government, but a type of society, and a manner of life which is in harmony with that type. To make it a type of society requires an advance along two lines. It involves, in the first place, the resolute elimination of all forms of special privilege, which favour some groups and depress others, whether their source be differences of environment, of education, or of pecuniary income. It involves, in the second place, the conversion of economic power, now often an irresponsible tyrant, into the servant of society, working within clearly defined limits, and accountable for its action to a public authority. . . . If, in this country, democracy falls, it will fall, not through any fortuitous combination of unfriendly circumstances, but from the insincerity of some of its professed defenders, and the timidity of the remainder. . . . If it stands, it will stand, not because it has hitherto stood, but because ordinary men and women were determined that it should, and threw themselves with energy into broadening its foundations. To broaden its foundations means, in the conditions of today, to destroy plutocracy and to set in its place an equalitarian society.'[1]

[1] Tawney, R. H., *Equality* (London, Allen & Unwin, revised ed. 1952), pp. 15–16.

The suggestions as to wage policy that follow are drafted, accordingly, in the belief not only that social equality is good in itself, but also that the future of democracy depends upon this broadening of its foundations; and that the broadening of those foundations means the 'destruction of plutocracy and the setting of an equalitarian society in its place'.

A wage and salary policy framed to suit such a philosophy would need first to promulgate certain general principles, and then to add to them specific indications as to the lines on which compromise between social principle and economic necessity should be effected. Such guidance in principle might take the form of policy declarations that, in proposals for wage advances, priority should be given to rates below a level to be from time to time prescribed; and that any advances above this level should be tapered off, perhaps with some further indications of the levels at which the tapering process should be accelerated. Already in certain public services, tapering has been practised, as in the Civil Service general pay addition of 1952 or in the awards to health service consultants in 1954; but there is no consistency of principle observed. Governments need to make up, and to declare, their minds on the merits and demerits of tapering, in respect not merely of the remuneration of their own employees, but equally as a lead to everyone concerned in wage and salary negotiations. In place of the vague, mutually contradictory statements quoted in Chapter IV of this book, we need a clear and consistent statement of the shape of income structure to be aimed at. Such a statement could, for example, take such forms as the following: 'priority to all advances in the under £8 a week class; increases in, say, the £800–£1,000 a year range normally to be tapered; further tapering above £2,500; no advances over £5,000.' These figures are, of course, purely illustrative. It is for governments to decide in the light of the political philosophies of the parties for which they speak, how far and how fast (if at all) they wish to travel in an equalitarian direction. Nor would any figures need to be interpreted rigidly; but some numerical terms must be used if any wage policy is to make sense at all.

It is easy to say that no government would dare to go to these lengths, for fear of the opposition of the trade unions (among which professional organizations must also be included). Obviously, no pains should be spared to win the sympathy of the trade union world for a wage policy designed to realize chosen social objectives; obviously, also, the chance of success in this would be greater for a government, the members of which had a history, in and out of office, of sympathetic relations with the unions. But to answer in advance that success is impossible is to make the very grave admission that in one large and important tract of social policy the government does not govern, but abdicates in favour of the trade unions; and to accept conditions which must continually threaten to frustrate every attempt at economic as well as social planning.

The broad outline of social policy having been determined, the next issue to be faced is the compatibility of this with the demands of the economic situation. Here again the principle on which compromise must be made is not difficult to define. Economic policy demands priority for development of whatever industries are deemed to be particularly vital; and economic policy demands also that in any industry there should be proper proportions of posts of varying degrees of responsibility. If these conditions cannot be satisfied in industries of serious national importance, the social objectives of wage policy may have to take second place.

This means that departures from a broadly equalitarian wage policy would in such circumstances be recognized as necessary. *But a case would have to be made for them.* That alone would constitute a remarkable difference from the present situation in which no case of any kind need ever be made for any wage bargain—at least not in terms of consistent and intelligent principles. Under the kind of arrangements proposed, wage rates out of line with the general pattern of social policy would be justified on one ground and one only: viz. inability to maintain recruitment. General policy, in fact, would be framed in terms of ethical and social policy; but these exceptions would represent unavoidable concessions to economic necessity.

It follows that 'adequate recruitment' would need to be sensibly defined. So far as differentials within a particular industry are concerned, this should not be too difficult. Within broad limits the ratios of technically skilled and supervisory to routine posts are set by the structure and customs of the industry concerned. At any one time these ratios may not indeed be optimal, but for the purposes of wage policy they can more or less be taken as given: when labour organization is effective, the unions can be trusted to keep a keen eye on any tendency to multiply unnecessarily the better-paid positions. Industries whose structure looks suspiciously top-heavy must be dealt with directly by appropriate special investigation; they cannot be put right indirectly by means of wage and salary policy.

The real difficulties arise in the definition of 'adequate' recruitment as between one industry and another. As we have seen, during periods of cumulative inflation and full employment, it is easy for practically every industry to represent itself as understaffed in every occupation.

In these conditions the supply-and-demand criterion makes no sense at all—and it is in fact nothing but an excellent instrument for perpetuating the inflation. One of the objects, however, of a considered wage policy is just to put a stop to this inflationary process. If that object is realized, an excess of vacancies over applications regains its traditional significance; and, in that event, in those areas of economic life (but only in those) where vital issues are not involved and in which there is accordingly no great need for economic planning, a short supply of labour in the strict sense of the economic textbooks could rank as at least *prima facie* evidence of economically inadequate wages.

These, however, can only be limited areas. Such is (and is long likely to be) the precarious condition of the British economy that even the most dogmatically *laissez-faire*-minded government is unlikely to abandon all economic planning in favour of completely free enterprise—to allow priorities of production to follow profit and profit only, even if it means that pits are closed, arable fields returned to grass, while building craftsmen become barmen and mill-workers domestic servants or shop girls. The scope and vigour of planning will, of course, depend upon the social and political philosophy of the government in power; but none can escape responsibility altogether for the pattern of production. It follows, therefore, that over a larger or smaller area of economic activity, every government must have some target figures of output in mind. Such targets (which for a number of years figured conspicuously in the annual Economic Surveys) imply, of course, a corresponding distribution of the labour forces; and it is that distribution which gives the required standard of 'adequate' recruitment. By that criterion an intelligible and precise meaning can be given to the concept of undermanning, which, as we have seen, is at present so devoid of precision as to be applicable almost indiscriminately everywhere.

There remain difficult issues in those cases in which an industry of national importance—let us say coal or steel—achieves a rising level of economical output of which it is justly proud. Is this or is it not good ground, within the framework of a generally equalitarian policy, for encouraging a higher wage-level than prevails in industries with a less distinguished record? The case for such discrimination can be argued both on ethical and on economic grounds. Ethically, the workers may claim special rewards for efforts that have resulted in an exceptional achievement; while economically, such rewards are, on the one hand, by definition feasible and should, on the other hand, have the valuable affect of encouraging others to aim at equally high standards.

Nevertheless, such deviations from the general wage pattern should be admitted only with caution and reluctance. They always raise difficulties. It is, for instance, always hard to determine how far allowance for special merit should go. Is it right that clerks on, say, the railways, should receive lower rates than their colleagues in the coal industry merely because coal has had an exceptionally successful year? The connection between the efforts of any individual employee and the total achievement of his industry is always notoriously slender: management and luck, as well as the conduct of his fellow-workers, come into the picture. For this reason it would seem best to resist claims for differential wages based on total industrial results, except in cases in which definite understaffing, as measured by the standards already indicated, can be shown to exist. This conclusion appears, moreover, the more reasonable, in view of the growing use of systems of payment by results, designed to link the pay of individual workers with their personal efforts. Payment by results, whenever this is practicable, rather than reclassification of wage and salary rates, seems in fact the right (in the double sense of both the 'accurate' and the 'just') way to recognize special achievement. It is, after all, a narrow view which would claim that the advantages accruing from the successful performance of a vital national industry should redound to the benefit of those who happen to work in that industry, rather than be spread over the community as a whole. Where, however (as may happen in industries that are privately owned), exceptional performance is synonymous with exceptional profit, any proposal to disregard overall results in wage determination carries the important corollary that, if the workers in an exceptionally productive industry are to forgo the fruits of their special position, the same rule must be applied to their employers also.

The broad picture then, as it would appear to a government which was equalitarian in philosophy and favourably disposed towards economic planning, would be as follows. Wage determinations would be conditioned by a programme of tapered increases subject to such modifications as might be required in order to meet shortage of labour—defined, in minor industries, chiefly in terms of demand and supply, and, in industries of major importance, in terms of planned estimates of desirable labour supply. Such a programme would have no legal or statutory basis. It would constitute, in the first instance, a departure-point for arbitrators and statutory wage councils, as well as terms of reference for courts of inquiry; and it would, for the first time, make it possible for those who serve in these capacities to tackle their jobs in a rational way. From this quarter it would react upon voluntary wage negotiators, with whom indeed it would already have

been discussed at all stages, and to whom it would need to be com-
mended in the most sympathetic possible terms.

Not less important is the attitude of the public at large—who have
to live on the wages and salaries agreed to by their union representatives, or fixed by arbitrators and statutory wage authorities. Here
there is without doubt a large job of public education to be done. The
public is ready enough to treat wage questions as matters of ethics:
indeed it is the man in the street's notions of justice which are
responsible for this practice. But the possibility that it may sometimes
be necessary, as a concession to economic stringency, in defiance of
prevailing conceptions of justice, to reward exceptionally highly
those who are employed in industries that happen to have rising
economic importance, is not likely to be so readily acceptable. To
appreciate the function of wage-rates as a mechanism for the distribution of labour involves sophisticated economic thinking, such as
does not come to most of us by the unaided light of nature or of
common sense.

Any wage policy which satisfies the demands both of social policy
and of economic necessity will need therefore to be intelligently
explained. But if that is courageously and frankly done, a policy on
the lines of that adumbrated here ought not to have difficulty in finding a sympathetic hearing—at least if we assume that it is presented
by a government which has a mandate from the electorate to follow a
generally equalitarian philosophy, and which can, therefore, expect a
considerable public to commend its social objectives. Occasional
anomalies are much less objectionable if they are recognized for what
they are—unavoidable concessions to necessity in the framework of
an otherwise acceptable policy. And, as has already been said, conflicts between economic necessity and social equalitarianism are not
likely in present circumstances to occur very often. On the contrary, as
long as near-full employment lasts economic forces will themselves be
pulling largely in the direction of equality. When abundant alternative opportunities are open, the dirty, the dangerous and the tedious
jobs will at last be in a position to demand the high pay which the
economists (in contradiction to all experience) have consistently
ascribed to them.

Indeed, it is apposite to reflect how little support can be found in
economic considerations for the more conspicuous inequalities of our
wage and salary system, and in particular, for the superior rewards of
those who hold the more skilled, responsible or interesting jobs in any
given industry. The spokesmen of professional associations and of
middle-class occupations generally are vociferous in their protests
against the reduction in the spread of earned incomes which has

occurred since the nineteen-thirties. Present differentials, it is constantly said, are not sufficient to compensate for the extra responsibilities carried at the higher levels: it does not pay, we are told, to
accept promotion. Nevertheless, one looks in vain for concrete evidence of the industries in which candidates are in fact reluctant to
accept promotion when opportunity offers: for examples of engine
cleaners who are no longer willing to become drivers, of headmaster-
ships offered in vain to assistant masters, or of potential doctors or
civil servants who prefer to go down the mines. Apart from a few
shortages—as of science teachers—it would seem that most of the
professions still enjoy a good supply of recruits. Today the middle and
professional classes are fighting back hard to recover the relative
advantages which they enjoyed twenty-five years ago; but their
strategy, in this battle, faces something of a dilemma. To claim a
superior standard of life explicitly on grounds of status is hardly in
keeping with the theoretically democratic temper of the age: and the
alternative economic argument—that incentives are inadequate to
maintain recruitment—will seldom stand against the facts.

The questionable assumption that differentials are *economically*
justified has indeed a most tenacious hold on the institutions and
ways of thought of our society. Economic incentives are constantly
treated as though they were the only motives known to man and
woman; and every virtue, no less than every skill, expects to be
bought for hard cash. If a policeman must be at once 'intelligent,
courteous and humane', that becomes, as a matter of course, an
argument for improving his remuneration;[1] and the same view
prevails as to, for example, the moral qualities required in the staffs
of approved schools and remand homes. Recruits to this service,
as the Committee which reviewed their conditions of employment
in 1946 had no difficulty in showing, need not only to be well
equipped by experience and training, but also to possess 'marked
qualities of patience, courage and resource';[2] and for these, it is
implied, an appropriately higher price must be paid. Occasionally,
where the non-acquisitive notions of an earlier age have left their
mark, these are indeed felt today to be an embarrassing legacy.
In the words of an American author, quoted by an unofficial British
committee: 'The current salary standards [in social work] have been
primarily influenced by the initial development of social work as a
voluntary or missionary type of occupation. Social work began as a
low-paid occupation where a considerable part of the compensation

[1] See p. 141.
[2] Home Office, Committee on Remuneration and Conditions of Service,
including Superannuation, in Approved Schools and Remand Homes (1946),
Report, p. 5.

was supposed to be of a non-pecuniary type. The altruism of social work pioneers and other less meritorious types of job satisfactions has obviously had a negative effect on salary standards.'[1] The Committee add their own comment that, 'The supply in this field of employment is lavish, due to the fact that so many people are motivated by a wish to serve their fellow citizens, and are *even* on occasion prepared to sacrifice well-paid positions in order to be able to do so.'[2]

Even the Church of England appears (notwithstanding the founder of Christianity's teaching that poverty is the passport to Heaven) to uphold this doctrine that everything, including the highest moral qualities, has its price. In a pamphlet, published in 1951, the fact that ministers of religion are expected to be 'men of outstanding character' is advanced in support of a plea for better pay for Anglican clergy—at a time when, according to figures quoted in the same paper, the 'average *net* income of an incumbent in charge of a Parish' exceeded 'average wages as reported by the *Ministry of Labour Gazette*' by approximately £75 per annum.[3] Seldom indeed does one find examples of the attitude of the priest who described himself and his wife as 'interested, and a little disgusted' by a correspondence appearing in the *Manchester Guardian* early in 1954 on the subject of clergy stipends—adding, 'My wife and I have two small children, who are being brought up happily, if frugally, on £360 per annum, augmented only by occasional gifts in kind from good-hearted parishioners. . . . It is true that I could possibly have earned two or three times my present salary, if I were employed in industry instead of by the Church. . . . But my wife and I knew all these things before I offered myself for ordination. We do not work, like Mr. Harrison's miner, for a fixed wage in return for so many

[1] Lurie, H. L., 'Criteria for Determining Salaries in Governmental and Voluntary Welfare Agencies', *The Compass* (June 1946), p. 27, quoted in *Salaries and Conditions of Work of Social Workers*, Report of the Joint Committee of the British Federation of Social Workers and the National Council of Social Service (London, NCSS, 1947), p. 46.

[2] *Salaries and Conditions of Work of Social Workers*, p. 46. Italics mine—B.W.

[3] *The Work and Revenues of the Church of England* (London, Church Information Board, 1951), p. 11. The reference is presumed to be to the Ministry's figure of average earnings which stood at 150s. 5d. for adult males in October 1950. The Church's acceptance of the values of the acquisitive society is still more plainly reflected in the following advertisement which appeared in *The Times* of 9 December 1953: 'The Church Commissioners invite applications for the early full-time appointment of Investment Manager of their Stock Exchange investments, which amount to over £100 million in value and include a large and growing portfolio of equities. Terms commensurate with responsibilities and according to applicant's experience are offered both as to salary and superannuation at levels usually paid by large Institutions and other investing bodies in the City.' The problem of combining the service of God and Mammon no longer, it would seem, presents any problem.

hours' work. We try, in our own humble way, to serve God for twenty-four hours in every day: and we are grateful to receive for our daily wants whatever the people think fit to give.'[1]

In a way, this implied association of money and merit is the obverse of the nineteenth-century attitude towards poverty. To the Victorians (and indeed to many Edwardians also) the poor were, as a rule, to blame for their own misfortune, and those who would relieve their distress ran grave risks of encouraging idleness. Even as late as 1907 it could be unblushingly stated that those of the poor 'whose indigence had not been produced by their own fault' were 'comparatively few in number'.[2] Today such sentiments are no longer publicized: few would undertake to demonstrate a negative correlation between poverty and moral quality; but the same relationship stated in positive terms seems to have become an established axiom—the implied major premise in fact of all modern professionalism.

Skilful manipulation of the mutual interaction of pay, prestige and professional competence is indeed one of the remarkable achievements of our age, which is distinguished for its pride in professionalism. Status, remuneration and training or professional skill are constantly discussed together;[3] and by a subtle blending of these elements, money is made to appear a measure of virtue. Ours is indeed not only an acquisitive society: it has surpassed itself in the way in which it has contrived to institutionalize, and to set the seal of social approbation upon, acquisitiveness. Status depends on pay: and pay and status together are presented as the guarantees not only of professional competence, but also of integrity, and indeed of every other virtue, as one occupation after another turns to good account methods originally devised by unions of manual workers to protect themselves against rapacious employers. That this development should have occurred is perhaps less surprising than that it should have been accepted without demur—even with cordiality—by the labour and trade union movements. Even in these quarters the doctrine that only the well paid can be relied upon to show themselves, as circumstances may require, courteous, humane, intelligent, skilful, courageous, resourceful, patient and of outstanding character passes unchallenged. Happily, however, institutionalized acquisitiveness (which certainly does less than justice to the social potentialities of our nature), is neither a permanent nor a universal feature of

[1] *Manchester Guardian*, 25 January 1954.

[2] Strachey, J. St. Loe, and others, *The Manufacture of Paupers* (London, Murray, 1907), p. 42.

[3] As, for instance, in the *Report on the Salaries and Conditions of Work of Social Workers* already quoted.

human society. Cultural habits are not irreversible; and in its modest way a wage policy which had the courage to admit that all satisfactions are not material might do something to reverse the trend.

IV

Wage policy is but one item in a comprehensive social programme: indeed it is only one item in the distributive chapters of social policy. The best and most admirable wage policy in the world cannot do everything: it cannot even, by itself, guarantee 'fair shares to all'. For that reason there are dangers in discussing wage policy in isolation from other measures; and it is necessary to add a word both as to limitations of the kind of programme here proposed, and as to its relation to other aspects of social policy. Three limitations in particular deserve notice.

First, a wage or salary is a payment made to an individual for his work. No wage policy can, therefore, do away with the cruel anomalies that result when the same income has to maintain a variable number of persons. One of the monstrous omissions of our society is its prolonged failure to provide for the needs of those who are unable to maintain themselves. As the late Eleanor Rathbone put it, some thirty years ago, '. . . wives and children appear only occasionally, together with butchers' meat and alcohol and tobacco, as part of the "comforts and decencies" which make up the British workman's standard of life and enable him to stand out against the lowering of his wage. I do not think it would be an exaggeration to say that, if the population of Great Britain consisted entirely of adult self-propagating bachelors and spinsters, nearly the whole output of writers on economic theory during the past fifty years might remain as it was written, except for a paragraph or phrase here and there, and those unessential to the main argument.'[1]

In the present century, the provision of old age and retirement pensions, and of family allowances, has done something to mitigate the hardships caused by disregard of the needs of the young and the old. But it is still true that the chief burden of poverty is carried by the young and the old; and it is still true also that the institution of dependency makes nonsense of all attempts to adjust wages to the cost of living. Indeed, as we have seen, one of the oddest features of contemporary wage discussions is the amount of time and effort spent on calculating a supposed living wage for an hypothetical

[1] Rathbone, Eleanor F., *The Disinherited Family* (London, Allen & Unwin, 1924), pp. 12–13.

13

average family in order to settle what thousands of families with membership above or below this average should have to live upon. It would be hardly more unrealistic to propose that in a school, in which the average age of the pupils was thirteen, but the actual ages ranged from eight to eighteen, the curriculum should be designed so as to be suitable throughout for thirteen-year-olds.

Second, no policy that is concerned with the fixing of wage and salary rates can take care of the domestic and social problems that arise from fluctuations in earnings under systems of payment by results. From such evidence as we have it appears that even from week to week these fluctuations are often very large; and neither the budgeting difficulties that result nor the effects on spending habits are perhaps sufficiently appreciated by salaried middle-class persons, accustomed to think in terms of incomes which are not only regular but often also move smoothly upwards along an incremental scale. To an exceptionally thrifty minority highly variable incomes may seem to present exceptional opportunity for saving, everything above the dependable minimum being firmly set aside; but human frailty being what it is, a light-hearted attitude of easy-come easy-go seems a more likely reaction. Indeed much of what is often critically described as the extravagance of working-class spending is to be explained in this way. Where incomes fluctuate widely, regular overheads must be kept within the narrow limits of what is sure to be available: the rest is windfall. Domestic repercussions, also, may result from this situation: at least, the house-keeping allowances made by husbands with highly variable incomes to their wives are likely to err on the conservative side, the husband reaping any incidental advantage. There are large social problems here, which will remain, whatever the principles on which wage and salary rates are determined.

The third limitation is as obvious as it is important; and it is this limitation which raises the major question of what is the appropriate place of wage and salary policy in a broader social programme. Wage policy is concerned only with gross earned incomes before deduction of direct taxes; whereas standards of living depend upon what people actually have to spend, not upon what they nominally earn. From the angle of class status or of social prestige, it may be said that it is actual, not theoretical, incomes which matter; and that, therefore, an alternative—and it is often suggested a better—road to social equality lies by way of a steeply progressive system of taxation. Gross incomes, earned as well as unearned, it is said, can be left to take care of themselves: excessive differences can easily be wiped out afterwards by the tax collector. And the equalizing process can be further speeded up by the development of social services—subsidized food and education, family allowances and so forth—which either offer equal absolute gains to all and so diminish proportional differences, or vary inversely with the means of the recipient.

In support of this view it can be shown that the really big reductions in the inequality of English social life which have occurred in recent years have come about in this way. Taxation has narrowed the gap between the highest and the lowest incomes by drastically lowering the level of the top. In 1938–9 the number of net (post-tax) incomes exceeding £6,000 a year amounted to 6,600: by 1950–1 it had fallen to sixty, though every £ was worth less than half its pre-war value.[1]

The dramatic nature of the change thus accomplished is not to be underestimated; nor does a plea that other measures also are necessary in any way detract from the virtues of what has been done in this way, or weaken the case for the continued use of a policy of redistribution by means of taxation on the one side, and social services on the other. Progressive taxation has done wonderful things in the way of democratizing English life; and, since very little attempt has up till now been made to use any methods of equalization other than this, it is not surprising that taxation has proved to be a more conspicuously successful instrument of equalization than any alternative. Nevertheless, for more reasons than one a redistributive taxation policy (although this, too, still has its place in the whole picture) needs today to be supplemented by other measures.

The first and foremost reason is that *some*thing has, in any case, to be done about wage policy. The difficulties and dangers described in the preceding pages are only too familiar; and they are not less real because the temptation to run away from them has been so feebly resisted. Neither on economic nor on social grounds can present practice be tolerated indefinitely. The crystallization of existing standards which results from the attempt to do justice in an ethical vacuum is bound to become more and more grotesque as time passes and conditions change. Economically it is never more than doubtfully viable; and in time it will become frankly ridiculous and lose even the appearance of justice. Sooner or later there must be changes of some kind, designed or undesigned. That is the primary argument for designing them.

Moreover, the effect of muddling along in the meantime without any coherent wage policy is to nullify the effectiveness of what is done elsewhere. As Lord Beveridge has forcefully pointed out, the great social programme conceived by him, and executed by the

[1] Central Statistical Office, *Annual Abstract of Statistics*, 1953, p. 244.

1945 Labour Government, which was to banish poverty for ever, has steadily been frittered away by the continued fall in the value of money. 'Every time a group of employers and a group of working people agree to raise the wages to be paid for the same product they are doing something to diminish the value of money, to make life harder for people living on pensions or on savings from the past. . . . There is no inherent mechanism in our present system which can with certainty prevent competitive sectional bargaining for wages from setting up a vicious spiral of rising prices under full employment.'[1] Owing to persistent inflation, the social services have, in looking-glass fashion, to run as fast as they possibly can in order to stay in the same place; and this they have never succeeded in doing. The poorest and the most unfortunate section of the community—pensioners and those who for one reason and another are unable to maintain themselves—have no champions to defend them comparable to the unions and professional associations which fight so successfully at all levels for their employed neighbours; and though no one disputes that in theory the rule that justice demands the preservation of existing standards applies also to these groups, no machinery exists to enforce the prompt execution of this principle in practice. It follows that, unless some method can be contrived of so managing wage changes as to avoid perpetual inflation, the use of tax revenues to finance a social service programme ceases to be an alternative method of implementing an equalitarian philosophy; for the efficiency of this device itself depends upon an effective wage policy.

Nor should it be forgotten that by no means all social services are in fact financed from progressive taxation. On the contrary, most of the money for national insurance benefits comes from the flat-rate contributions of insured persons and their employers—from a tax, that is to say, which is severely regressive in its incidence. When the real value of insurance benefits has been reduced beyond bearing by inflation, and those contributions have to be raised, the effect of the whole operation cannot by any stretch of the imagination be described as an equalizing process. In these conditions it is the lower-paid wage earners, together with all those employers who fail to pass their contributions into the price of what they sell, who carry the main burden of relieving the hardships of pensioners. The facile assumption that everything that is commonly labelled as a 'social service' involves a transfer from rich to poor is quite untrue.

And the primary purpose of taxation, when all is said, is not to

[1] Lord Beveridge, as reported in the *Manchester Guardian*, 23 October 1953.

modify the distribution of income. The primary purpose is to raise the funds required for the expenses of government; and, in the total of these expenses, those services which raise the relative standard of living of the lower income groups (known to a less squeamish age simply as 'the poor') play a relatively modest part. Military expenditure is much the most formidable item in the bill; and the impact of progressive taxation upon distribution is, therefore, largely a by-product of wars, hot or cold. This is hardly a happy situation for an equalitarian policy; for, it means that the security of a desirable pattern of distribution is contingent upon the continuance of extremely undesirable international relations. To put the point concretely, the opportunity for lightening taxation that would follow any relaxation of international tensions becomes automatically an occasion for an aggravation of the inequalities in the distribution of wealth. Never was this more apparent than in the budget of the Labour Government which took office at the end of the Second World War. With money to burn after the end of the fighting, the first budget of the first Labour Government ever to command a parliamentary majority made reductions in the rates of direct taxation, the effect of which was to add £25 a year to those with gross incomes of £300 a year and £357 a year to those with incomes of £20,000—a consequence which must have made the Chancellor's socialist forbears turn in their graves.[1]

At the higher levels of income the present situation is indeed at once ludicrous and calculated to produce ill-will all round. Its absurdity was well illustrated by the dilemma which faced the Government when in 1953 it wished to increase the salaries of the judiciary. The original intention was that the judges should receive a net, tax-free increase of £1,000 a year; but the proposal to exempt even so eminent a group as this from the obligation to pay income tax and surtax like other people met with such violent opposition that it had to be abandoned. When it became known that the gross salary of the Lord Chancellor would have to be raised by at least £30,000 a year if he was to enjoy a net increment of £1,000 at the tax rates of 1952–3, and that for the Lords of Appeal and other superior judges the corresponding increase would be over £5,000 a year, the discrepancy proved too grotesque to be tolerable; and in the end the Lord Chancellor had to be content with a gross increase of £2,000 and the other judges with an extra £3,000, yielding them (at the rates of 1953–4) only about £250 and £725 per annum respectively. But these figures only high-lighted a condition which occurs in greater or less degree whenever high-level salaries are

[1] Figures relate to married couples without children.

increased—the condition that an employer must make a present of several hundreds, if not thousands, to the Inland Revenue in order that his employee may receive a clear advance of a few pounds a week.

That these large differences between actual and nominal salaries create a sense of irritation, if not of injustice, in the minds of the recipients hardly needs to be demonstrated. The fact that you are said to receive a certain income naturally fosters the belief that you have a right at least to something of that order; and this in turn creates continual pressure to find some way of bridging the gap—as by tax-free schemes of superannuation and so forth. Such pressure (which is by no means unsuccessful) is a continual threat to the equalizing effects of progressive taxation. Nor is it any less easy to understand the ill-will provoked, amongst those accustomed only to modest figures, by the practice of making very large gross additions to already high salaries. Apart from anything else, the facts of these cases are widely misunderstood. When in the spring of 1954 it was announced that the basic rate for consultants was to be increased by £400 per annum at the minimum, tapered to £350 at the maximum, giving a scale of £2,100 to £3,100, the comment that these increases alone amounted to as much as the rate payable to many wage-earners (railway guards, for instance) for a full week's work apart from overtime, was not uncommonly heard: the public at large, not unnaturally, takes such figures at their face value, and does not trouble to consider the substantial corrections to be made on account of differential rates of taxation.

These misunderstandings, and the bitterness and envy that go with them, would be obviated if it was not thought necessary to maintain the extreme inequalities in the present structure of gross wages and salaries. These inequalities are ill-adapted to the climate of a democratic and socially integrated community: guilty knowledge of this is indeed betrayed by the persistent efforts, to which attention has been drawn in these pages, to keep the measure of these inequalities dark. At the very least, the modern habit of assessing the value of a man's work in ethical terms should carry this one corollary— that in this, as in other affairs, it matters as much that justice should be manifest as that it should be done.

Index

191